THE PSYCHOLOGY MAJOR

THE PSYCHOLOGY MAJOR

CAREER OPTIONS AND STRATEGIES FOR SUCCESS

Third Edition

R. Eric Landrum
Stephen F. Davis

PEARSON

Prentice
Hall

Upper Saddle River, New Jersey 07458

Library of Congress Cataloging in Publication Data

Landrum, R. Eric.
   The psychology major: career options and strategies for success / R. Eric Landrum, Stephen F. Davis.—3rd ed.
      p. cm.
   Includes bibliographical references and index.
   ISBN–13: 978–0–13–198751–7 (pbk.)
   ISBN–10: 0–13–198751–8 (pbk.)
      1.   Psychology—Vocational guidance.   I. Davis, Stephen F. II. Title.

BF76.L36 2006
150.23'73—dc22   2005037087

Editorial Director: Leah Jewell
Executive Editor: Jessica Mosher
Editorial Assistant: William Grieco
Senior Marketing Manager: Jeanette Moyer
Marketing Assistant: Alexandra Trum
Assistant Managing Editor: Maureen Richardson
Production Liaison: Randy Pettit
Manufacturing Buyer: Sherry Lewis
Cover Design: Jayne Conte
Cover Illustration/Photo: Getty Images, Inc.
Director, Image Resource Center: Melinda Reo
Manager, Rights and Permissions: Zina Arabia
Manager, Visual Research: Beth Brenzel
Manager, Cover Visual Research & Permissions: Karen Sanatar
Composition/Full-Service Project Management: GGS Book Services
Printer/Binder: Bradford & Bigelow
Typeface: 9.5/11 Helvetica

Credits and acknowledgments borrowed from other sources and reproduced, with permission, in this textbook appear on appropriate page within text.

Pearson Education LTD., London
Pearson Education Singapore, Pte. Ltd
Pearson Education, Canada, Ltd
Pearson Education–Japan
Pearson Education Australia PTY, Limited

Pearson Education North Asia Ltd
Pearson Educación de Mexico, S.A. de C.V.
Pearson Education Malaysia, Pte. Ltd
Pearson Education, Upper Saddle River, New Jersey

10 9 8 7 6 5 4 3 2 1
ISBN 0-13-198751-8

Contents

Preface to the Third Edition

We originally wrote this book because we saw a need for a resource in our classrooms, a resource that was not available elsewhere (demonstrating, once again, that necessity is the mother of invention). Our goal for this text was and continues to be to provide strategies for success that will allow students to achieve their career goals, whatever they may be. Also, we wanted to provide some fundamental tips and advice that can be useful to *all* students, but especially useful for psychology majors.

So why did we revise this book again? First, thanks to colleagues and students around the country, the book has been modestly successful, and thus there was an opportunity for a third edition. Second, it gave us a chance to improve upon a solid foundation with some major updates and expansions. Third, we wanted to add new features and new examples that make reading more engaging and the book more valuable to the students and for our colleagues.

Our basic approach to writing this book was to provide immediately useful and helpful information to students majoring in psychology or thinking about majoring in psychology. The approach of this book is applied—to provide students with practical, timely, up-to-date information that helps them. We think there are a number of benefits to be gained by using this text. First, it fulfills a need—to our knowledge no book exists that presents this mix of knowledge in such an easy-to-read and easy-to-use format. This text standardizes and catalogs much of the practical advice that professors often give to students on a one-to-one basis—this book does not replace that interaction, but it helps to supplement it. We provide tips on how to do well in all classes, how to find research ideas, and how to write papers in APA format. Also, the book contains up-to-date career information that faculty might not normally have at their fingertips, including the latest salary figures for a number of psychology-related jobs and occupations. Other benefits include the coverage of ethics for undergraduate students, sections on self-reflection, and an overview of disciplines related to psychology. These features are important perspectives that may not often be shared with the new or prospective psychology major.

We have worked hard on this revision of the textbook. We have split previous chapters into two and expanded the coverage. We have added completely new chapters. We have added many new examples and new success stories. The references have been completely overhauled and updated. In particular, you will find a number of new "value-added" features—in fact, although the page count has increased about 60%, the paperback edition helps to keep the cost of the book at the lowest possible level. Below are some of the major changes and additions to the third edition:

- In this edition we continue with our "Success Stories" by adding new stories where appropriate. Faculty members told us stories, sometimes about themselves and sometimes about their students that lend a more personal perspective to the text material. We hope that this narrative approach engages the reader further in understanding why the chapter topics are important and how these issues truly influence student success.

- We continue to update the book thoroughly as new information becomes available. Consider the reference section. The second edition contained 183 references. In this revision, we deleted 35 references but added 75 new references. Of these 75 new references, 80% were from the year 2000 or later. We try to stay on top of this rapidly changing landscape so that faculty and students don't have to.

- We significantly enhanced the usefulness of this book for students by including many more examples. For instance, we often encourage students to work hard and garner strong letters of recommendation, but do students know what a good letter looks like? We have included sample letters for recommendation for those applying for good jobs as well as those applying for graduate school. We also have included a sample resume and a sample curriculum vita for students. Additionally, we have included a sample personal statement so students can see an example of how the principles presented in this book can be put into practice.

Who might use this textbook? As a primary text, it is appropriate for courses such as "Careers in Psychology," "Introduction to the Psychology Major," "The Professional Psychologist," or courses with similar titles and content. This book provides a thorough overview of the discipline, career options (both with and without a graduate degree), strategies for success in and out of the classroom, and coverage of critical issues in psychology. It is also an excellent complimentary text for a number of courses in the psychology curriculum. This book will be helpful for: (1) any course that requires students to conduct research and write papers in APA format, (2) any course that discusses potential careers and earnings in psychology, and (3) any course that covers the opportunities for psychology majors and the ethical implications for being a psychologist. Specifically, this book makes a good supplemental text for research methods/experimental psychology courses, any capstone course, introductory courses, careers courses, etc. The unique mix and coverage of topics makes this text useful in a variety of teaching situations.

Projects such as this one do not occur in a vacuum. We would like to thank Jessica Mosher at Prentice Hall for seeing the value and potential in a third edition of the book; her efforts occurred in the right place at the right time. We would also like to thank Kerri Scott for all of her hard work. Additionally, we appreciate the efforts of Babitha Balan at GGS Book Services for making every page look good. We also want to thank our colleagues who have helped shape the direction of this third edition—whether through formal reviews, e-mails, conversations at conferences, etc.—you have greatly helped confirm the value and necessity of such a book. Finally, we dedicate this book to our students—past, present, and future—our students are the reason we wrote the book, and it continues to be our honor and privilege to teach and profess in a manner that positively influences others' lives. Thank you for allowing us to maximize the opportunity.

R.E.L. & S.F.D.

THE PSYCHOLOGY MAJOR

CHAPTER 1

Why College?

If you are reading this book, the odds are that you are in an elite group. We wrote this book primarily for two audiences: (a) college students thinking about majoring in psychology; and (b) college students who have already declared psychology as their major. Not only do we present up-to-date information about careers in psychology (both with a bachelor's degree and with graduate training), but also provide valuable strategies to get the most out of your undergraduate experience and maximize your chances for success.

WHO GOES TO COLLEGE

The demand for a college education continues to grow. In 1975, 63% of adults had a high school diploma and 14% had obtained a bachelor's degree. By 2000, 84% of adults had a high school diploma and 26% had a bachelor's degree or higher (Day & Newburger, 2002). There are ample opportunities to meet these goals, with 4,182 degree-granting institutions in the United States. However, there appears to be a growing demand for these opportunities—total enrollment in degree-granting institutions for Fall 2000 was 15,312,289; for Fall 2012, the projected total enrollment is 17,673,000—an increase of 15.4% (National Center for Education Statistics, 2003). This book is designed to help you make the most of your undergraduate education to maximize your opportunities for future success, whatever that route may be. With this number of people attending and completing college, how will you stand out? If you follow the advice in this book, you will know what to do to stand out from the crowd!

PUBLIC EXPECTATIONS CONCERNING COLLEGE

Students clearly have multiple goals they want to accomplish when going to college, but the public has high expectations about what students should learn. A 2003 survey conducted by the *Chronicle of Higher Education* identified the public's views on higher education as well as highlighted the important roles for a college to perform. For instance, 91% of those surveyed agreed or strongly agreed with the statement "colleges and universities are one of the most valuable resources in the U.S." When presented with the statement "college graduates today are well prepared for the work force," 56% agree or strongly agreed. Interestingly, when presented with the statement "a graduate-school or professional-school degree will soon be more important than a four-year degree for success in the U.S.," 64% agreed or strongly agreed with that statement. If you believe that your future may include graduate school, many chapters of this book will be particularly helpful to you.

It is clear that the public expects much, not only from college graduates but from the colleges also. In the same Chronicle of Higher Education (2003) survey, respondents rated the importance of the various roles colleges fulfill. Table 1.1 presents the results of that portion of the survey.

It is interesting to note that the public expects colleges and universities to succeed in many areas. Whereas career concerns top the list, we also expect college graduates to be well-rounded citizens who can make important contributions, such as learning about the world through research or helping teach our children. No wonder obtaining a college degree takes at least 4 years! Before exploring the college experience specific to psychology, let us look at why students choose to go to college, how they choose a college, and their expectations after they get to college.

STUDENT EXPECTATIONS ABOUT GOING TO COLLEGE

In a survey of Fall 1999 freshmen (Chronicle of Higher Education, 2001), the top five reasons for deciding to go to college were (a) to be able to get a better job; (b) to learn more about things that interest me; (c) to get training for a better career; (d) to be able to make more money; and

Chapter 1: Why College?

2

TABLE 1.1 Importance Ratings for Roles Colleges Are Expected to Perform

Survey Item	Percentage Rating "Very Important" or "Important"
Prepare its undergraduate students for a career	92%
Provide education to adults so they qualify for better jobs	90%
Prepare future leaders of society	88%
Offer a broad-based general education to undergraduate students	88%
Prepare students to be responsible citizens	85%
Prepare undergraduate students for graduate or professional school	85%
Discover more about the world through research	84%
Help elementary and high schools do a better job teaching children	83%
Teaching students how to cope with a rapidly changing world	83%
Teach students to get along with people from different backgrounds	80%
Help students develop good values and ethical positions	81%
Prepare students from minority groups to become successful	77%
Conduct research that will make American businesses more competitive	70%
Enroll students from all parts of the country	70%
Help local businesses and industries in the area be successful	63%
Help attract new business to local region	62%
Provide useful information to the public on issues affecting their daily lives	62%
Improve the image of the state in which it is located	60%
Promote international understanding by encouraging students to study in other countries	56%
Provide cultural events to the community	60%
Play athletics for the entertainment of the community	35%

Source: The Chronicle survey of public opinion on higher education (2003, May 2). *The Chronicle of Higher Education*, p. A11.

(e) to gain a general education and appreciation of ideas. Psychology is an excellent choice! As you will see throughout this book, psychology majors can get good jobs with a bachelor's degree; they learn about human behavior (what could possibly be more interesting than our own behavior?); they can prepare to go on to graduate school so that they can receive training for additional careers. In general, college graduates do make more money than nongraduates do (more on this later), and psychology at the undergraduate level tends to focus on general education and the appreciation of ideas, particularly from a critical thinking perspective.

As students enter college, what is the highest degree they plan to attain? From the survey of Fall 1999 freshmen, 26.7% indicated that the bachelor's degree was the highest degree they planned to achieve; 40.1% reported the master's degree, and 14.2% stated the Ph.D. or Ed.D. (doctoral degrees, or doctorates). The remaining 18% reported other degrees and less than 1% indicated that they did not intend to achieve a higher degree. As you think about your own choices, you may be interested to know some reasons students cite for selecting a particular college or university (Chronicle of Higher Education, 2001). The top five reasons they rated as "very important" in selecting a specific college were (a) college has a very good academic reputation, (b) graduates get good jobs, (c) size of college, (d) offered financial assistance, and (e) low tuition. As a recipient of a college degree, you will be in an elite group, but you are not alone; in 2000–2001 there were 1,244,171 bachelor's degrees awarded in the United States. In the same year (the latest data available at the time of this writing), 73,534 bachelor's degrees in psychology were awarded (National Center for Education Statistics, 2003). You will hear more about this in Chapter 3.

Success Stories

Dr. Anita Rosenfield
Yavapai College

One Thanksgiving I decided to volunteer at the local Salvation Army rather than go to friends or relatives. Tables were set up with nice linen cloths, and volunteers picked up the food from various food centers to serve to those who came to eat. I was at a condiment table with a young lady who was majoring in child development at a community college where I had taught. One of her brothers was also with us. Her parents and other brother were at the dessert table. The young man told me that he and his brother were both high school dropouts—however, a few years back their father had decided to sell his business and go to college. When he got his AS, he went on to major in business and computers at Cal Poly Pomona, and his sons were so impressed they decided to enroll at the same community college. They were both going to graduate in the spring and had already been accepted into 4-year programs, and their father was planning to get his master's in International Business at LaVerne University.

As the evening moved on, the three siblings walked back and forth from the condiment table to where their parents were. Then the father came over to me. He put his hand on my shoulder and said he hadn't recognized me—but I was the first professor he had when he started at the community college. We had had several long talks about what he had done and what he planned to do and his fears about whether he could succeed. I had encouraged him to continue with his studies, telling him that he was doing extremely well (which he was!). That night, he told me he had thought about dropping out, but because of my encouragement, he decided to continue with his studies. Because of that, his sons and his daughter were successfully getting through college, and he was going on for his master's. It seems that his motivation and my encouragement changed the course of a family.

That's my favorite success story!

DESIRABLE SKILLS AND ABILITIES

Indeed, graduates need to be ready for a variety of work situations and experiences. Chen (2004) reports that the average college graduate will have eight different jobs that will require work in three different professions or occupations. What types of skills and abilities will lead to success during a lifetime of work and career change? Table 1.2 presents the workplace competencies and foundation skills identified by the Secretary's Commission on Achieving Necessary Skills (SCANS) report as presented by the National Centre for Vocational Education Research (2004).

However, even though we want college graduates to come away with these skills and abilities (and apparently so does the public), there is more to a college education than vocational training. An undergraduate education fosters lifelong learning and a sense of civic responsibility. Perhaps Chen (2004) says it better: "Put simply, the objective of liberal education is to produce thinkers, not workers; the education should be useful—but not utilitarian. It is therefore not so much a question of *what* is taught but of *how* it is taught. The question is not so much about *subjects*, but about *processes*" [italics in original], p. 3. We will revisit this idea before the end of this chapter.

THE COVERT CURRICULUM

Drew Appleby writes about the two distinct curricula of an undergraduate education (Appleby, 2001). The curriculum of coursework to complete toward the undergraduate degree is called the *overt curriculum*. When a college or university describes their classes, prerequisites, and

---

TABLE 1.2 Necessary Skills for Workplace Know-How

Workplace competencies

Effective workers can productively use:

- Resources—they know how to allocate time, money, materials, space, and staff
- Interpersonal skills—they can work in teams, teach others, serve customers, lead, negotiate, and work well with people from culturally diverse backgrounds
- Information—they can acquire and evaluate data, organize and maintain files, interpret and communicate, and use computers to process information
- Systems—they understand social, organizational, and technological systems; they can monitor and correct performance; and they can design or improve systems
- Technology—they can select equipment and tools, apply technology to specific tasks, and maintain and troubleshoot equipment

Foundation skills

Competent workers in the high-performance workplace need:

- Basic skills—reading, writing, arithmetic and mathematics, speaking, and listening
- Thinking skills—the ability to learn, to reason, to think creatively, to make decisions, and to solve problems
- Personal qualities—individual responsibility, self-esteem and self-management, sociability, and integrity

---

Source: National Centre for Vocational Education Research (2004). *Generic skills for the new economy.* In: Siena College (Ed.), Liberal education and the new economy. Loudonville, NY: Siena College.

other requirements, they are describing the overt curriculum. However, Appleby and others (e.g., Hettich, 1998) discuss the less obvious or *covert curriculum*. According to Appleby, "colleges and universities often call these 'lifelong learning skills' because they refer not to the specific information that students acquire during their formal education (i.e., the contents of their education), but to how successfully they can continue to acquire information after their formal education has ended (i.e., the processes they developed as they acquired the contents of their education)" (2001, p. 28). In other words, the covert curriculum addresses *how* to learn, as opposed to *what* to learn. The skills presented below (with brief descriptions) should be useful in the lifelong pursuit of knowledge.

Reading with comprehension and the ability to identify major points. People employed in management positions are constantly in search of new ideas and methods to help them perform their jobs more successfully. They understand they must keep up with the current literature and innovations in their profession and obtain relevant information from other sources.

Speaking and writing in a clear, organized, and persuasive manner. The ability to communicate in a clear, organized, and persuasive manner is one of the most crucial characteristics of successfully employed people. The inability to do so leaves others confused about what we have written or said (because we are unclear), convinced that we do not know what we are talking or writing about (because we are unorganized), and unlikely to do what we ask them to do (because we are not persuasive).

Writing in a particular style. Not only do you need to be able to write clearly, but be able to write in a particular style. Psychologists use the *Publication Manual of the American Psychological Association.* Although future employers may not require writing in this particular style, the ability to follow the format guidelines of businesses and clients and the ability to follow precise instructions is an important ability.

Listening attentively. Successful employees listen carefully and attentively to their supervisors' instructions, understand what these instructions mean (or ask for clarification to improve their understanding), and then carry out these instructions in an accurate and complete manner.

Taking accurate notes. Employees must often listen to others and accurately remember what they hear. This process can take place in a one-on-one situation or in groups. Unless the amount of information provided is small or the employee's memory is large, it is wise to take notes.

Mastering efficient memory strategies. All jobs require employees to remember things (e.g., customer's names, meeting dates and times, locations of important information, etc.). Memory refers to the ability to select, store, and use information, and these skills are vital to effective and efficient workplace behavior. The results of a lack of memory skills are confusion, disorganization, and incompetence.

Developing critical thinking skills. Employees must not only be able to remember vital information (i.e., *retention*), they must *comprehend* it so they can communicate it to others in an understandable manner. They must *apply* the information they comprehend in order to solve problems in the workplace. They must *analyze* large, complex problems or sources of information into smaller, more manageable units. They must locate, gather, and *synthesize* (i.e., combine) information from a variety of different sources into new and creative ideas. Finally, they must *evaluate* ideas and methods by applying appropriate criteria to determine their value or usefulness.

Submitting assignments on time and in acceptable form. Employers pay their employees to perform jobs accurately, completely, and in a timely manner. Employees are terminated if they cannot perform their jobs (i.e., their work is incorrect, incomplete, and/or late).

Behaving in a responsible, punctual, mature, and respectful manner. Employees who fail to show up for work (or often late), or whose behaviors are immature or disrespectful are seldom employed for long.

Managing stress and conflict successfully. Employees are often exposed to stressful working conditions and must work with less-than-perfect fellow employees. Stress and conflict management are essential skills that successful employees possess.

Organizing the physical environment to maximize efficiency. Employees must be able to organize their physical environments so they can perform their jobs competently and efficiently. Poor organizational skills often result in appearing confused, making mistakes, and losing important information.

Observing, evaluating the attitudes and behaviors of role models. Successful employees quickly learn the culture of their organization by observing their supervisors and other successful employees. Learning which behaviors to avoid and learning which behaviors to imitate is a crucial skill for an employee who wishes to remain with an organization, receive above average salary increases, and earn promotions.

Maintaining an accurate planner or calendar. Successful employees in today's fast-paced world must be capable of managing their time and controlling their complicated schedules. Behaving in a temporally clueless manner (e.g., forgetting meetings, neglecting appointments, and missing deadlines) is a signpost on the road to the unemployment office.

Working as a productive member of a team. Employers pay employees to perform complex tasks that almost always require some degree of teamwork—very few people work alone. The ability to work as a productive member of a successful team and to be seen as a "team player" requires a set of crucial skills and characteristics that must be acquired through practice.

Interacting successfully with a wide variety of people. The working world is filled with people who differ in many ways. Successful employees are those who have developed the ability to interact in a congenial and productive manner with a wide variety of people (e.g., a supervisor who is older, a client of a different race, or a coworker with a different sexual orientation).

Seeking feedback about performance and using it to improve future performance. Employees are hired to perform certain duties. Successful employees gain rewards such as promotions, raises; unsuccessful employees remain at lower positions and pay levels or are terminated. Savvy employees understand that their performance must satisfy not only their own standards of quality, but also the standards of their supervisor(s).

Accepting responsibility for your own behavior and attitudes. Being able to act in a responsible manner is the cornerstone of personal growth and professional maturity in any occupation. College is the perfect time to learn how to take responsibility for your own actions (rather than blaming your failures on others), and to understand that it is the way you interpret external circumstances that determines how you will respond to them, not the circumstances themselves.

Utilize technology. Future employees need to be technologically sophisticated in order to qualify for many jobs. The ability to word process, use spreadsheets, understand databases, work with statistical programs, and do library searches using bibliographic databases are important aspects of technological literacy.

As you can see, no one course could accomplish all of those goals. However, by carefully examining this list, you might better understand why college teachers structure their courses the way they do. Over the course of your undergraduate education, hopefully you will have multiple chances to develop and sharpen these skills and abilities from the covert curriculum.

THE CIVIC, LIBERAL ARTS VALUE OF A COLLEGE EDUCATION

Earlier we indicated that your college education is not all about the accumulation of skills and abilities to get you a job. There are larger goals of an undergraduate education. All universities attempt to produce better-educated citizens, who are capable of using higher order critical thinking skills. "One of the major characteristics of a 'liberal' or 'liberal arts' education is that it is not focused on a specific career, but aims instead to provide an environment both within the curriculum and outside it that helps students to learn how to *think*, how to be *creative*, how to be *flexible*, how to get on with others—and how to go on learning for the rest of their lives" [italics in original] (Chen, 2004, p. 2).

Over 150 years ago, John Henry Newman (1852) communicated this idea quite well (see Table 1.3).

THE FINANCIAL VALUE OF A COLLEGE EDUCATION

We have already explored many of the reasons for coming to college, whether it is to obtain a good job or to improve yourself or to become a better citizen or to gain critical thinking skills or to master the covert curriculum. These are all appropriate motivations, but so is the motivation to improve your financial standing. Money is not everything in life, but it sure helps. We would be remiss if not addressing this important issue.

TABLE 1.3 The Aim of a University Education

If then a practical end must be assigned to a University course, I say it is that of training good members of society. Its art is the art of social life, and its end is fitness for the world. It neither confines its views to particular professions on one hand, nor creates heroes or inspires genius on the other. Works indeed of genius fall under no art; heroic minds come under no rule; a University is not a birthplace of poets or of immortal authors, of founders of schools, leaders of colonies, or conquerors of nations. It does not promise a generation of Aristotles or Newtons, of Napoleons or Washingtons, of Raphaels or Shakespeares, though such miracles it has before now contained within its precincts. Nor is it content on the other hand with forming the critic or the experimentalist, the economist or the engineer, although such too it includes within its scope. But a university training is the great ordinary means to a great but ordinary end; it aims at raising the intellectual tone of society, at cultivating the public mind, at purifying the national taste, at supplying true principles to popular enthusiasm and fixed aims to popular aspiration, at giving enlargement and sobriety to the ideas of the age, at facilitating the exercise of political power, and refining the intercourse of private life. It is the education which gives a [person] a clear, conscious view of their own opinions and judgements, a truth in developing them, an eloquence in expressing them, and a force in urging them."

Source: John Henry Newman (1852).

TABLE 1.4 Estimates of Average Annual Earnings and Synthetic Work-Life Earnings for Full-Time, Year-Round Workers by Educational Attainment

Educational Attainment	Average Annual Earnings	Synthetic Work-Life Earnings
Doctoral degree	$89,400	$3.4 million
Professional degree	$109,600	$4.4 million
Master's degree	$62,300	$2.5 million
Bachelor's degree	$52,200	$2.1 million
Associate's degree	$38,200	$1.6 million
Some college	$36,800	$1.5 million
High school graduate	$30,400	$1.2 million
Not high school graduate	$18,900	$1.0 million

Notes: Professional degrees include M.D. (physician), J.D. (lawyer), D.D.S. (dentist), and D.V.M. (veterinarian). Synthetic work-life earnings are estimates of total earnings spanning 40 years (ages 25 to 64), adjusting for age and experience over time.

Source: Day, J. C. & Newburger, E. C. (2002). *The big payoff: Educational attainment and synthetic estimates of work-life earnings* (Publication P23-210). Washington, DC: U.S. Census Bureau.

In later chapters of this book we will discuss the specifics of what you can earn with the various degrees in psychology, including specialty areas. For now, let us focus on the general benefit of staying in college. The U.S. Census Bureau has completed some fascinating work looking at one's level of educational attainment and earnings, both an average year's earnings and a projected level of earnings over a 40-year career (from ages 25 to 64). These latter projected earnings over a working career are called synthetic earnings, and they are based on 1999 dollars. How much more money can you expect to make with a college degree compared to a high school diploma? Is there much financial advantage to getting a master's degree compared to a bachelor's degree? These types of questions are answered in Table 1.4.

Again, it is important to reiterate that financial reasons alone should not dictate your life decisions—do you really want to be quite miserable while making a good income? However, these data should be useful as one component of your decision-making process. Also, if you are in the middle of your sophomore year in college and having a hard time staying motivated, the information in Table 1.4 might be helpful. For instance, you might think about getting your associate's degree (an intermediate degree that can typically be earned in 2 years) if you are too burned out to finish the bachelor's degree. And remember, there are over 4,100 colleges and universities in the United States—if you drop out and decide to come back, there will be opportunities to do so.

Success Stories

Dr. Salvador Macias, III
University of South Carolina-Sumter

I am a second generation Mexican American . . . my grandparents moved to New Mexico, then on to California in the 1920s just before my father was born. He was one of eight children, only a few of whom (especially the younger ones) graduated high school (my father earned his GED in the Army). I am the first one in our extended family to have graduated college (though some older cousins did attend a year or two). I believe that one of my younger cousins has a master's degree (some 35 grandchildren in the family, I have lost touch with some!), and there are a few in the next generation who have earned baccalaureate degrees (I'm proud to say that two of my three children have, one is now in a Ph.D. program in Chemistry, and the youngest is a senior in college this year!).

My parents just "assumed" that I would attend college, so I pretty much grew up with that plan. When I was 15, my father died unexpectedly; I was the oldest of nine children . . . and our future was in some doubt, but it was still assumed that I would attend college. In my senior in high school (Catholic school, southern California) I applied to UCLA . . . but in March! Obviously, my application was too late, and was forwarded on to UC Riverside, probably the best thing that ever happened to me! At that time it had about 5,000 students, classes beyond the freshmen level were fairly small, and I got to know many of my professors on a personal level.

One professor in particular, Austin H. Riesen (who became my advisor and undergraduate mentor), was especially important to my academic development. I first came to know him in a somewhat circuitous fashion. A friend of mine worked in his lab observing monkeys . . . they were short of help, this work was absolutely fascinating to me . . . and I was brought into the research team. At that time I was a biology major, but quickly added psychology, stayed in Riesen's lab for a couple of years, branched out into a few other labs as volunteer, paid assistant, received academic credit, etc. I am convinced that had my application to UCLA been accepted I would have, at best, floundered along, maybe eventually graduating . . . but would not have had the opportunity or courage to approach a professor and ask to participate in an ongoing research program! Having had such easy access to my professors, even playing on some softball teams with a few, having it become normal that they would know my name . . . etc., I'm sure is what is responsible for me discovering a passion for psychology, and the opportunity to develop sufficient academic skills to handle (even wish for) graduate school.

OH, YOU DON'T HAVE TO GO TO COLLEGE . . .

Better pay typically comes with more education. However, to be fair and balanced, if pay is your primary consideration, we should to point out that you can have a top-paying job without a bachelor's degree at all. Banerji (1998) reported the median salaries of occupations that do not require a degree: millwrights ($60,000), electrical equipment/household appliance repairers ($52,000), tool-and-die makers ($50,000), advertising and business salespeople ($45,000), and rail- and water-transportation workers ($45,000). In fact, we probably all know of some individuals who have done quite well without a college education. In fact, we often hear success stories about older individuals who did quite well without finishing high school. However, these stories seem to be the exception and not the rule. Banerji points out that although most of these occupations do not require an advanced degree, some do require formal training beyond a high school education. One way or other, additional education and training is probably in a high school graduate's future, whether it is through higher education, the military, or the professional trades.

Exercise #1: Should I Stay In College?

We assume that you are reading this book because you are already in college. However, you should know that a great many students start college but never finish. Even though this first chapter (and the rest of this book) will make persuasive arguments for continuing your college education, some students do drop out. The table below presents two types of information based on previous research: (a) campus characteristics that helped to keep students in school and (b) campus characteristics that did not help students stay in school. For this exercise, circle the items in both categories that you think would affect you—both positively and negatively. Being familiar with the items on this list may alert you to positive situations to pursue and negative situations to avoid.

Positive Campus Characteristics	Negative Campus Characteristics
Caring attitude of faculty and staff	Inadequate academic advising
Consistent high quality of teaching	Conflict between class schedule and job
Adequate financial aid programs	Inadequate financial aid
Consistent high quality of advising	Inadequate counseling support system

Positive Campus Characteristics	Negative Campus Characteristics
Encouragement of student involvement in campus life	Inadequate personal contact between students and faculty
Excellent career planning services	Inadequate curricular offerings
Admissions practices geared to recruiting students likely to persist to graduation	Inadequate part-time employment
Overall concern for student-institutional congruence or "fit"	Inadequate academic support services, learning centers, and similar resources
Excellent counseling services	Lack of faculty care and concern
System of identifying potential dropouts (early alert system)	Inadequate extracurricular activities
	Inadequate opportunity for cultural and social growth
	Lack of staff care and concern for students
	Unsatisfactory living accommodations
	Inadequate career planning services
	Insufficient intellectual stimulation or challenge
	Quality of teaching not consistently high
	Restrictive rules and regulations governing student behavior

Source: Cowart, S. C. (1987). *What works in student retention in state colleges and universities.* Washington, DC: American Association of State Colleges and Universities. (ERIC Document Reproduction Service No. ED347928).

Knowing about these factors may help you to anticipate negative situations and increase your chances for success during your undergraduate education. Be sure to take advantage of the services available on your campus.

CHAPTER 2

Why Psychology?

Are you the type of person who might be interested in any of the following?

- Would you like to study the mental processes that help us acquire and remember information so we can improve our everyday memory?
- Would you like to help people with behavioral disorders help themselves to achieve a better quality of life?
- Would you like to work with communities and neighborhoods to help them plan for the future?
- Would you like to understand those factors that facilitate teaching so that teachers can be taught techniques to improve student learning?
- Would you like to use the information we have about health and behavior to promote wellness and prevent illness? Would you like to improve the coping strategies of persons under stress?
- Would you like to study the brain and begin to understand the changes that occur with the use of drugs or the onset of brain injury or trauma?
- Would you like to better understand why people behave differently in a group from how they behave when alone and why personal decisions are affected by the context in which they are made?

If any of these questions interest you, then psychology may be a good fit as a major! In fact, a general interest in and a passion for understanding of human behavior goes a long way in motivating people to explore whether psychology is the major for them.

THOUGHTS ABOUT THE PSYCHOLOGY MAJOR

At the undergraduate level, many students select psychology as a major because of their interest in becoming a psychologist. If you study this book carefully, talk to students majoring in psychology, and listen to your psychology professors, you will quickly understand that you will not be qualified to be a psychologist at the conclusion of your undergraduate training. It is best to think of your undergraduate education in psychology as learning about psychology, not learning "to do" psychology. McGovern, Furumoto, Halpern, Kimble, and McKeachie (1991) made this point clear when they stated that "a liberal arts education in general, and the study of psychology in particular, is a preparation for lifelong learning, thinking, and action; it emphasizes specialized and general knowledge and skills" (p. 600). A quality undergraduate education in psychology should prepare you to be a citizen and a critical thinker (qualities mentioned in Chapter 1)—the professional functioning of a psychologist comes after specialized work and training at the graduate level.

A guide written by students for students suggested the following about choosing a major: "If you choose a major that truly interests you and pushes you to learn, you'll gain a huge set of skills that you can then use in any career. It sounds so idealistic, but it's true. Employers don't expect you to start your first job knowing exactly how to do it—on-the-job training is a core learning component that almost all careers offer. But employers do expect you to be a well-rounded person, have solid writing and communication skills, and the ability and training to learn new things and excel at them" (Natavi Guides, 2002, p. 17).

Even though the bachelor's degree in psychology is not a professional degree, it is still a good choice to produce a well-rounded, well-educated citizen and person. Why? Although psychology departments at colleges and universities differ, McGovern et al. (1991) identified common goals for undergraduate students to accomplish. These goals include:

A knowledge base—there is a wide array of information in psychology that you need to understand to be a student of human behavior.

Thinking skills—critical thinking and reasoning, analysis of outcomes through experimental methods and statistics give psychology students the tools to make reasoned decisions.

Language skills—as scientists, psychologists must be able to communicate findings to the broader scientific community; students must develop reading, writing, and presentation skills.

Information gathering and synthesis—psychology students need to be able to gather information from a number of sources (e.g., library, computerized databases, the Internet) and be able to synthesize this information into coherent lines of reasoning.

Research methods and statistical skills—the development of quantitative and qualitative methods of data analysis and interpretation is central to the discipline.

Interpersonal skills—psychology students need to be sensitive to the diversity of the environment in which they live and be able to use this increased sensitivity and self-knowledge to monitor their own behavior.

History of psychology—psychology majors need to understand the contexts out of which popular ideas and people have emerged—George Santayana once said, "Those who do not know history are doomed to repeat it."

Ethics and values—psychology majors need to understand the ethical treatment of research participants, to understand conflicts of interest, and to generate options that maximize human dignity, human welfare, and the maintenance of academic and scientific integrity.

Success Stories

Dr. Sophia Pierroutsakos
Furman University

I majored in Psychology in college with a clinical future in mind. I finally decided that wasn't for me, and for whatever reason, didn't explore other options within the field. So, as graduation approached, I spent more time with my political science minor, did an internship in political science, and planned to go to grad school in political science. That next fall, I was taking a few graduate night courses in international relations and had a huge stack of graduate school information packets and applications at home. It suddenly became clear to me that political science was NOT it for me, and that I really needed to finish exploring psychology. After all, I knew there was much more to it than clinical so why didn't I spend some time learning more about the options? I talked to some of my undergraduate Psych professors, looked through lots of journals, and began to realize that developmental psychology was a better fit for me. I will never forget the day I took this huge stack of political science grad applications and materials to the recycling bin. It was difficult to go back to some of my letter writers and ask them to write me a NEW set of letters, for psychology this time. I am sure some of them thought I was flaky.

The regular GRE testing dates had passed, so I had to drive 6 hours to a central testing site and pay a large fee to be tested. I stopped at one of the grad schools I was interested in along the way. I walked in, talked to the graduate dean, described my interests, and he sent me down the hall to meet the person who ended up being my advisor for my master's and Ph.D. (but I didn't know that then). I applied to several schools, got into several, got a great offer from one of the top programs in developmental psych, and worked with the person I met on the way to take my GREs! Now, I am a faculty member at a liberal arts university and I teach and do research with the help of undergraduates. I love working with all kinds of students, but especially enjoy seeing a student discover their love of developmental psychology as somewhat of a surprise, like I did.

As I was finishing up undergrad, I don't think any of my professors would have guessed I would end up being a developmental psychologist. (I was going to be a political scientist, remember?)

But, I have realized since that it makes a lot of sense giving my interests up until then. I just had to be patient about finding a good career path for me, and be willing to talk to lots of people, and ask myself some deep questions. It wasn't easy telling my letter writers that I had completely changed my mind. But, it was the right thing to do!

How has this experience affected my advising of psychology majors? I encourage them to keep talking through things, with as many different people as they would like, because those conversations are essential to finding and making a good choice. But I also remind them that they can change their mind as they go, so they don't feel paralyzed by their fear of making the WRONG choice. Political Science wasn't right for me, but I had to walk a bit down that road before I realized it.

AREAS OF SPECIALIZATION WITHIN PSYCHOLOGY

The skills and abilities that a student can attain in a psychology major are impressive. These skills and abilities help to explain, in part, the growing popularity of this major. Students seem to be initially attracted to psychology by courses in the areas of abnormal psychology, personality, developmental psychology, and educational psychology. Students are also attracted to the major because of the applicability of the subject matter—human behavior! For instance, although some students enter college declaring psychology as their major, often psychology departments see increases in the number of majors following completion of the introductory/general psychology course. Introductory psychology is a challenging course, and many departments have very talented instructors teaching the course. Talented instructors can make interesting subject matter come alive—perhaps another reason for the popularity of psychology.

In the introductory course, students are introduced to the various areas and specializations in psychology; the options are staggering. As a psychology major, you will receive a good grounding in the basics of psychology, taking courses that emphasize the development of skills and abilities (e.g., research methods and statistics) while also accumulating a knowledge base (e.g., developmental psychology, social psychology, history and systems). Even if you recently completed an introductory course, it is hard to remember all the options. To our knowledge, there is no "official" list of the major areas of psychology; we compiled our list from a number of sources. Within most of these areas, there are opportunities to specialize even further—more on this later. Technically speaking, though, the American Psychological Association (APA) recognizes only four "specialties"—clinical, counseling, school, and industrial/organizational psychology (APA, 1997a). All the remaining areas are considered subfields or areas of concentration. For the sake of clarity, however, we will just call the specializations with psychology "areas." Some of the major areas, with brief descriptions, are listed below (APA, 1996, 1997c; Lefton, 1997).

Clinical psychologists assess and treat mental, emotional, and behavioral disorders. These disorders range from short-term crises, such as difficulties resulting from adolescent rebellion, to more severe, chronic conditions, such as schizophrenia. Some clinical psychologists treat specific problems exclusively, such as phobias or clinical depression. Others focus on specific populations: youngsters, ethnic minority groups, gays and lesbians, and the elderly, for instance.

Cognitive psychologists are interested in thought processes, especially relations among learning, memory, and perception. As researchers, they focus primarily on mental processes that influence the acquisition and use of knowledge as well as the ability to reason, the process by which people generate logical and coherent ideas, evaluate situations, and reach conclusions.

Community psychologists strengthen existing social support networks and stimulate the formation of new networks to effect social change. A goal of community psychologists is to help individuals and their neighborhoods or communities to grow, develop, and plan for the future. Community psychologists are concerned with behavior in natural settings, such as the home, the neighborhood, and the workplace, and they seek to understand the factors that contribute to normal and abnormal behaviors in these settings.

Counseling psychologists help people accommodate to change or make changes in their lifestyle. For example, they provide vocational and career assessment and guidance or help someone come to terms with the death of a loved one. They help students adjust to college and help people to stop smoking or overeating. They also consult with physicians on physical problems that have underlying psychological causes. Counseling psychologists provide assessment of and counseling for personal, career, and educational problems, and often use research to evaluate the effectiveness of treatment.

Developmental psychologists study the psychological development of the human being that takes place throughout life. They are interested in the description, measurement, and explanation of age-related changes in behavior: stages of development, universal traits and individual differences, and abnormal changes in development. Until recently, the primary focus was on childhood and adolescence—the most formative years. However, as life expectancy in this country approaches 80 years, developmental psychologists are becoming increasingly interested in aging, especially in researching and developing ways to help elderly people stay as independent as possible.

Educational psychologists concentrate on the conditions under which effective teaching and learning take place. They consider a variety of factors, such as human abilities, student motivation, and the effect on the classroom of the diversity of race, ethnicity, and culture. Educational psychologists help to design the methods and materials used to educate students of all ages.

Engineering psychologists conduct research on how people work best with machines. For example, how can a computer be designed to prevent fatigue and eye strain? What arrangement of an assembly line makes production most efficient? What is a reasonable workload? Most engineering psychologists work in industry, but some are employed by the government. They are often known as *human factors specialists*.

Environmental psychologists examine the relation between psychology and the physical environment, including homes, offices, urban or rural areas. Although some environmental psychologists do basic research examining people's attitudes toward different environments or a person's sense of personal space, others do applied research, such as evaluating a new office design or assessing the impact of building a new power plant in a particular environment.

Experimental or general psychologists use the experimental approach to understand basic elements of behavior and mental processes. They focus on basic research, and their interests often overlap with fields outside psychology (e.g., biology, computer science, mathematics, sociology). Areas of study include motivation, thinking, attention, learning and memory, sensory and perceptual processes, physiology, genetics, and neurology. Experimental psychologists study the basic processes by which we encode, store, retrieve, express, and apply knowledge.

Forensic psychologists apply psychological principles to legal issues. Their expertise is often essential in court. They can, for example, help a judge decide which parent should have custody of a child or evaluate a defendant's mental competence to stand trial. Some forensic psychologists are trained in both psychology and the law.

Health psychologists are interested in how biological, psychological, and social factors affect health and illness. They identify the kinds of medical treatment people seek and get, how patients handle illness, why some people do not follow medical advice, and the most effective ways to control pain or to change poor health habits. They also develop health care strategies that foster emotional and physical well-being. Health psychologists also investigate issues that affect a large segment of society, and they develop and implement programs to deal with these problems.

Industrial/organizational (I/O) psychologists apply psychological principles and research methods to the workplace in the interest of improving productivity and the quality of work life. An I/O psychologist's research interests might include organizational structure, worker productivity and job satisfaction, consumer behavior, selection, placement training, and development of personnel, and human–machine interactions. Many I/O psychologists serve as human resources specialists, who help organizations with staffing, training, and employee development and management in such areas as strategic planning, quality management, and coping with organizational change.

Neuropsychologists explore the relations between brain systems and behavior. For example, neuropsychologists may study how the brain creates and stores memories, or how various diseases and injuries of the brain affect emotion, perception, and behavior. Neuropsychologists frequently help design tasks to study normal brain functions with new imaging techniques, such as positron emission tomography (PET); single photon emission computed tomography (SPECT); and functional magnetic resonance imaging (fMRI). Neuropsychologists also assess and treat people.

Quantitative and measurement psychologists focus on methods and techniques for acquiring and analyzing psychological data. Some of these professionals develop new methods for performing analyses; others create research strategies to assess the effect of social and educational programs and psychological treatment. They develop and evaluate mathematical models for psychological tests, and propose methods for evaluating the quality and fairness of the tests.

School psychologists work directly with public and private schools. They assess and counsel students, consult with parents and school staff, and conduct behavioral interventions when appropriate. School psychologists help educators and other school personnel promote the intellectual, social, and emotional development of children. School psychologists are also involved in creating environments that enhance learning and positive mental health.

Social psychologists study how a person's mental life and behavior are shaped by interactions with other people. They are interested in all aspects of interpersonal relationships, including both individual and group influences; they seek ways to improve such interactions. For example, their research helps us understand how people form attitudes toward others, and when these attitudes are harmful—as in the case of prejudice—they suggest ways to change them. Social psychologists study individuals as well as groups, observable behaviors, and private thought.

As you can see, it is quite a list! Typically, you will not specialize in a particular area at the undergraduate level. There may be "tracks" or "concentrations" for you, but your bachelor's degree will be in psychology; it will not be a bachelor's degree in experimental psychology or neuropsychology. Your area of specialization becomes much more important if you elect to attend graduate school. In fact, if you decide to pursue a graduate degree in psychology, not only will you probably specialize in one of the areas presented, but your degree may come from a program that specializes even further. For a sense of those different levels of specialization, Table 2.1 presents a listing of master's degrees and/or doctoral degrees that can be earned in psychology programs in the United States.

Table 2.1 also shows there are specializations within specializations in psychology. For instance, if you have always wanted to become a clinical psychologist, which type? Will it be clinical, clinical mental health counseling, clinical neuropsychology, clinical child, clinical community, or clinical school? (Clinical respecialization is a special degree for those who already have a Ph.D. but want to go back to school to get a degree in clinical psychology.) Even areas such as developmental, education, and experimental psychology have subspecialties. At this point, it is not necessary to know exactly which area of psychology you want to study—what is important is that you begin to understand the vast opportunities and diversity that psychology has to offer. With all of the choices available you may ask, "Where do I begin in selecting courses as a psychology major, and what can I do with a bachelor's degree?" Those questions sound like ones that you might ask of your academic advisor or your mentor—more on these important roles later.

WHO MAJORS IN PSYCHOLOGY

Psychology continues to be an extremely popular choice, both for students enrolled in its courses and psychology majors. Departments offering degrees in psychology are readily available. According to the National Center for Education Statistics (2003), for the 2000–2001 school year, there were 169 departments offering associate's degrees, 1,286 departments offering bachelor's degrees, 605 departments offering master's degrees, and 260 departments offering doctoral degrees in psychology. These psychology departments generate a great deal

TABLE 2.1 Master's and Doctoral Degrees Obtainable from Psychology Programs

Adolescence and youth	Counseling—secondary school	Marriage and family therapy
Adult development	Counseling—vocational	Mathematical
Aging	Curriculum and instruction	Medical psychology
AIDS intervention or research	Developmental	Mental health
Applied	Developmental psychobiology	Mental retardation
Applied developmental	Developmental—comparative	Minority mental health
Applied social	Developmental—exceptional	Neuropsychology
Art therapy	Doctoral preparation	Neuroscience
Behavior therapy	Early childhood education	Organizational
Behavioral analysis	Ecological	Parent education
Behavioral genetics	Educational	Pastoral counseling
Behavioral medicine	Educational administration	Pediatric psychology
Behavioral neuroscience	Educational measurement	Personality
Behavioral science	Educational policy analysis	Personnel and guidance
Behavioral science—applied	Educational research and evaluation	Phenomenological
Child development	Engineering	Physiological
Child psychopathology	Environmental	Preclinical
Clinical	Evolutionary/sociobiology	Primate behavior
Clinical assessment	Experimental psychopathology	Professional
Clinical neuropsychology	Experimental—animal behavior	Program evaluation
Clinical respecialization	Experimental—general	Psychobiology
Clinical—child	Forensic	Psycholinguistics
Clinical—community	General	Psychological assessment
Clinical—school	Group psychotherapy	Psychology of women
Cognitive	Health psychology	Psychometrics
College counseling	Helping services	Psychopharmacology
College counseling, administration	History and systems	Psychotherapy and psychoanalysis
College teaching	Human development/family studies	Public policy
Community	Human factors	Quantitative (measurement)
Community rehabilitation counseling	Human relations	Quantitative methods
Community—clinical	Human services	Reading
Community—rural	Human services administration	Rehabilitation
Community—school	Human sexuality	Research methodology
Comparative	Humanistic	School
Computer applications	Industrial/organizational	School psychometry
Conditioning	Interdisciplinary psychology	Sensation and perception
Consulting psychology	Law and psychology	Social
Consumer	Learning	Sociocultural perspectives
Counseling and guidance	Learning disabilities	Special education
Counseling	Learning—animal	Sports
Counseling psychology	Learning—human	Statistics
Counseling—colleges, universities	Life-span development	Substance abuse
Counseling—elementary school	Marriage and family	Supervision
Counseling—marriage and family		

Source: American Psychological Association (2000). *Graduate study in psychology* (34th ed.). Washington, DC: Author.

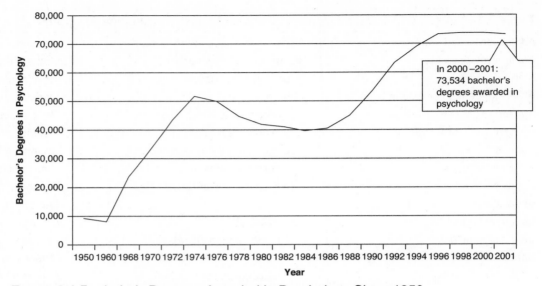

FIGURE 2.1 Bachelor's Degrees Awarded in Psychology Since 1950

Note: For clarity in the figure, the odd-numbered years from 1967 to 1999 have been omitted.

Source: National Center for Education Statistics (2003). *Digest of education statistics 2002* (Publication NCES 2003-060). Washington, DC: U.S. Department of Education.

of student interest. For instance, during the 1999–2000 academic year, 100,000 students were enrolled at 2-year institutions, 349,000 students were enrolled at 4-year institutions, and 74,000 students were enrolled in graduate programs in psychology. Thus, about 3.4% of all students enrolled in higher education are psychology majors.

The number of students choosing to major in psychology also continues to grow. There have been over 70,000 bachelor's degrees in psychology awarded every year since 1994–1995 (National Center for Education Statistics, 2003). In 1980–1981, there were 41,068 bachelor's degrees in psychology awarded; 20 years later in 2000–2001 (the latest year available), there were 73,534 bachelor's degrees awarded—a 79% increase! To see the historical trend in the awarding of bachelor's degrees in psychology, see Figure 2.1.

One of the recurring themes that you will be asked to consider throughout this book is this—what will you do, as an undergraduate, to make yourself competitive with 70,000+ graduates in psychology each year? It doesn't matter if you go the good job route or the graduate school route—the competition will be heavy for premium opportunities along both routes. The rest of this book is dedicated to alerting you to the opportunities available. We also focus on skills and abilities that you can develop while you are still an undergraduate.

DESIRABLE SKILLS AND ABILITIES FOR THE PSYCHOLOGY MAJOR

So what are those skills, abilities, and traits that employers want you to acquire en route to your baccalaureate degree (with a special emphasis on a bachelor's degree in psychology)? The listing below, assembled from many sources (Appleby, 1998b; Butler, 1997; Edwards & Smith, 1988; Lloyd, Kennedy, & Dewey, 1997; United States Department of Labor, 1991a), should start to give you some idea of the skills and abilities you are expected to possess.

Utilizing resources: scheduling, using a budget, assigning space, and managing a staff

Working effectively with others: demonstrating teamwork, teaching new skills to others, fulfilling customer needs, leadership, negotiation, sensitivity to diversity

Acquiring and using information: acquiring, interpreting, organizing, maintaining, and evaluating information; knowing how to learn

Utilizing technology to solve problems: familiarity with new and emerging technologies, awareness of applications to work use

Communication: reading and comprehending complex materials, clear writing, listening carefully and accurately, speaking articulately and persuasively

Computation/numeracy: ability to perform mathematical operations, measurement skills; possess analytical skills, ability for word processing, e-mail, Internet

Problem-solving: decision-making, learning, reasoning; understanding symbols, tables, and graphs

Personal qualities/traits: responsibility, self-esteem, appropriate social skills, self-management and awareness, integrity, hard working, tolerance for stress and ambiguity, outgoing personality

Flexibility: use of creative thinking, adaptable, ability to be a critical thinker

Proficiency in field of study: good grades, understand psychological ideas and how they are applied

What is the benefit of knowing this information? As you pursue your undergraduate career, try to arrange your curriculum choices to give yourself the opportunity to acquire as many of these skills and abilities as possible. You will not be able to master every one of them—at least not during your undergraduate years. These are skills and abilities you might aspire to—design your undergraduate coursework so that, as you complete the coursework, you acquire proficiency in many of the above areas. Realize, however, that some of these items are more "teachable" or "learnable" than others. With the right coursework, a teacher can improve your computational/statistical ability, but a teacher is less able to influence some of your traits (e.g., your personality).

This list of skills and abilities is impressive. As an undergraduate, it would be difficult to achieve all of those skills and abilities to any significant level of proficiency. So which ones are the *most* important? If you have to choose certain skills and abilities to concentrate on, what should they be? First, you want to honestly evaluate your current strengths and weaknesses; seek out opportunities to improve on your weaknesses. We sometimes tell students: You need to have good oral communication skills before you leave this university. Where and with whom do you want to hone this skill—with us, where the absolute worst thing that can happen in a supportive environment is that you get one bad grade, or on the job, where a bad performance might cost you your job, your security, your home, your car, etc.? College is the place to improve what you are not good at—not the place to avoid your weaknesses altogether. Students who fear math courses often take the minimum number of credits required when they should be working to strengthen their math skills. A similar pattern often occurs with writing. If you have difficulty in writing, or are not confident in your writing ability, the last thing you need to do is avoid all courses that involve writing. You might be able to graduate that way, but you may not be very employable.

THE IMPORTANCE OF ADVISING AND MENTORING

At some universities, advising is divided into categories: academic advising and career advising. Academic advising focuses on the curricular demands of the major and addresses such issues as course scheduling and availability, student success in academic courses, meeting prerequisites, and graduation requirements. Career advising emphasizes the student's short- and long-term goals and takes the form of multiple discussions between the student and advisor over the course of an academic career. It is during these career-advising sessions that much of the information provided in this book would be imparted. For example, questions about employment opportunities with a bachelor's degree and graduate school options are often discussed during career advising. This book helps provide resource information to the psychology major and will help you prepare for meetings with your academic advisor.

Lunneborg and Baker (1986) described four types of advising models that exist on college campuses:

Central model: centralized, all-campus advising office completes advising for all majors; no psychology faculty formally involved in advising.

No-faculty model: undeclared majors are advised at a centralized office; after declaring a major, majors are advised in the psychology department in the departmental advising office; advised in department, but not by faculty (e.g., peer advisors).

Part-faculty model: undeclared majors advised at centralized office; then majors declaring psychology are assigned to all psychology faculty members.

All-faculty model: almost all psychology faculty advise majors from the first year through the last year.

It is important to determine the model used in your psychology department. Academic and career advising-based decisions are ultimately your responsibility; the institution shares some responsibility in providing accurate information about academic and career choices, satisfaction with the major, progress toward the degree, and interest in the profession. It is hard to imagine a psychology department in any college or university where you will not be able to find someone to help you—the key may be in finding out *whom* to ask. By the way, Lunneborg and Baker (1986) found that students preferred the all-faculty model with smaller numbers of majors.

In order to maximize your gain when meeting with your advisor, Appleby (1998a) suggests the following:

- Learn your advisor's name, office location, office hours, phone number, and e-mail address.
- Meet with your advisor regularly to plan next semester's schedule (academic advising) and to discuss future plans and how to accomplish them (career advising).
- For academic advising sessions regarding registration, be aware of the courses you have to take, the courses you have already taken, and the courses offered for next semester. Have prepared a tentative schedule of classes you think is feasible.
- Be open and honest about your career goals with your advisor.
- Consult with your advisor when you are in academic difficulty, when you want to add or drop a class, when you might be thinking about changing your major, or when you might be thinking about withdrawing from school or transferring to another college or university.
- Accept responsibility for the academic and career decisions that you make.

At times, you may be surprised by the reactions of your advisor(s); he or she has your best interests at heart. That is, if your best option is to withdraw from school, your advisor will probably not try to talk you out of it. In making that big a decision, however, an advisor may suggest that you seek additional input, such as from trusted friends, a career guidance center, counseling center, etc. If you are miserable as a psychology major, why remain in the major? As academics, we really do have your best interests in mind—we want you to be satisfied with, and successful in, your college experience. Many students fail to take advantage of the advising opportunities afforded to them—be sure that you are not one of those students!

The role of the mentor has long been acknowledged as important at the graduate student level, but there is increasing emphasis on mentoring for undergraduate-level students. Hammer (2003) recently highlighted the importance of being mentored for undergraduate students in psychology: "A strong mentor serves as a guide for your professional development and challenges you to take advantage of important opportunities. A mentor has your best interests at heart, puts time and effort into you as an individual, and is someone you can trust. A mentor is the first person you think of when you need a letter of recommendation, some advice on an academic decision, or direction on a research project. You can think of a mentor as your 'go-to' professor" (p. 4).

More specifically, what would you expect a mentor to do for you? In a national survey of graduate students in a mentoring relationship, the items in Table 2.2 were evaluated using an agreement scale. Not only does this table provide specific functions of mentors, but it also communicates the relative importance of these tasks.

Is a mentor the same as an advisor? Not necessarily. They could be the same person, or not. The mentor is more of a long-term guide who helps you to succeed and fulfill your goals. Your mentor might very well also be your academic advisor. However, you might have one faculty member be an academic advisor, and another be your mentor. There are some advantages to this approach. First, you would gain multiple perspectives on issues relevant to you. Second, it would allow you to build important relationships with multiple faculty. Third, it would allow you to cultivate relationships with professionals that might lead to letters of recommendation, which will be important for pursuing either a good job or graduate school.

TABLE 2.2 Mean Ratings of Mentoring Functions

Mentor Function	Mean
Provided direct training or instruction for me	4.50
Offered me acceptance, support, and encouragement	4.46
Served as a role model for me	4.26
Sponsored me for desirable positions such as assistantships, practica, or internship	3.86
Proved opportunities for me to engage in research	3.76
Helped me to gain greater exposure and visibility	3.61
Served to protect me	3.46
Provided personal guidance and counsel for me	3.46
Served as a friend	3.36

Notes: Each statement began with "My mentor. . ." Responses were based on a 5-point Likert-type scale, from 1 = *strongly disagree* to 5 = *strongly agree.*

Source: Clark, R. A., Harden, S. L., & Johnson, W. B. (2000). Mentor relationships in clinical psychology doctoral training: Results of a national survey. *Teaching of Psychology, 27,* 262–268.

You can begin to see how important a mentor can be in your professional development. In selecting a mentor, you may wish to use the information provided in Table 2.3 that indicates the most frequently mentioned personality characteristics of mentors. Although this study was completed with clinical students enrolled in a doctoral program, we believe these are desirable characteristics of all mentors. The more matches between the top of the list and potential faculty mentors, the better your chances (we think) of developing a mutually beneficial relationship.

TABLE 2.3 Most Frequently Mentioned Personality Characteristics of Mentors

Characteristic	Frequency
Supportive	111
Intelligent	104
Knowledgeable	73
Ethical	56
Caring	54
Humorous	50
Encouraging	49
Honest	39
Empathic	39
Approachable	38
Accepting	35
Warm	33
Available	33
Genuine	33
Dedicated	30

Note: Clinical psychology doctoral students with mentors (*N* = 521) were asked to list the three most important personality characteristics of their most significant faculty member. Frequency represents the number of times each characteristic was mentioned.

Source: Clark, R. A., Harden, S. L., & Johnson, W. B. (2000). Mentor relationships in clinical psychology doctoral training: Results of a national survey. *Teaching of Psychology, 27,* 262–268.

WHY THE PSYCHOLOGY MAJOR IS A GOOD CHOICE

Completion of a rigorous undergraduate program in psychology affords students with a host of developed and honed skills that they can apply to the marketplace (with a bachelor's degree) or to graduate school (for a master's degree or a doctorate). Successful graduates of undergraduate psychology leave with many of these skills and abilities:

- Scientific literacy in reading and writing
- Strong analytical skills and statistical/computer familiarity
- Interpersonal awareness and self-monitoring/management skills
- Communication skills and the ability to work in groups
- Problem-solving and information-finding skills
- Critical thinking and higher order analysis capabilities
- Research and measurement skills

More than likely, the opportunities to acquire these skills exist in your psychology department. Some of these skills will be honed and sharpened in the classroom and by performing class-related tasks, but others are better learned outside the classroom from experiences gained as a research assistant, internship, or teaching assistant. This book is designed for one primary purpose—to help you get the most out of your undergraduate psychology major experience. If *you* don't take advantage of the opportunities that surround you, someone else will.

Exercise #2: Psychology Survey

Below is a survey that your first author uses when teaching the "Introduction to the Psychology Major" course at Boise State University. It was designed specifically for this course. However, it also addresses many of the topics in this book. Before reading any further, complete this survey now, and at the end of the book we will revisit this survey and see if there have been any changes.

Survey Items	Please circle one answer for each question				
	Strongly Disagree	Moderately Disagree	Neutral	Moderately Agree	Strongly Agree
I feel prepared for any type of post-B.A./B.S. career	1	2	3	4	5
I know the information necessary to apply for graduate programs in psychology	1	2	3	4	5
I am certain I will be able to work in a psychology-related job	1	2	3	4	5
I understand the course requirements for the psychology major at this university	1	2	3	4	5
I am familiar with the jobs a B.A./B.S.-level psychologist can attain	1	2	3	4	5
I feel prepared to apply for graduate school	1	2	3	4	5
I understand the course requirements for the psychology minor at this university	1	2	3	4	5
I know about the opportunities in psychology that I can experience outside of the classroom	1	2	3	4	5
I am committed to the psychology major	1	2	3	4	5
I know how to find information about psychology on the Internet	1	2	3	4	5
I understand the importance of math and science in psychology	1	2	3	4	5
I know how to find information about psychology using PsycINFO	1	2	3	4	5
I have a good understanding of the study skills needed for success in college	1	2	3	4	5
I am familiar with the type of careers graduates from this program have attained	1	2	3	4	5
I understand the ethical implications of studying psychology and doing psychological research	1	2	3	4	5
Letters of recommendation are an important part of the post-B.A./B.S. process	1	2	3	4	5
I understand some of the disciplines related to psychology	1	2	3	4	5
After this course, I think I'll still be interested in majoring in psychology	1	2	3	4	5
I want a career that is psychology-related	1	2	3	4	5

Which term below best reflects your current feeling toward being a psychology major? (Circle one)

Very negative	Somewhat negative	Uncertain	Somewhat positive	Very positive

CHAPTER 3

Careers with a Bachelor's Degree in Psychology

Early in your undergraduate career, it is important to think about your future career goals—those goals influence the decisions you make today. If there is a particular area in psychology that you would like to work in after graduation, the coursework you take now should be related to the skills and abilities you will need on the job. This chapter is about the options you have as a bachelor's-level psychology graduate. You may be surprised at the opportunities that are available, but you also need to recognize the challenges and limitations.

THE UNDERGRADUATE CURRICULUM

As you think about selecting a particular college or university, or as you ponder the decision you have already made, how much did the curriculum (the courses required and recommended by the psychology department and the university) influence your decision? Although the overall reputation of the institution probably influenced your decision, your choice of psychology as a major was probably not made on the basis of a particular course offered by the department. You may be surprised, but psychologists care deeply about the undergraduate curriculum! This interest has a long history (Holder, Leavitt, & McKenna, 1958; Menges & Trumpeter, 1972; Messer, Griggs, & Jackson, 1999; Wolfle, 1947), and psychologists continue to study and tweak the curriculum to meet the needs of students and employers (Perlman & McCann, 1998a, 1998b). This research on curriculum offerings specifically addresses current practices, and what skills and abilities students need to succeed after college. Although students may not give the curriculum much thought, it provides the intellectual foundation on which you can achieve an education in psychology. A good curriculum meets the needs of students who want to work as a bachelor's-level psychology graduate as well as students who go on to graduate school.

While in school, however, it is important to be thinking ahead to the transitions to be made at the conclusion of your undergraduate training (more on this at the end of the chapter). For instance, your first author is fond of telling his students "the point of coming to Boise State is to leave Boise State." The transition from college to work continues to receive scrutiny by researchers. Consider this idea offered by Holton (1998), as cited in Hettich (2004): "The paradox is that although the *knowledge* acquired in college is critical to graduates' success, the *process* of succeeding in school is very different from the process of succeeding at work. Many of the skills students developed to be successful in education processes and the behaviors for which they were rewarded are not the ones they need to be successful at work. Worse yet, the culture of education is so different that when seniors continue to have the same expectations of their employers that they did of their college and professors, they are greatly disappointed with their jobs and make costly career mistakes. Despite their best attempts to make adjustments, they cannot adjust for educational conditioning because they are not conscious of it" [italics in original] (p. 4).

Serious consideration has been given to the learning goals and outcomes of psychology majors. An APA task force designed to explore and articulate these learning goals and outcomes developed a list of 10 goals and outcomes that describe the knowledge, skills, and abilities developed within the psychology major and enhanced by the psychology major. These learning goals and outcomes are presented in Table 3.1.

TABLE 3.1 Undergraduate Psychology Learning Goals and Outcomes

Knowledge, Skills, and Values Consistent with the Science and Application of Psychology	Knowledge, Skills, and Values Consistent with Liberal Arts Education that Are Further Developed in Psychology
1. Knowledge base of psychology—students will demonstrate familiarity with the major concepts, theoretical perspectives, empirical findings, and historical trends in psychology	6. Information and technological literacy—students will demonstrate information competence and the ability to use computers and other technology for many purposes
2. Research methods in psychology—students will understand and apply basic research methods in psychology, including research design, data analysis, and interpretation	7. Communication skills—students will be able to communicate effectively in a variety of formats
3. Critical thinking skills in psychology—students will respect and use critical and creative thinking, skeptical inquiry, and, when possible, the scientific approach to solve problems related to behavior and mental processes	8. Sociocultural and international awareness—students will recognize, understand, and respect the complexity of sociocultural and international diversity
4. Application of psychology—students will understand and apply psychological principles to personal, social, and organizational issues	9. Personal development—students will develop insight into their own and others' behavior and mental process and apply effective strategies for self-management and self-improvement
5. Values in psychology—students will be able to weigh evidence, tolerate ambiguity, act ethically, and reflect other values that are the underpinnings of psychology as a discipline	10. Career planning and development—students will emerge from the major with realistic ideas about how to implement their psychological knowledge, skills, and values in occupational pursuits in a variety of settings

Source: Task Force on Undergraduate Psychology Major Competencies (2002, March). *Undergraduate psychology major learning goals and outcomes: A report.* Washington, DC: American Psychological Association.

As you can see, this is an impressive list! Given a thoughtful curriculum, by the time you have completed your undergraduate education you should be improving in all of these areas.

WHAT EMPLOYERS WANT, AND WHAT THEY PAY

Researchers continue to study those job skills that employers who hire bachelor's degree psychology majors value. Three sources of information demonstrate a convergence in what employers are looking for—social and personal skills, the ability to work in groups, flexibility, etc. Table 3.2 presents three perspectives on employer-desired job skills and highlights the convergence. Given the differing methodologies used to draw conclusions, the emphasis on communication skills, flexibility/adaptability, interpersonal dynamics, ability to work as a team, and other skills and abilities emerge across the studies. It is important for students and faculty alike to understand the importance of this list, and to ensure that faculty members strive, in part, to design curricular experiences that allow students to acquire and hone many of the skills presented in Table 3.2.

We have already mentioned in a previous chapter the overall value of a bachelor's degree. But what about a bachelor's degree in psychology? You should note that this information is difficult to come by, and the information that is available comes from various sources, such as the National Association of Colleges and Employers (NACE) and the Bureau of Labor Statistics. According to Murray (2002a), the NACE average starting salary for psychology majors in 2001–2002 was $29,952. The Bureau of Labor Statistics has starting salaries ranging from $21,900 to $27,200 for 2001 psychology majors. And a third source pegs the average starting salary at $25,000 for 1999 psychology majors. First, it is important to note that these are average *starting* salaries. Second, the diverse employment opportunities for psychology graduates compounds the difficulty in collecting accurate salary information. Lastly, as in all professions, you will most likely start at the bottom and have to work your way up. So, although

---

TABLE 3.2 What Employers Want from Those with a Bachelor's Degree in Psychology

---

Jobweb (2001)—What Employers Want—Top 10 Qualities Employers Seek

Communication skills (verbal and written)	Strong work ethic
Honesty/integrity	Analytical skills
Teamwork skills	Flexibility/adaptability
Interpersonal skills	Computer skills
Motivation/initiative	Self-confidence

Appleby (2000)—Job Skills Valued by Employers Who Interview Psychology Majors

Social skills	Information gathering/processing skills
Personal skills	Numerical/computer/psychometric skills
Communication skills	

Landrum and Harrold (2003)—Employer's Perception of Importance—Top 10 Skills and Abilities

Listening skills	Focus on customers/clients
Ability to work with others as part of a work team	Interpersonal relationship skills
Getting along with others	Adaptability to changing situations
Desire and willingness to learn	Ability to suggest solutions to problems
Willingness to learn new, important skills	Problem-solving skills

---

these salary figures may be a bit disappointing, remember that they are average starting figures—it will be up to you to make them go up! Of course these starting salaries will vary by region of the country, job demands, experience, etc. We do not present these numbers to lower your enthusiasm for psychology; however, we feel it is important that you make an informed decision about majoring in psychology.

Hopefully, we have convinced you of the importance of the curriculum and its connection to what employers want. Next, see if there is a careers course available at your institution. For example, at Boise State University, one course that orients the student to the major as well as career opportunities is called "Introduction to the Psychology Major." At Emporia State University, the course is called "The Professional Psychologist." Buckalew and Lewis (1982) called for such courses to be made available to let students know about the career opportunities and choices available to them. Kennedy and Lloyd (1998) completed an evaluation of Georgia Southern University's "Careers in Psychology" course and found that students in the course clarified career goals and were most satisfied with the topics tied to careers and graduate school. Dodson, Chastain, and Landrum (1996) also evaluated a psychology seminar course at Boise State and found that students changed their way of thinking about psychology because of the course. For instance, students often changed the terminal degree they were planning to pursue (e.g., from a doctorate to a master's degree), and they changed their strategies for seeking financial aid for graduate education (they became aware of more opportunities for funding). If your university has a careers course, seriously consider taking it—if it is not available, suggest it to a student-friendly faculty member (perhaps it can be taught as a special-topics or one-time offering). Also, your local Psi Chi chapter or Psychology Club might consider inviting faculty members to give talks about career opportunities in psychology.

CAREERS WITH A BACHELOR'S DEGREE

You may be surprised to discover the variety of opportunities available to you with a bachelor's degree in psychology. For some reason, faculty sometimes present this career path as a bleak alternative (as compared with going to graduate school); the majority of most graduates, however, *do not* pursue graduate training. However, we do want to be realistic about the opportunities. You will *not* be able to be a practicing psychologist without an advanced degree in psychology. With your bachelor's degree, you can obtain jobs both within psychology (usually in a support staff-type of role) and related to the discipline of psychology. There are also a number of opportunities to apply your undergraduate training in psychology in areas that are not directly related to psychology but that involve some components of human behavior. If you stop to think about it, there are very few, if any, jobs or careers that do not involve or would not benefit from a greater understanding of human behavior.

What can you do with a bachelor's degree in psychology? Before we address some of the specific job opportunities available, let us review the primary work activities of bachelor's degree holders. According to the APA Research Office (2003), 44% work in management sales and administration; 24% in professional services; 13% in teaching; 11% in computer applications; and 8% in research and development. These data are based on the results of a 1999 survey of bachelor's-level degree recipients. Where do they work? This same survey found that 48% work for for-profit companies, 13% work for educational institutions, 12% work for nonprofit organizations, 11% work for state or local government, 6% work for universities and colleges, 6% are self-employed, and 4% work for the federal government. As you can see, the variety of tasks and settings is vast, including many business applications. We will make these opportunities even clearer later in the chapter when potential job descriptions are presented.

Employers have different expectations about what you can do based on your level of education. Pinkus and Korn (1973) found that BA-level employers expect their applicants to be generalists, with favorable personality traits and some type of field experience, preferably a supervised situation. Experience is important! You need to take advantage of the opportunities available to you in your psychology department. Even at the bachelor's level (and especially if you have intentions of going to graduate school), being a good (or even great) "book-student" is not enough. Straight A's and a 4.0 GPA are not enough to convince an employer to hand you a job. Although people will be somewhat interested in what you know, they also want to know what you can do and what you have done.

What are the careers related to psychology that are available to the bachelor's-level psychology major? As you explore your opportunities for employment with a bachelor's degree, it would be helpful to know some of the choices available and what some of the job titles are. Table 3.3 presents a sampling of job titles relevant to students with a bachelor's degree in psychology. These titles were obtained from a variety of sources (Appleby, 1999; Aubrecht, 2001; Lloyd, 1997a, 1997b; Occupational Outlook Handbook, 1998a; Shepard, 1996).

TABLE 3.3 Sampling of Job Titles Relevant to Those with a Bachelor's Degree in Psychology

Related to Psychology	Related to Business	Other Areas
Academic advisor	Administrative assistant	Activity director
Alcohol/drug abuse counselor	Advertising agent	Assistant youth coordinator
Behavior analyst	Advertising trainee	Camp staff director
Career counselor	Affirmative action representative	College admissions officer
Career planning and placement counselor	Airline reservations clerk	Community organizer
Case management aide	Bank management	Community recreation worker
Case worker	Claims specialist	Community relations officer
Child care worker	Customer relations	Congressional aide
Child protection worker	Customer service representative	Crime prevention coordinator
Community outreach worker	Employee counselor	Director of alumni relations
Community support worker	Employee relations assistant	Director of fund-raising
Corrections officer	Energy researcher	Driving instructor
Counselor aide	Events coordinator	Educational coordinator
Day care center supervisor	Financial researcher	Fast-food restaurant manager
Director of volunteer services	Hotel management	Foster home parent
Eligibility worker	Human relations director	Film researcher/copywriter

(continued)

TABLE 3.3 Sampling of Job Titles Relevant to Those with a Bachelor's Degree in Psychology *(continued)*

Related to Psychology	Related to Business	Other Areas
Employment counselor	Human resources recruiter	Historical research assistant
Family services worker	Insurance agent	Hospital patient service representative
Gerontology aide	Insurance claims/underwriter	Juvenile probation officer
Group home coordinator	Intelligence officer	Laboratory assistant
Housing/student life coordinator	Job analyst	Neighborhood outreach worker
Life skill counselor	Loan officer	Newspaper reporter
Mental health technician	Lobbying organizer	Nursing home administrator
Mental retardation unit manager	Management trainee	Park and recreation director
Parole officer	Marketing representative	Private tutor
Political campaign worker	Marketing researcher	Research assistant
Probation officer	Media buyer	Security officer
Program manager	Occupational analyst	Statistical assistant
Public affairs coordinator	Office manager	Statistical reports compiler
Public relations specialist	Personnel worker/administrator	Task force coordinator
Publications researcher	Property management	Teaching
Radio/TV research assistant	Public information officer	Technical writer
Rehabilitation advisor	Sales representative	Vocational rehabilitation counselor
Residential counselor	Small business owner	Volunteer coordinator
Residential youth counselor	Staff training and development	Work activity program director
Social services assistant	Store manager	Youth minister
Social services director		
Social work assistant		
Urban planning research assistant		
Veteran's advisor		

Success Stories

Candace Brown
Boise State University Alumnus

I've been interested in Forensic Psychology ever since I decided to major in Psychology (about 8 years ago). I had planned on getting my doctorate in Forensic Psychology, but after moving to Boise from Minnesota, decided I wasn't ready to move across the country again (most of the decent Forensic Psychology colleges were back East). While in school, I tried to learn as much as I could about different positions in the Boise area regarding hours, type of work, pay, qualifications, etc.

When I graduated in 2000, I started applying places and realized that a B.S. in Psychology isn't going to get you much pay—at least if you want to work in the field! I took a job as a Vocational Evaluator, where I administered different types of tests to people with physical, mental, and/or emotional disabilities. The work itself was very interesting and I gained wonderful skills, but unfortunately, the company wasn't running very well and there was a great lack of respect for our manager and a lack of organization among my office members. I thought long and hard about what I wanted to do as a career and thought I would pursue a corporate training degree. I knew corporate trainers made a lot of money and I started a graduate program at Boise State. That lasted one semester, when I realized that doing something just for the money is a bad idea! I had become frustrated at making so little and at the time, I was willing to sacrifice my true interests. I had also always been interested in law (though I didn't want to be an attorney) and thought it sounded very interesting—maybe I could work in criminal law and satisfy that craving! Having my bachelor's degree helped me get into the program and I graduated with my Paralegal certificate in May of this year. I love working as a Paralegal and without my bachelor's degree, I wouldn't have gotten many of the opportunities I have—my current job, for one! I feel that the opportunities are endless.

I wish when I was obtaining my degree that I had done an internship. It wasn't required when I was in the Psychology program and because I had to work to pay all my own bills, I didn't feel it would be worth it to take time out from work to do it. I think it would have been well worth it—to gain some job skills and make connections. If an internship is not possible because of work duties, I would work extra hard at talking to as many people as you can in the field and learn about various types of jobs. When I thought of Psychology, I thought in a very narrow scope, so it's important to check things out and keep an open mind!

I feel like employers really value someone with a degree because it shows a sense of commitment and the ability to follow through. Many jobs today require some sort of degree, no matter what it's in, so don't ever feel that it's a waste of time. One thing I suggest, though, is to maybe try to be somewhat specific in your career goals. I graduated not really knowing what I wanted to do and because the major is so general, it can be hard to set yourself apart from all the other graduates out there. Even if you do volunteer work, make yourself unique and network, network, network!

The best advice I can give on finding a good job is to keep an open mind. Even if you want to stay in a specific area, like Boise, check out what's going on in other parts of the country! It will help you know what the trends are, what salaries are like and may give you some ideas of certain companies, organizations, etc. to look at when job searching. I think the most important thing is to not get frustrated, but also be realistic. You're probably not going to make $40,000 per year fresh out of school, or maybe I was just looking in the wrong places! For me, once I got into a more specific career field, things started falling into place. Just focus on what's important and what your interests are and go for it! Sometimes our priorities change, but it's important to always do something you enjoy!

CAREER OPTIONS, JOB DESCRIPTIONS, AND THE AMAZING O*NET

O*NET stands for Occupational Information Network, which is a comprehensive database of work attributes and job characteristics. O*NET incorporates much of the information that was formerly available from the *Dictionary of Occupational Titles* (which is no longer published). Quite simply, O*NET is an amazing tool that anyone with Internet access (online.onetcenter.org) can use. Covering over 1,000 occupations, O*NET provides detailed information about each job, including knowledge, skills, and abilities needed, interests, general work activities, and a work context. It also provides links to salary information.

All occupations are organized using O*NET-SOC codes (SOC stands for standard occupational classification). In the example job descriptions included in this chapter, we have also included the O*NET-SOC codes so that if you want more information about a particular job, you can use that code at online.onetcenter.org to instantly access detailed information. This system is well designed and user-friendly. What kind of detailed information is available about each job? In the exercise at the end of this chapter, we include a complete sample listing for a recreational therapist. What is that? As you will see from the sample, a great deal of detail is available. You can examine not only the tasks of that job, but the knowledge required, skills necessary, abilities used, typical work activities, the context of work, training expected, general interest of those in the job, work styles, work values, related occupations, and a link to wage information!

Although it is rather long, in the following pages we present some of the job titles and brief descriptions of over 100 jobs that are related to psychology, related to business, and other jobs (similar to the organization of Table 3.3). Our feeling is that if you want to explore your career options, you need to know a bit about the actual careers. You will note that we have also included the O*NET-SOC code with each occupation—if you want to obtain complete data about a particular job (as with the example in Exercise #3)—you can visit online.onetcenter.org and directly enter this code. You should also note that the organization of jobs into three categories (psychology-related, business-related, and other) is our classification and not from O*NET. As you will see in the table, this is somewhat arbitrary at times. Our goal is to present the information as organized as we can, to facilitate your use of the information.

WHAT ABOUT THE ASSOCIATE'S DEGREE?

At some colleges and universities, students can graduate with an associate's degree in psychology. Unfortunately there is very little national information about this degree, jobs available to associate's degree holders, salaries, etc. A comprehensive review found few published works (e.g., APA, 1986; Kerchhoff & Bell, 1998; Taylor & Hardy, 1996). Taylor and Hardy's (1996) study was of associate's degree holders from one university. They found that the types of jobs held with this degree include "human resources worker, crisis intervention associate, rehabilitation worker, child welfare worker, psychiatric technician, correctional officer, police officer, child care assistant, mental health technician, aide to geriatric clients, and social welfare worker" (p. 960). In a careers pamphlet from APA (1986), the occupations typical for an associate's degree recipient were described in these categories:

Human services—training to work in social welfare agencies, correctional facilities, or agencies serving special populations such as the elderly, the physically handicapped, and the mentally handicapped.

Mental health—training for employment in mental hospitals, mental health clinics, community mental health centers, counseling centers, and crisis intervention units.

Drug and alcohol rehabilitation counseling—training to work under supervision as a counseling aide or paraprofessional counselor to people under treatment for abusing drugs or alcohol.

Early childhood education—training for a job as a teacher's aide or a child care assistant in a preschool, day-care center, Head Start program, or other service for young children.

The information about salary levels of associate's degree holders is extremely limited, also coming from the Taylor and Hardy (1996) study of one institution's associate's degree graduates. They found that entry-level salaries for holders of the associate's degree ranged from $9,600 to $14,000, with salaries $4,000–$8,000 higher in the eastern and western coastal states. Although the associate's degree is a popular option for some students, unfortunately there is very little national data collected on this topic that might be helpful for students considering this option. It does seem clear that "people employed in these settings with associate degree training are supervised by a psychologist, social worker, or teacher" (APA, 1986, p. 19). At the end of the 2000–2001 year, 1,544 associate's degrees in psychology were awarded (National Center for Education Statistics, 2003).

BECOMING A FRESHMAN AGAIN

At the beginning of this chapter we alluded to the challenges in making the transition from college to the world of work. In the next chapter, we will explore the strategies you can use to land that good job with a bachelor's degree. But for now, it's worth considering the challenges you have ahead. Paul Hettich has studied this issue of transitions, and not only clearly identifies the

TABLE 3.4 Career Options and Occupational Descriptions

Psychology-Related Job Titles, Brief Descriptions, and O*NET-SOC Codes

11-3042.00—Training and Development Managers—Plan, direct, or coordinate the training and development activities and staff of an organization.

11-9031.00—Education Administrators, Preschool and Child Care Center/Program—Plan, direct, or coordinate the academic and nonacademic activities of preschool and child care centers or programs.

11-9111.00—Medical and Health Services Managers—Plan, direct, or coordinate medicine and health services in hospitals, clinics, managed care organizations, public health agencies, or similar organizations.

11-9151.00—Social and Community Service Managers—Plan, organize, or coordinate the activities of a social service program or community outreach organization. Oversee the program or organization's budget and policies regarding participant involvement, program requirements, and benefits. Work may involve directing social workers, counselors, or probation officers.

13-1071.01—Employment Interviewers, Private or Public Employment Service—Interview job applicants in employment office and refer them to prospective employers for consideration. Search application files, notify selected applicants of job openings, and refer qualified applicants to prospective employers. Contact employers to verify referral results. Record and evaluate various pertinent data.

13-1073.00—Training and Development Specialists—Conduct training and development programs for employees.

19-4061.00—Social Science Research Assistants—Assist social scientists in laboratory, survey, and other social research. May perform publication activities, laboratory analysis, quality control, or data management. Normally these individuals work under the direct supervision of a social scientist and assist in those activities that are more routine.

19-4092.00—Forensic Science Technicians—Collect, identify, classify, and analyze physical evidence related to criminal investigations. Perform tests on weapons or substances, such as fiber, hair, and tissue to determine significance to investigation. May testify as expert witnesses on evidence or crime laboratory techniques. May serve as specialists in area of expertise, such as ballistics, fingerprinting, handwriting, or biochemistry.

21-1011.00—Substance Abuse and Behavioral Disorder Counselors—Counsel and advise individuals with alcohol, tobacco, drug, or other problems, such as gambling and eating disorders. May counsel individuals, families, or groups or engage in prevention programs.

21-1012.00—Educational, Vocational, and School Counselors—Counsel individuals and provide group educational and vocational guidance services.

21-1014.00—Mental Health Counselors—Counsel with emphasis on prevention. Work with individuals and groups to promote optimum mental health. May help individuals deal with addictions and substance abuse; family, parenting, and marital problems; suicide; stress management; problems with self-esteem; and issues associated with aging and mental and emotional health.

21-1015.00—Rehabilitation Counselors—Counsel individuals to maximize the independence and employability of persons coping with personal, social, and vocational difficulties that result from birth defects, illness, disease, accidents, or the stress of daily life. Coordinate activities for residents of care and treatment facilities. Assess client needs and design and implement rehabilitation programs that may include personal and vocational counseling, training, and job placement.

21-1021.00—Child, Family, and School Social Workers—Provide social services and assistance to improve the social and psychological functioning of children and their families and to maximize the family well-being and the academic functioning of children. May assist single parents, arrange adoptions, and find foster homes for abandoned or abused children. In schools, they address such problems as teenage pregnancy, misbehavior, and truancy. May also advise teachers on how to deal with problem children.

21-1022.00—Medical and Public Health Social Workers—Provide persons, families, or vulnerable populations with the psychosocial support needed to cope with chronic, acute, or terminal illnesses, such as Alzheimer's, cancer, or AIDS. Services include advising family caregivers, providing patient education and counseling, and making necessary referrals for other social services.

21-1023.00—Mental Health and Substance Abuse Social Workers—Assess and treat individuals with mental, emotional, or substance abuse problems, including abuse of alcohol, tobacco, and/or other drugs. Activities may include individual and group therapy, crisis intervention, case management, client advocacy, prevention, and education.

21-1091.00—Health Educators—Promote, maintain, and improve individual and community health by assisting individuals and communities to adopt healthy behaviors. Collect and analyze data to identify community needs prior to planning, implementing, monitoring, and evaluating programs designed to encourage healthy lifestyles, policies, and environments. May also serve as a resource to assist individuals, other professionals, or the community, and may administer fiscal resources for health education programs.

(continued)

TABLE 3.4 (continued)

21-1092.00—Probation Officers and Correctional Treatment Specialists—Provide social services to assist in rehabilitation of law offenders in custody or on probation or parole. Make recommendations for actions involving formulation of rehabilitation plan and treatment of offender, including conditional release and education and employment stipulations.

21-1093.00—Social and Human Service Assistants—Assist professionals from a wide variety of fields, such as psychology, rehabilitation, or social work, to provide client services, as well as support for families. May assist clients in identifying available benefits and social and community services and help clients obtain them. May assist social workers with developing, organizing, and conducting programs to prevent and resolve problems relevant to substance abuse, human relationships, rehabilitation, or adult daycare.

25-1194.00—Vocational Education Teachers Postsecondary—Teach or instruct vocational or occupational subjects at the postsecondary level (but at less than the baccalaureate) to students who have graduated or left high school. Includes correspondence school instructors; industrial, commercial, and government training instructors; and adult education teachers and instructors who prepare persons to operate industrial machinery and equipment and transportation and communications equipment. Teaching may take place in public or private schools whose primary business is education or in a school associated with an organization whose primary business is other than education.

25-3011.00—Adult Literacy, Remedial Education, and GED Teachers and Instructors—Teach or instruct out-of-school youths and adults in remedial education classes, preparatory classes for the General Educational Development test, literacy, or English as a Second Language. Teaching may or may not take place in a traditional educational institution.

25-3021.00—Self-Enrichment Education Teachers—Teach or instruct courses other than those that normally lead to an occupational objective or degree. Courses may include self-improvement, nonvocational, and nonacademic subjects. Teaching may or may not take place in a traditional educational institution.

25-9031.00—Instructional Coordinators—Develop instructional material, coordinate educational content, and incorporate current technology in specialized fields that provide guidelines to educators and instructors for developing curricula and conducting courses.

25-9041.00—Teacher Assistants—Perform duties that are instructional in nature or deliver direct services to students or parents. Serve in a position for which a teacher or another professional has ultimate responsibility for the design and implementation of educational programs and services.

29-1122.00—Occupational Therapists—Assess, plan, organize, and participate in rehabilitative programs that help restore vocational, homemaking, and daily living skills, as well as general independence, to disabled persons.

29-1125.00—Recreational Therapists—Plan, direct, or coordinate medically approved recreation programs for patients in hospitals, nursing homes, or other institutions. Activities include sports, trips, dramatics, social activities, and arts and crafts. May assess a patient's condition and recommend appropriate recreational activity.

29-2053.00—Psychiatric Technicians—Care for mentally impaired or emotionally disturbed individuals, following physician instructions and hospital procedures. Monitor patients' physical and emotional well-being and report to medical staff. May participate in rehabilitation and treatment programs, help with personal hygiene, and administer oral medications and hypodermic injections.

29-9011.00—Occupational Health and Safety Specialists—Review, evaluate, and analyze work environments and design programs and procedures to control, eliminate, and prevent disease or injury caused by chemical, physical, and biological agents or ergonomic factors. May conduct inspections and enforce adherence to laws and regulations governing the health and safety of individuals. May be employed in the public or private sector.

29-9091.00—Athletic Trainers—Evaluate, advise, and treat athletes to assist recovery from injury, avoid injury, or maintain peak physical fitness.

31-1013.00—Psychiatric Aides—Assist mentally impaired or emotionally disturbed patients, working under direction of nursing and medical staff.

31-2011.00—Occupational Therapist Assistants—Assist occupational therapists in providing occupational therapy treatments and procedures. May, in accordance with state laws, assist in development of treatment plans, carry out routine functions, direct activity programs, and document the progress of treatments. Generally requires formal training.

33-3012.00—Correctional Officers and Jailers—Guard inmates in penal or rehabilitative institution in accordance with established regulations and procedures. May guard prisoners in transit between jail, courtroom, prison, or other point. Includes deputy sheriffs and police who spend the majority of their time guarding prisoners in correctional institutions.

33-3021.03—Criminal Investigators and Special Agents—Investigate alleged or suspected criminal violations of federal, state, or local laws to determine if evidence is sufficient to recommend prosecution.

TABLE 3.4 (continued)

33-3021.04—Child Support, Missing Persons, and Unemployment Insurance Fraud Investigators—Conduct investigations to locate, arrest, and return fugitives and persons wanted for nonpayment of support payments and unemployment insurance fraud, and to locate missing persons.

39-9011.00—Child Care Workers—Attend to children at schools, businesses, private households, and child care institutions. Perform a variety of tasks, such as dressing, feeding, bathing, and overseeing play.

39-9021.00—Personal and Home Care Aides—Assist elderly or disabled adults with daily living activities at the person's home or in a daytime nonresidential facility. Duties performed at a place of residence may include keeping house (making beds, doing laundry, washing dishes) and preparing meals. May provide meals and supervised activities at nonresidential care facilities. May advise families, the elderly, and the disabled on such things as nutrition, cleanliness, and household utilities.

39-9041.00—Residential Advisors—Coordinate activities for residents of boarding schools, college fraternities or sororities, college dormitories, or similar establishments. Order supplies and determine need for maintenance, repairs, and furnishings. May maintain household records and assign rooms. May refer residents to counseling resources if needed.

43-4061.01—Claims Takers, Unemployment Benefits—Interview unemployed workers and compile data to determine eligibility for unemployment benefits.

43-4061.02—Welfare Eligibility Workers and Interviewers—Interview and investigate applicants and recipients to determine eligibility for use of social programs and agency resources. Duties include recording and evaluating personal and financial data obtained from individuals; initiating procedures to grant, modify, deny, or terminate eligibility for various aid programs; authorizing grant amounts; and preparing reports. These workers generally receive specialized training and assist social service caseworkers.

43-9111.00—Statistical Assistants—Compile and compute data according to statistical formulas for use in statistical studies. May perform actuarial computations and compile charts and graphs for use by actuaries. Includes actuarial clerks.

Business-Related Job Titles, Brief Descriptions, and O*NET-SOC Codes

11-1021.00—General and Operations Managers—Plan, direct, or coordinate the operations of companies or public and private sector organizations. Duties and responsibilities include formulating policies, managing daily operations, and planning the use of materials and human resources, but are too diverse and general in nature to be classified in any one functional area of management or administration, such as personnel, purchasing, or administrative services. Includes owners and managers who head small business establishments whose duties are primarily managerial.

11-2011.00—Advertising and Promotions Managers—Plan and direct advertising policies and programs or produce collateral materials, such as posters, contests, coupons, or giveaways, to create extra interest in the purchase of a product or service for a department, an entire organization, or on an account basis.

11-2021.00—Marketing Managers—Determine the demand for products and services offered by a firm and its competitors and identify potential customers. Develop pricing strategies with the goal of maximizing the firm's profits or share of the market while ensuring the firm's customers are satisfied. Oversee product development or monitor trends that indicate the need for new products and services.

11-2022.00—Sales Managers—Direct the actual distribution or movement of a product or service to the customer. Coordinate sales distribution by establishing sales territories, quotas, and goals and establish training programs for sales representatives. Analyze sales statistics gathered by staff to determine sales potential and inventory requirements and monitor the preferences of customers.

11-2031.00—Public Relations Managers—Plan and direct public relations programs designed to create and maintain a favorable public image for employer or client; or if engaged in fund-raising, plan and direct activities to solicit and maintain funds for special projects and nonprofit organizations.

11-3011.00—Administrative Services Managers—Plan, direct, or coordinate supportive services of an organization, such as recordkeeping, mail distribution, telephone operator/receptionist, and other office support services. May oversee facilities planning and maintenance and custodial operations.

11-9141.00—Property, Real Estate, and Community Association Managers—Plan, direct, or coordinate selling, buying, leasing, or governance activities of commercial, industrial, or residential real estate properties.

13-1031.01—Claims Examiners, Property and Casualty Insurance—Review settled insurance claims to determine that payments and settlements have been made in accordance with company practices and procedures. Report overpayments, underpayments, and other irregularities. Confer with legal counsel on claims requiring litigation.

13-1031.02—Insurance Adjusters, Examiners, and Investigators—Investigate, analyze, and determine the extent of insurance company's liability concerning personal, casualty, or property loss or damages, and attempt to effect settlement with

(continued)

TABLE 3.4 (continued)

claimants. Correspond with or interview medical specialists, agents, witnesses, or claimants to compile information. Calculate benefit payments and approve payment of claims within a certain monetary limit.

13-1032.00—Insurance Appraisers, Auto Damage—Appraise automobile or other vehicle damage to determine cost of repair for insurance claim settlement and seek agreement with automotive repair shop on cost of repair. Prepare insurance forms to indicate repair cost or cost estimates and recommendations.

13-1071.00—Employment, Recruitment, and Placement Specialists—Recruit and place workers.

13-1071.02—Personnel Recruiters—Seek out, interview, and screen applicants to fill existing and future job openings and promote career opportunities within an organization.

13-1072.00—Compensation, Benefits, and Job Analysis Specialists—Conduct programs of compensation and benefits and job analysis for employer. May specialize in specific areas, such as position classification and pension programs.

13-1121.00—Meeting and Convention Planners—Coordinate activities of staff and convention personnel to make arrangements for group meetings and conventions.

13-2021.01—Assessors—Appraise real and personal property to determine its fair value. May assess taxes in accordance with prescribed schedules.

13-2021.02—Appraisers, Real Estate—Appraise real property to determine its value for purchase, sales, investment, mortgage, or loan purposes.

13-2031.00—Budget Analysts—Examine budget estimates for completeness, accuracy, and conformance with procedures and regulations. Analyze budgeting and accounting reports for the purpose of maintaining expenditure controls.

13-2041.00—Credit Analysts—Analyze current credit data and financial statements of individuals or firms to determine the degree of risk involved in extending credit or lending money. Prepare reports with this credit information for use in decision-making.

13-2051.00—Financial Analysts—Conduct quantitative analyses of information affecting investment programs of public or private institutions.

13-2053.00—Insurance Underwriters—Review individual applications for insurance to evaluate degree of risk involved and determine acceptance of applications.

13-2061.00—Financial Examiners—Enforce or ensure compliance with laws and regulations governing financial and securities institutions and financial and real estate transactions. May examine, verify correctness of, or establish authenticity of records.

13-2072.00—Loan Officers—Evaluate, authorize, or recommend approval of commercial, real estate, or credit loans. Advise borrowers on financial status and methods of payments. Includes mortgage loan officers and agents, collection analysts, loan servicing officers, and loan underwriters.

19-3021.00—Market Research Analysts—Research market conditions in local, regional, or national areas to determine potential sales of a product or service. May gather information on competitors, prices, sales, and methods of marketing and distribution. May use survey results to create a marketing campaign based on regional preferences and buying habits.

41-1011.00—First-Line Supervisors/Managers of Retail Sales Workers—Directly supervise sales workers in a retail establishment or department. Duties may include management functions, such as purchasing, budgeting, accounting, and personnel work, in addition to supervisory duties.

41-2031.00—Retail Salespersons—Sell merchandise, such as furniture, motor vehicles, appliances, or apparel in a retail establishment.

41-3011.00—Advertising Sales Agents—Sell or solicit advertising, including graphic arts, advertising space in publications, custom-made signs, or TV and radio advertising time. May obtain leases for outdoor advertising sites or persuade retailers to use sales promotion display items.

41-3021.00—Insurance Sales Agents—Sell life, property, casualty, health, automotive, or other types of insurance. May refer clients to independent brokers, work as an independent broker, or be employed by an insurance company.

41-4011.03—Sales Representatives, Electrical/Electronic—Sell electrical, electronic, or related products or services, such as communication equipment, radiographic-inspection equipment and services, ultrasonic equipment, electronics parts, computers, and EDP systems.

41-4011.05—Sales Representatives, Medical—Sell medical equipment, products, and services. Does not include pharmaceutical sales representatives.

41-9022.00—Real Estate Sales Agents—Rent, buy, or sell property for clients. Perform duties, such as study property listings, interview prospective clients, accompany clients to property site, discuss conditions of sale, and draw up real estate contracts. Includes agents who represent the buyer.

TABLE 3.4 (continued)

43-1011.01—First-Line Supervisors, Customer Service—Supervise and coordinate activities of workers involved in providing customer service.

43-1011.02—First-Line Supervisors, Administrative Support—Supervise and coordinate activities of workers involved in providing administrative support.

43-4051.00—Customer Service Representatives—Interact with customers to provide information in response to inquiries about products and services and to handle and resolve complaints.

43-4161.00—Human Resources Assistants, Except Payroll and Timekeeping—Compile and keep personnel records. Record data for each employee, such as address, weekly earnings, absences, amount of sales or production, supervisory reports on ability, and date of and reason for termination. Compile and type reports from employment records. File employment records. Search employee files and furnish information to authorized persons.

Other Job Titles, Brief Descriptions, and O*NET-SOC Codes

13-1041.01—Environmental Compliance Inspectors—Inspect and investigate sources of pollution to protect the public and environment and ensure conformance with federal, state, and local regulations and ordinances.

13-1041.02—Licensing Examiners and Inspectors—Examine, evaluate, and investigate eligibility for, conformity with, or liability under licenses or permits.

13-1051.00—Cost Estimators—Prepare cost estimates for product manufacturing, construction projects, or services to aid management in bidding on or determining price of product or service. May specialize according to particular service performed or type of product manufactured.

15-1081.00—Network Systems and Data Communications Analysts—Analyze, design, test, and evaluate network systems, such as local area networks (LAN), wide area networks (WAN), Internet, intranet, and other data communications systems. Perform network modeling, analysis, and planning. Research and recommend network and data communications hardware and software. Includes telecommunications specialists who deal with the interfacing of computer and communications equipment. May supervise computer programmers.

15-2031.00—Operations Research Analysts—Formulate and apply mathematical modeling and other optimizing methods using a computer to develop and interpret information that assists management with decision making, policy formulation, or other managerial functions. May develop related software, service, or products. Frequently concentrates on collecting and analyzing data and developing decision support software. May develop and supply optimal time, cost, or logistics networks for program evaluation, review, or implementation.

15-2091.00—Mathematical Technicians—Apply standardized mathematical formulas, principles, and methodology to technological problems in engineering and physical sciences in relation to specific industrial and research objectives, processes, equipment, and products.

17-2111.01—Industrial Safety and Health Engineers—Plan, implement, and coordinate safety programs, requiring application of engineering principles and technology, to prevent or correct unsafe environmental working conditions.

17-2111.03—Product Safety Engineers—Develop and conduct tests to evaluate product safety levels and recommend measures to reduce or eliminate hazards.

19-3051.00—Urban and Regional Planners—Develop comprehensive plans and programs for use of land and physical facilities of local jurisdictions, such as towns, cities, counties, and metropolitan areas.

19-4091.00—Environmental Science and Protection Technicians, Including Health—Performs laboratory and field tests to monitor the environment and investigate sources of pollution, including those that affect health. Under direction of an environmental scientist or specialist, may collect samples of gases, soil, water, and other materials for testing and take corrective actions as assigned.

21-2021.00—Directors, Religious Activities and Education—Direct and coordinate activities of a denominational group to meet religious needs of students. Plan, direct, or coordinate church school programs designed to promote religious education among church membership. May provide counseling and guidance relative to marital, health, financial, and religious problems.

25-4011.00—Archivists—Appraise, edit, and direct safekeeping of permanent records and historically valuable documents. Participate in research activities based on archival materials.

25-4012.00—Curators—Administer affairs of museum and conduct research programs. Direct instructional, research, and public service activities of institution.

25-4013.00—Museum Technicians and Conservators—Prepare specimens, such as fossils, skeletal parts, lace, and textiles, for museum collection and exhibits. May restore documents or install, arrange, and exhibit materials.

(continued)

TABLE 3.4 (continued)

25-4031.00—Library Technicians—Assist librarians by helping readers in the use of library catalogs, databases, and indexes to locate books and other materials; and by answering questions that require only brief consultation of standard reference. Compile records; sort and shelve books; remove or repair damaged books; register patrons; check materials in and out of the circulation process. Replace materials in shelving area (stacks) or files. Includes bookmobile drivers who operate bookmobiles or light trucks that pull trailers to specific locations on a predetermined schedule and assist with providing services in mobile libraries.

27-2012.03—Program Directors—Direct and coordinate activities of personnel engaged in preparation of radio or television station program schedules and programs, such as sports or news.

27-2012.05—Technical Directors/Managers—Coordinate activities of technical departments, such as taping, editing, engineering, and maintenance, to produce radio or television programs.

27-3021.00—Broadcast News Analysts—Analyze, interpret, and broadcast news received from various sources.

27-3022.00—Reporters and Correspondents—Collect and analyze facts about newsworthy events by interview, investigation, or observation. Report and write stories for newspaper, news magazine, radio, or television.

27-3031.00—Public Relations Specialists—Engage in promoting or creating goodwill for individuals, groups, or organizations by writing or selecting favorable publicity material and releasing it through various communications media. May prepare and arrange displays, and make speeches.

27-3041.00—Editors—Perform variety of editorial duties, such as laying out, indexing, and revising content of written materials, in preparation for final publication.

27-3042.00—Technical Writers—Write technical materials, such as equipment manuals, appendices, or operating and maintenance instructions. May assist in layout work.

27-3043.04—Copy Writers—Write advertising copy for use by publication or broadcast media to promote sale of goods and services.

29-2051.00—Dietetic Technicians—Assist dietitians in the provision of food service and nutritional programs. Under the supervision of dietitians, may plan and produce meals based on established guidelines, teach principles of food and nutrition, or counsel individuals.

29-2071.00—Medical Records and Health Information Technicians—Compile, process, and maintain medical records of hospital and clinic patients in a manner consistent with medical, administrative, ethical, legal, and regulatory requirements of the health care system. Process, maintain, compile, and report patient information for health requirements and standards.

31-1011.00—Home Health Aides—Provide routine, personal health care, such as bathing, dressing, or grooming, to elderly, convalescent, or disabled persons in the home of patients or in a residential care facility.

31-1012.00—Nursing Aides, Orderlies, and Attendants—Provide basic patient care under direction of nursing staff. Perform duties, such as feed, bathe, dress, groom, or move patients, or change linens.

31-9096.00—Veterinary Assistants and Laboratory Animal Caretakers—Feed, water, and examine pets and other nonfarm animals for signs of illness, disease, or injury in laboratories and animal hospitals and clinics. Clean and disinfect cages and work areas, and sterilize laboratory and surgical equipment. May provide routine post-operative care, administer medication orally or topically, or prepare samples for laboratory examination under the supervision of veterinary or laboratory animal technologists or technicians, veterinarians, or scientists.

33-9021.00—Private Detectives and Investigators—Detect occurrences of unlawful acts or infractions of rules in private establishment, or seek, examine, and compile information for client.

33-9032.00—Security Guards—Guard, patrol, or monitor premises to prevent theft, violence, or infractions of rules.

39-9032.00—Recreation Workers—Conduct recreation activities with groups in public, private, or volunteer agencies or recreation facilities. Organize and promote activities, such as arts and crafts, sports, games, music, dramatics, social recreation, camping, and hobbies, taking into account the needs and interests of individual members.

43-4111.00—Interviewers, Except Eligibility and Loan—Interview persons by telephone, mail, in person, or by other means for the purpose of completing forms, applications, or questionnaires. Ask specific questions, record answers, and assist persons with completing form. May sort, classify, and file forms.

43-6011.00—Executive Secretaries and Administrative Assistants—Provide high-level administrative support by conducting research, preparing statistical reports, handling information requests, and performing clerical functions such as preparing correspondence, receiving visitors, arranging conference calls, and scheduling meetings. May also train and supervise lower-level clerical staff.

TABLE 3.4 (continued)

43-9011.00—Computer Operators—Monitor and control electronic computer and peripheral electronic data processing equipment to process business, scientific, engineering, and other data according to operating instructions. May enter commands at a computer terminal and set controls on computer and peripheral devices. Monitor and respond to operating and error messages.

53-6041.00—Traffic Technicians—Conduct field studies to determine traffic volume, speed, effectiveness of signals, adequacy of lighting, and other factors influencing traffic conditions, under direction of traffic engineer.

Source: National O*NET™ Consortium (2001, May). *O*NET occupational listings.* Raleigh, NC: Author.

parameters, but also offers tips for how to deal with this challenge. Table 3.5 highlights the differences between college and the workplace.

The challenges are numerous! In thinking about how to prepare for this transition, Hettich (2004, pp. 8–9) provides concrete advice on strategies you can pursue while still an undergraduate student. His suggestions include:

- Complete courses that focus directly on specific organizational aspects of the workplace, such as management, leadership, communication and group skills, organizational behavior, the sociology of organizations, career planning, and human resources.
- Enroll in workshops, seminars, or courses that focus on self-development, leadership, conflict management, team building, interpersonal communication, time management, stress management, and similar professional skills.
- Join clubs, sports, and campus organizations where collaboration, teamwork, conflict, communication, and leadership are practiced as constructive tools.
- Complete internships and perform volunteer work.

TABLE 3.5 Graduates Perceived Differences Between College and Workplace

College	Workplace
Frequent and concrete feedback	Feedback infrequent and not specific
Some freedom to set a schedule	Less freedom or control over schedule
Frequent breaks and time off	Limited time off
Choose performance level	"A" level work expected continuously
Correct answers usually available	Few right answers
Passive participation permitted	Active participation in initiative expected
Independent thinking supported	Independent thinking often discouraged
Environment of personal support	Usually less personal support
Focus on personal development	Focus on getting results for organization
Structured courses and curriculum	Much less structure, fewer directions
Few changes in routine	Often constant and unexpected changes
Personal control over time	Responds to supervisor's directions
Individual effort and performance	Often, team effort and performance
Intellectual challenge	Organizational and people challenges
Acquisition of knowledge	Acquisition and application of knowledge
Professors	Supervisors

Source: Hettich, P. I. (2004, April). *From college to corporate culture: You're a freshman again.* Paper presented at the Midwestern Psychological Association meeting, Chicago, IL. Adapted from Holton (1998).

- Collect evidence of curricular and cocurricular achievements, including papers, projects, awards, and performance evaluations, and organize them in an electronic portfolio that monitors personal progress and serves as a tool in job searches.
- Recognize that grades, test scores, and GPAs are often skewed predictors of intelligence in the workplace.
- Remember that teachers cannot give students all the answers because we do not know them.

There are multiple opportunities for success in the workplace, but there are matching challenges as well. We hope this chapter has alerted you to some of the opportunities; the next chapter provides strategies for how to pursue the career that you want. If financial considerations are your primary objective, many areas of psychology may not satisfy your needs. Serious career exploration and an understanding of your own value system will help you find a suitable career match. Other chapters of this book also help you to find where your "niche" might be. Our suggestion—be as honest as you can with yourself from the start, and you will probably have less grief in the long run. You are employable with a bachelor's degree in psychology! Combs (2000, p. 14) bluntly summarizes the relationship between selecting your major and getting a good job: "No matter what you major in, if you can't answer the phone, make a presentation, do a spreadsheet, or write a business letter, nobody needs you."

Exercise #3: The O*Net System

Previously in this chapter we presented brief job descriptions of over 100 potential occupations of interest for psychology majors. This information comes from the O*NET system (Occupational Information Network). For each occupation, there is actually detailed information available, covering numerous job-related areas. Below we have re-created the information available for one position, recreational therapist. For this exercise, visit the O*NET Web site (online.onetcenter.org) and explore job occupations that interest you. There are even tools available to help you explore what your career interests are.

Summary Report for:
29-1125.00 - Recreational Therapists

Plan, direct, or coordinate medically approved recreation programs for patients in hospitals, nursing homes, or other institutions. Activities include sports, trips, dramatics, social activities, and arts and crafts. May assess a patient's condition and recommend appropriate recreational activity.

TASKS

- Observe, analyze, and record patients' participation, reactions, and progress during treatment sessions, modifying treatment programs as needed.
- Develop treatment plan to meet needs of patient, based on needs assessment, patient interests, and objectives of therapy.
- Encourage clients with special needs and circumstances to acquire new skills and get involved in health-promoting leisure activities, such as sports, games, arts and crafts, and gardening.
- Counsel and encourage patients to develop leisure activities.

- Confer with members of treatment team to plan and evaluate therapy programs.
- Conduct therapy sessions to improve patients' mental and physical well-being.
- Instruct patient in activities and techniques, such as sports, dance, music, art or relaxation techniques, designed to meet their specific physical or psychological needs.
- Obtain information from medical records, medical staff, family members, and the patients themselves to assess patients' capabilities, needs, and interests.
- Plan, organize, direct, and participate in treatment programs and activities to facilitate patients' rehabilitation, help them integrate into the community, and prevent further medical problems.
- Prepare and submit reports and charts to treatment team to reflect patients' reactions and evidence of progress or regression.

KNOWLEDGE

Psychology—Knowledge of human behavior and performance; individual differences in ability, personality, and interests; learning and motivation; psychological research methods; and the assessment and treatment of behavioral and affective disorders.

Customer and Personal Service—Knowledge of principles and processes for providing customer and personal services. This includes customer needs assessment, meeting quality standards for services, and evaluation of customer satisfaction.

Therapy and Counseling—Knowledge of principles, methods, and procedures for diagnosis, treatment, and rehabilitation of physical and mental dysfunctions, and for career counseling and guidance.

Sociology and Anthropology—Knowledge of group behavior and dynamics, societal trends and influences, human migrations, ethnicity, cultures and their history and origins.

Education and Training—Knowledge of principles and methods for curriculum and training design, teaching and instruction for individuals and groups, and the measurement of training effects.

English Language—Knowledge of the structure and content of the English language including the meaning and spelling of words, rules of composition, and grammar.

Fine Arts—Knowledge of the theory and techniques required to compose, produce, and perform works of music, dance, visual arts, drama, and sculpture.

SKILLS

Social Perceptiveness—Being aware of others' reactions and understanding why they react as they do.

Active Listening—Giving full attention to what other people are saying, taking time to understand the points being made, asking questions as appropriate, and not interrupting at inappropriate times.

Writing—Communicating effectively in writing as appropriate for the needs of the audience.

Speaking—Talking to others to convey information effectively.

Reading Comprehension—Understanding written sentences and paragraphs in work-related documents.

Monitoring—Monitoring/Assessing performance of yourself, other individuals, or organizations to make improvements or take corrective action.

Service Orientation—Actively looking for ways to help people.

Coordination—Adjusting actions in relation to others' actions.

Time Management—Managing one's own time and the time of others.

Learning Strategies—Selecting and using training/instructional methods and procedures appropriate for the situation when learning or teaching new things.

ABILITIES

Oral Expression—The ability to communicate information and ideas in speaking so others will understand.

Oral Comprehension—The ability to listen to and understand information and ideas presented through spoken words and sentences.

Inductive Reasoning—The ability to combine pieces of information to form general rules or conclusions (includes finding a relationship among seemingly unrelated events).

Problem Sensitivity—The ability to tell when something is wrong or is likely to go wrong. It does not involve solving the problem, only recognizing there is a problem.

Speech Clarity—The ability to speak clearly so others can understand you.

Near Vision—The ability to see details at close range (within a few feet of the observer).

Written Expression—The ability to communicate information and ideas in writing so others will understand.

Deductive Reasoning—The ability to apply general rules to specific problems to produce answers that make sense.

Originality—The ability to come up with unusual or clever ideas about a given topic or situation, or to develop creative ways to solve a problem.

Written Comprehension—The ability to read and understand information and ideas presented in writing.

WORK ACTIVITIES

Assisting and Caring for Others—Providing personal assistance, medical attention, emotional support, or other personal care to others such as coworkers, customers, or patients.

Scheduling Work and Activities—Scheduling events, programs, and activities, as well as the work of others.

Getting Information—Observing, receiving, and otherwise obtaining information from all relevant sources.

Thinking Creatively—Developing, designing, or creating new applications, ideas, relationships, systems, or products, including artistic contributions.

Monitor Processes, Materials, or Surroundings—Monitoring and reviewing information from materials, events, or the environment, to detect or assess problems.

Organizing, Planning, and Prioritizing Work—Developing specific goals and plans to prioritize, organize, and accomplish your work.

Identifying Objects, Actions, and Events—Identifying information by categorizing, estimating, recognizing differences or similarities, and detecting changes in circumstances or events.

Communicating with Supervisors, Peers, or Subordinates—Providing information to supervisors, coworkers, and subordinates by telephone, in written form, e-mail, or in person.

Making Decisions and Solving Problems—Analyzing information and evaluating results to choose the best solution and solve problems.

Documenting/Recording Information—Entering, transcribing, recording, storing, or maintaining information in written or electronic/magnetic form.

WORK CONTEXT

Face-to-Face Discussions—How often do you have to have face-to-face discussions with individuals or teams in this job?

Work with Work Group or Team—How important is it to work with others in a group or team in this job?

Contact with Others—How much does this job require the worker to be in contact with others (face-to-face, by telephone, or otherwise) in order to perform it?

Physical Proximity—To what extent does this job require the worker to perform job tasks in close physical proximity to other people?

Deal with Physically Aggressive People—How frequently does this job require the worker to deal with physical aggression of violent individuals?

Structured versus Unstructured Work—To what extent is this job structured for the worker, rather than allowing the worker to determine tasks, priorities, and goals?

Freedom to Make Decisions—How much decision-making freedom, without supervision, does the job offer?

Telephone—How often do you have telephone conversations in this job?

Exposed to Disease or Infections—How often does this job require exposure to disease/infections?

Time Pressure—How often does this job require the worker to meet strict deadlines?

Job Zone

Title	Job Zone Four: Considerable Preparation Needed
Overall Experience	A minimum of two to four years of work-related skill, knowledge, or experience is needed for these occupations. For example, an accountant must complete four years of college and work for several years in accounting to be considered qualified.
Job Training	Employees in these occupations usually need several years of work-related experience, on-the-job training, and/or vocational training.
Job Zone Examples	Many of these occupations involve coordinating, supervising, managing, or training others. Examples include accountants, chefs and head cooks, computer programmers, historians, pharmacists, and police detectives.
SVP Range	(7.0 to < 8.0)
Education	Most of these occupations require a four-year bachelor's degree, but some do not.

Interests

Social—Social occupations frequently involve working with, communicating with, and teaching people. These occupations often involve helping or providing service to others.

Artistic—Artistic occupations frequently involve working with forms, designs, and patterns. They often require self-expression and the work can be done without following a clear set of rules.

Realistic—Realistic occupations frequently involve work activities that include practical, hands-on problems and solutions. They often deal with plants, animals, and real-world materials like wood, tools, and machinery. Many of the occupations require working outside, and do not involve a lot of paperwork or working closely with others.

Work Styles

Concern for Others—Job requires being sensitive to others' needs and feelings and being understanding and helpful on the job.

Self-control—Job requires maintaining composure, keeping emotions in check, controlling anger, and avoiding aggressive behavior, even in very difficult situations.

Cooperation—Job requires being pleasant with others on the job and displaying a good-natured, cooperative attitude.

Integrity—Job requires being honest and ethical.

Social Orientation—Job requires preferring to work with others rather than alone, and being personally connected with others on the job.

Adaptability/Flexibility—Job requires being open to change (positive or negative) and to considerable variety in the workplace.

Dependability—Job requires being reliable, responsible, and dependable, and fulfilling obligations.

Innovation—Job requires creativity and alternative thinking to develop new ideas for and answers to work-related problems.

Stress Tolerance—Job requires accepting criticism and dealing calmly and effectively with high stress situations.

Leadership—Job requires a willingness to lead, take charge, and offer opinions and direction.

Work Values

Achievement—Occupations that satisfy this work value are results oriented and allow employees to use their strongest abilities, giving them a feeling of accomplishment. Corresponding needs are Ability Utilization and Achievement.

Relationships—Occupations that satisfy this work value allow employees to provide service to others and work with coworkers in a friendly noncompetitive environment. Corresponding needs are Coworkers, Moral Values and Social Service.

Related Occupations

O*NET-SOC Code	O*NET-SOC Title	Reports (help)		
21-1021.00	Child, Family, and School Social Workers	Summary	Details	Custom
29-1122.00	Occupational Therapists	Summary	Details	Custom
29-1123.00	Physical Therapists	Summary	Details	Custom

CHAPTER 4

Pursuing Bachelor's-Level Options

If you have been following along until now, you know something about the opportunities afforded to you by your undergraduate education. You also know that a college-to-career transition may be more difficult than expected. Most undergraduate psychology majors do *not* go to graduate school, but they pursue a good job with their bachelor's degree in psychology. This chapter is dedicated to providing you with tips and ideas on how to facilitate your job search. In it you will find tips on preparing your resume, interviewing skills and potential questions, and strategies for securing strong letters of recommendation. We did not design these materials to provide comprehensive information on every job application situation—there are plenty of good resources available, both in print and on the Internet.

THE COMPLEXITY OF FINDING A JOB

At first glance, the job search may seem overwhelming. There are many components to the job search, each with its own level of importance, and each having consequences if not satisfactorily completed. In this chapter we are going to take you through, step by step, the basic components you need for the job application process. It appears that this process is one that you will revisit from time to time. According to Chen (2004), college graduates will have eight different jobs during their lifetime, which will require work in three different professions or occupations. As an undergraduate, you can start to build toward your future career searches. You can start a resume. You can participate in activities that not only help you build a strong resume, but also help you build mentoring relationships that can lead to letters of recommendation. You can also take classes and participate in class projects that help build interpersonal skills (highly valued by employers, by the way) that will lead to success on interviews. What do we mean by interpersonal skills? Yancey, Clarkson, Baxa, and Clarkson (2003) articulated a cogent list of interpersonal competencies: (a) effectively translating and conveying information, (b) being able to accurately interpret other people's emotions, (c) being sensitive to other people's feelings, (d) calmly arriving at resolutions to conflict, (e) avoiding gossip, and (f) being polite. Focus on these interpersonal skills while you are an undergraduate, and you'll be well on your way to success.

In some situations, you will be asked to fill out a job application. Be sure to take every step of this process seriously. Your application tells the employer about (a) your work habits, (b) how well you follow instructions, (c) your character, (d) your personal achievements, (e) your job performance, and (f) your potential (Idaho Department of Labor, 1998). Instructions from the Idaho Department of Labor (1998) also emphasize that neatness counts. You also need to be completely accurate and honest, double-check your application, and notify those persons whom you plan to use as references. The information available about psychology baccalaureates in particular suggests that the three most successful methods of finding jobs were through classified advertisements (21%), a family member or friend (9%), or submitted unsolicited resumes (7%) (Waters, 1998). Landrum (1998) suggests that you tap into connections that you might already have. Former employers, family connections, and others can be extremely helpful in getting your "foot-in-the-door." Internships often lead to possible job opportunities after graduation; you get a look at how it would be to work in that environment, and the employer gets a sneak peek at your work habits, skill, and potential. It is also important to remember that you are not going to get the perfect job with the perfect salary the first time you apply. You need to be patient as you build your own set of skills and abilities, establish your track record, hone your work ethic, and develop your work history.

Success Stories

Dr. Edie Woods
Madonna University

[A story from one of Edie's students.] May 1, 2004 was one day that I will never forget because it was the day that I *finally* graduated with high honors and received my BS in Psychology! I emphasized the word finally because it took me approximately 20 years to complete my undergraduate years.

My childhood was filled with overwhelming loneliness. By the time I was 15 years old I became a teenage runaway. I tried to go back to school to finish high school. I can remember as far back as being in first grade and feeling that I was lost. By the time I was half way through my senior year in high school I was placed in a tenth grade math class. I walked out of that math class, and I walked out of the high school. I never went back to that high school and no one ever asked me why. I did find the strength to go back to night school a few years later and I was able to complete my high school education. I began classes at a local community college and by the time I was 19 I was married. Within the first year of my marriage I was being physically abused and I eventually dropped out of college. I was missing too many classes because of the abuse. I was divorced and became a single mother to two children that were both under the age of five. I was in the process of slowly trying to rebuild my life. I started taking classes again at the local college that I had previously attended. I was remarried at the age of 28 and had my third child a few years later. I was in the process of going back to college but I unexpectedly became a full-time stepmother to my husband's three young children.

I spent most of my days during the spring and summer of 2000 helping my mother who was dying from cancer. I remember looking at my mother one day and I thought about how rapidly her life had changed when her cancer came out of remission. I thought about how I would want to look back on my life if I was in my mother's place. I knew without a doubt that I wanted to go back and finish working on my degree. It was a very exciting time for me when I walked back into Madonna University as a full-time student. Within that first month back at school my father had a massive heart attack and passed away in the snow in his backyard. I was devastated by his unexpected death. Nineteen days later the man who called me "his bride" for 20 years filed for divorce and I never saw it coming. I really wasn't sure how I was going to continue with my classes, but with my own inner determination and strength, and with the support and understanding of some of my professors I was encouraged to continue.

As I was walking up to the stage on the day of my graduation, three of my professors that I have a tremendous amount of respect for were all standing at the bottom of the stage. Each person in his or her own unique way had helped me make it to that day. My children were all there to see me graduate, too. I am currently working on my masters in clinical psychology. I do know that it's never too late and one is never too old to follow one's dream.

PREPARING YOUR RESUME, WITH SAMPLES

Because there are many resume preparation books on the market and Web sites dedicated to this process, we will provide some general tips and ideas to help you prepare a superior resume. A resume should answer two important questions for a potential employer: (1) what can you do for me (answered in career objectives) and (2) why should you be considered for this job (answered in educational history and work experience) (La Sierra University, 2000). The resume continues to be an important tool in determining whether a job applicant gets an interview with an employer (Coxford, 1998). Lore (1997) found that only one interview is granted for every 200 resumes received by the average employer. Lore goes on to suggest that resumes are typically scanned in 10 to 20 seconds, and not thoroughly read. Thus, an employer's decision is going to be made on the first impression of the resume, which means that the top half of the first page is critical. If the first few lines do not catch the interest of the reader, then the opportunity is lost.

Lore (1997) suggests two general sections of the resume. In the first section, make the claims and assertions about your abilities, qualities, and achievements. In the second section, present the evidence in support of the statements you made in the first section. Within these two sections, you will have multiple parts of the resume. Some of these parts (Coxford, 1998) should include the sections given in Table 4.1.

If you have just received your bachelor's degree in psychology, you may have a rela-tively short resume. That's OK—take that opportunity to go into some detail about the experiences you have had. Table 4.2 contains a list of action verbs you can use to accurately describe the types of duties and responsibilities you held as an undergraduate (and before, if applicable). A number of resources are available that provide tips on resume preparation. Taken from Career-Mosaic (1997) and JobWeb (2001), Table 4.3 offers some of the most common resume tips. These are the basics that must be mastered prior to sending out your resume to anyone.

Some of these suggestions are based on the practice of companies that scan resumes; you do not want to do anything on paper that will make it more difficult for companies to read scanned copies of your resume. In fact, if you really want to be prepared, scan a copy of your resume yourself, and then print the file on your computer. Can you read all of the print? Is the font readable, or too small? Making sure your scanned resume is readable would demonstrate an impressive level of attention to detail to any employer. The practice of sending a resume via e-mail is a requirement that is becoming much more prevalent. It is the obligation of the person sending the resume to make sure that his or her computer system/program is compatible with that of the company (generally speaking, Microsoft Word is the dominant word processor today—avoid WordPerfect or Microsoft Works files). If the company cannot open a resume, they typically do not send an e-mail or give you a call to let you know.

On the following pages, you will find some sample resumes from undergraduate psychology majors (Figure 4.1). Note that the identities of the actual persons have been changed. You will note that these two resumes are from students in different parts of their careers. You would be surprised at the variability of resumes submitted to organizations.

By the way, never, ever, fabricate information on your resume. Odds are, it will come back to haunt you eventually, even if you get away with it for a while. Read on page 50 for a very public example of this type of mistake.

TABLE 4.1 Potential Resume Sections

Name, address, city, state, phone number, and e-mail address where you can be reached

Position objective statement and summary of qualifications

Employment and education history, including professional training and affiliations

Military service history (if applicable)

Licenses and certificates (if applicable)

Knowledge of foreign languages

Publications and professional presentations

Special accomplishments

Statement that references and work sample are available upon request

TABLE 4.2 Action Verbs

accelerated	attained	compared	determined	exempted	illustrated	localized	penalized
acclimated	attracted	compiled	developed	exercised	illuminated	located	perceived
accompanied	audited	completed	devised	expanded	implemented	maintained	performed
accomplished	augmented	complied	devoted	expedited	improved	managed	permitted
achieved	authored	composed	diagrammed	explained	improvised	mapped	persuaded
acquired	authorized	computed	directed	exposed	inaugurated	marketed	phased out
acted	automated	conceived	disclosed	extended	indoctrinated	maximized	pinpointed
activated	awarded	conceptualized	discounted	extracted	increased	measured	pioneered
actuated	avail	concluded	discovered	extrapolated	incurred	mediated	placed
adapted	balanced	condensed	dispatched	facilitated	induced	merchandised	planned
added	bargained	conducted	displayed	familiarized	influenced	merged	polled
addressed	borrowed	conferred	dissembled	fashioned	informed	met	prepared
adhered	bought	consolidated	distinguished	fielded	initiated	minimized	presented
adjusted	broadened	constructed	distributed	figured	innovated	modeled	preserved
administered	budgeted	consulted	diversified	financed	inquired	moderated	presided
admitted	built	contracted	divested	fit	inspected	modernized	prevented
adopted	calculated	contrasted	documented	focused	inspired	modified	priced
advanced	canvassed	contributed	doubled	forecasted	installed	monitored	printed
advertised	capitalized	contrived	drafted	formalized	instigated	motivated	prioritized
advised	captured	controlled	earned	formed	instilled	moved	probed
advocated	carried out	converted	eased	formulated	instituted	multiplied	processed
aided	cast	convinced	edited	fortified	instructed	named	procured
aired	cataloged	coordinated	effected	found	insured	narrated	produced
affected	centralized	corrected	elected	founded	interfaced	negotiated	profiled
allocated	challenged	corresponded	eliminated	framed	interpreted	noticed	programmed
altered	chaired	counseled	employed	fulfilled	interviewed	nurtured	projected
amended	changed	counted	enabled	functioned	introduced	observed	promoted
amplified	channeled	created	encouraged	furnished	invented	obtained	prompted
analyzed	charted	critiqued	endorsed	gained	inventoried	offered	proposed
answered	checked	cultivated	enforced	gathered	invested	offset	proved
anticipated	chose	cut	engaged	gauged	investigated	opened	provided
appointed	circulated	debugged	engineered	gave	invited	operated	publicized
appraised	clarified	decided	enhanced	generated	involved	operationalized	published
approached	classified	decentralized	enlarged	governed	isolated	orchestrated	purchased
approved	cleared	decreased	enriched	graded	issued	ordered	pursued
arbitrated	closed	deferred	entered	granted	joined	organized	quantified
arranged	co-authored	defined	entertained	greeted	judged	oriented	quoted
ascertained	cold called	delegated	established	grouped	launched	originated	raised
asked	collaborated	delivered	estimated	guided	lectured	overhauled	ranked
assembled	collected	demonstrated	evaluated	handled	led	oversaw	rated
assigned	combined	depreciated	examined	headed	lightened	paid	reacted
assumed	commissioned	described	exceeded	hired	liquidated	participated	read
assessed	committed	designated	exchanged	hosted	litigated	passed	received
assisted	communicated	designed	executed	identified	lobbied	patterned	recommended

TABLE 4.2 (*Contd.*)

reconciled	remedied	retrieved	sold	stressed	systematized	translated	viewed
recorded	remodeled	revamped	solved	structured	tabulated	transported	visited
recovered	renegotiated	revealed	spearheaded	studied	tailored	traveled	weighed
recruited	reorganized	reversed	specified	submitted	targeted	treated	welcomed
rectified	replaced	reviewed	speculated	substantiated	taught	tripled	widened
redesigned	repaired	revised	spoke	substituted	terminated	uncovered	witnessed
reduced	reported	revitalized	spread	suggested	tested	undertook	won
referred	represented	rewarded	stabilized	summarized	testified	unified	worked
refined	requested	routed	staffed	superseded	tightened	united	wrote
regained	researched	safeguarded	staged	supervised	took	updated	
regulated	resolved	salvaged	standardized	supplied	traced	upgraded	
rehabilitated	responded	saved	steered	supported	traded	used	
reinforced	restored	scheduled	stimulated	surpassed	trained	utilized	
reinstated	restructured	screened	strategize	surveyed	transacted	validated	
rejected	resulted	secured	streamlined	synchronized	transferred	valued	
related	retained	simplified	strengthened	synthesized	transformed	verified	

Source: TMP Worldwide (1998). Action verbs to enhance your resume. Retrieved September 28, 1998 from http://www.aboutwork.com/rescov/resinfo/verbs.html.

TABLE 4.3 Resume Preparation Tips

Make the first impression count. A good resume may get you to the next stage of the process. A poor resume may stop you from going anywhere.

Keep your resume current. Make sure it has your new phone number, e-mail address, etc.

Make sure others proofread your resume before you show it to potential employers. Typographical and grammatical errors are **unacceptable**. Mistakes in your resume will cost you the opportunity to advance in the employment process.

Have your resume reviewed and critiqued by a career counselor, and also have your mentor in psychology review your resume for you.

Run a spell check and grammar check on your computer before showing your resume to anyone.

Find a competent friend (an English major would be handy here) to do a grammar review of your resume.

Then ask another friend to proofread it. The more sets of eyes that examine your resume, the better.

Be concise—try to limit yourself to 1–2 pages. If the employer sets a page limit, follow it exactly.

Use white or off-white paper.

Use standard size, 8.5"×11" paper.

Print on one side of the paper, using a font size between 10 and 14 points.

Use a nondecorative font (like Arial or Times New Roman), choose one font, and stick to it.

Avoid italics, script, and underlined words.

Don't use horizontal or vertical line, or shading.

Don't fold or staple your resume; if you must mail it, mail it in a large envelope.

Electronic resumes have different formatting demands. Many Web sites can assist you in the process of preparing a Web-friendly resume. It probably is worth noting that it is the *student's* responsibility to make sure that the company's equipment is compatible when sending an electronic resume.

Sheila A. Cardonicci

1234 Main Street   Boise, ID 83725   208-555-1212 (home)   208-555-2121 (cell)

thisisafakename@hotmail.com

Education

Boise State University - Boise, ID
B.A., Psychology May 2002
G.P.A.: 3.6/4.0 Major G.P.A.

Honors

Dean's List 2 Terms
Psi Chi - National Honor Society for Psychology

Summary of Qualifications

Trained in research methodologies and experienced in SPSS.
Three years experience as a research assistant.
Computer skills: SPSS software, Microsoft WordPerfect, Word, Power Point, Excel, Internet, Front Page, database searches, Pathways, and CdWeb.

Relevant Work Experience

3/03 to current
Medical Information Specialist for Saint Alphonsus Cancer Treatment Center Responsibilities: greeting and registering patients, scheduling appointments, filing and preparing patient charts for physicians, answering telephones, intranet searches, unit clerk experience and being receptive to the patient's needs.
Salary: $10.35/hour

8/02 to 5/03
Research coordinator for Dr. Jamie Goldenberg, Boise State University Responsibilities: conducting breast cancer behavior research experiments while corresponding with Mountain State Tumor Institute, entering and analyzing data using SPSS, creating measures, budgeting federal grant, generating a comprehensive literature review on breast cancer and breast self-exams, training and supervising undergraduate research assistants, presenting research, scheduling participants for research studies, and conducting psychological experiments.
Manuscript in progress Salary: $12.00/hour

5/00 to 3/03
Assistant Director for Precious Gifts Preschool
Responsibilities: employee payroll, managing accounts receivable and customer service, and assistant teacher.
Salary: $12.00/hour

FIGURE 4.1 Sample Resumes from Undergraduate Psychology Majors

Education Experience

1/01 to 5/02
Boise State University- Boise, ID Research Assistant
Performed Psych-Lit data collection, entry, and analysis, conducted psychological literature reviews and experiments, presented at the Boise State University Undergraduate Research Conference, Spring of 2002
Manuscript in progress

1/02 to 5/02
Boise State University - Boise, ID Teaching Assistant
Maintained two office hours weekly for tutoring, conducted study groups, proctored exams in the absence of the professor, presented guest lecture on Development to introductory psychology class

James Jorgensen

Current and Permanent Address:
5678 Elm Street
Boise, ID 83725
(208) 555-1212

OBJECTIVE

Seeking admittance to graduate studies in Marriage and Family Counseling for Fall 2004. Future employment objectives include counseling licensing, then employment in a group practice, government agency or public sector company.

EDUCATION

Bachelor of Arts - Psychology, December 2003
Boise State University, Boise, ID
GPA: 3.81/3.91 Major
Dean's List

Reed College 1976-1977
Portland, OR
GPA: 2.33

Mills College 1975-1976 and 1977-1978
Oakland, CA
GPA: 2.56

PERSONAL QUALIFICATIONS AND SKILLS

- Excellent interpersonal skills and ability to relate well with people from all walks of life.
- Highly motivated to succeed in graduate school and counseling profession due to maturity and life experiences; conscientious.
- Excellent written and oral communication skills.
- Computer literate; experienced with Psychlit, Microsoft Word, Word Perfect, Internet, Excel, DOS and Macintosh.
- Able to interpret statistical data and reports.
- Leadership abilities in academic arenas, employment and community service positions, and social activities.

EMPLOYMENT

Intern. Boise Police Department Victims' Services, Boise, ID (1/2002- 5/2002) Worked twelve hours per week with the staff Victim Witness Coordinators in case management; attended weekly interagency meetings for new cases; attended intake meetings and court hearings for victims and their families.

Volunteer. Boise School District, White Pine Elementary, Boise, ID (9/1999-present) Assisted in classroom tutoring and academic activities; held chairman positions twice for all-school functions.

Volunteer. Lakewood Guild, Boise, ID. (1998-1999). Held position of President of local community organization of 900 Lakewood homes in fund-raising for charitable donations, including running monthly meetings, organizing committees for various fund-raising events, publishing monthly newsletters and filing all legal and tax documents for this non-profit organization.

Volunteer. Cathedral of the Rockies Methodist Church, Boise, ID (9/1995-6/1996). Held position of head teacher for pre-school Sunday school program including lesson planning and weekly implementation, and directing department monthly meetings.

Accountant. Accountants-on-Call, Palo Alto, CA (5/1987-7/1992). Specialized in accounting positions at major firms in the San Francisco bay area that were relocating in-house accounting departments to other cities. These companies included Hewlett-Packard, Apple Computer, Alumax, and other corporations.

Manager of Finance. Nelson, Coulson and Associates, Inc., Denver, CO (9/1983-5/1987) Supervised and managed accounting department for large engineering consulting firm with one hundred million in annual revenues, including generating all financial reports, budgets and projections, weekly payroll, and managing one million dollar bank line-of-credit.

REFERENCES
Available Upon Request

U. of Notre Dame Football Coach Quits After Résumé Fabrications Are Disclosed

By WELCH SUGGS

George J. O'Leary, hired December 9 to coach the University of Notre Dame's football team, resigned late Thursday after admitting that he had lied about his academic and athletic background.

Mr. O'Leary's résumé and profiles of him published by Notre Dame and by the Georgia Institute of Technology, where he had coached since 1994, said that he had earned a master's degree in education at New York University in 1972. But officials there said they had no record of his receiving any degrees. Mr. O'Leary also claimed to have played football for three years at the University of New Hampshire, but a spokesman there said he was never on the team's roster.

After *The Union Leader* of Manchester, N.H., published an article on Thursday saying he had never played at New Hampshire, Mr. O'Leary tendered his resignation. On Friday, he released a statement confirming that at the beginning of his coaching career, he had lied about the matter and about his master's degree.

Many years ago, as a young married father, I sought to pursue my dream as a football coach," Mr. O'Leary said. "In seeking employment, I prepared a résumé that contained inaccuracies regarding my completion of course work for a master's degree and also my level of participation in football at my alma mater. These statements were never stricken from my résumé or biographical sketch in later years."

Mr. O'Leary began his college coaching career at Syracuse University, in 1980. A 1986 biographical sketch of him in the university's football media guide claims he earned three varsity letters at New Hampshire but does not mention an NYU degree. In 1987, he moved to Georgia Tech to be the Yellow Jackets' defensive coordinator, and in 1992 he and Georgia Tech's head coach, Bobby Ross, were hired by the San Diego Chargers, of the National Football League. In 1994, he returned to Georgia Tech as the head coach, a job he retained until Notre Dame hired him this month.

The biographies also say that Mr. O'Leary graduated from New Hampshire in 1968, when in fact he graduated in 1969, according to the spokesman.

Notre Dame's athletics director, Kevin White, had moved very quickly to hire Mr. O'Leary after firing the previous coach, Bob Davie, less than a week before. Mr. White reportedly contacted several other coaches, including Mike Bellotti of the University of Oregon and Tyrone Willingham of Stanford University, before coming to terms with the Georgia Tech coach.

I understand that these inaccuracies represent a very human failing," Mr. White said in a statement released Friday. "Nonetheless, they constitute a breach of trust that makes it impossible for us to go forward with our relationship."

Mr. White said he would resume the coaching search immediately.

Source: The Chronicle of Higher Education, Monday, December 17, 2001.

LETTERS OF RECOMMENDATION, WITH A SAMPLE

In many job application situations, you may be asked for one or more letters of recommendation (and letters of recommendation are a more typical requirement for graduate school applications, covered later). Plous (1998a) suggests that you should ask for recommendations from people who (a) have worked closely with you, (b) have known you long enough to know you fairly well, (c) have some expertise, (d) are senior and well known, if possible (e.g., department chair), (e) have a positive opinion of you and your abilities, and (f) have a warm and supportive personal style. Landrum (1998) and Wilson (1998) also emphasize that when you ask a faculty member or other professional for a letter of recommendation, ask for a *strong* letter of recommendation. Most faculty members would rather not write a letter than write a weak letter of recommendation. How do you ask for a strong letter—just like that—"Would you be willing to write me a strong letter of recommendation?"

Plous (1998a) also recommends that you give your letter writers plenty of lead time, at least 3 or 4 weeks. Then, about 1 week before the deadline, give your letter writer a gentle reminder about the upcoming due date for the letter of recommendation. You will want to provide your letter writers with a complete packet of materials—this packet needs to be well organized in order for all the letters to get where they need to go and get there on time. Table 4.4 includes some of the items you might be asked to provide.

How do you secure those strong letters of recommendation? You must be more than a good book student. Being involved outside of the classroom gives you well-rounded experiences; it also gives your letter writers something to write about. Future chapters highlight many of the ways you can become involved in your psychology education outside of the classroom. Table 4.5 from Appleby (1998) lists, in order of importance, ideas on how to secure a **strong** letter of recommendation.

TABLE 4.4 Items to be Included in Your Request for Letters of Recommendation

Current copy of your academic transcript; usually an unofficial or "student" copy is fine.

Copy of your academic vita that lists your achievements and accomplishments in the discipline (see Chapter 6) or a resume that summarizes your job history, skills, and abilities (see this chapter).

Pre-addressed (stamped) envelope for each letter, whether it goes back to you (the student), or goes directly to the place of employment (or graduate school); does this envelope need to be signed on the back? Remind your letter writers if it needs to be sealed and signed.

Any forms that the letter writer might be asked to submit with the letter. Be sure to sign the form where you need to, and sign the waiver.

Cover sheet to the letter writer that includes contact information if your letter writer needs to reach you, when you will submit your application (you don't want the letters to arrive before your application), the deadline for each letter, your career aspirations (i.e., personal statement will do), and information you would like emphasized in the letter.

Source: Plous, S. (1998a). Advice on letters of recommendation. Retrieved September 28, 1998, at http://www.wesleyan.edu/spn/recitips.htm.

TABLE 4.5 Strategies for Securing a Strong Letter of Recommendation

Deal effectively with a variety of people

Display appropriate interpersonal skills

Listen carefully and accurately

Show initiative and persistence

Exhibit effective time management

Hold high ethical standards and expect the same of others

Handle conflict successfully

TABLE 4.5 (*Contd.*)

Speak articulately and persuasively

Work productively as a member of a team

Plan and carry out projects successfully

Think logically and creatively

Remain open-minded during controversies

Identify and actualize personal potential

Write clearly and precisely

Adapt to organizational rules and procedures

Comprehend and retain key points from written materials

Gather and organize information from multiple sources

When faculty members are asked to write a strong letter of recommendation, and the student is a strong student, the letter is easy (and often a pleasure) to write. However, when faculty members are pressed to write for a student who is not so strong, what is not said in the letter may be as important as what is said. Figure 4.2, shows a sample of an actual letter the first author has written. The names and other identifying factors have been changed. The details in this letter make it valuable to those requesting the letter. Would you like this type of letter written about you?

INTERVIEW SKILLS, QUESTIONS, AND KNOCKOUT FACTORS

So you have written your resume, the resume did its job, and now you have landed that valuable interview. Before the interview, you need to do your homework—learn as much as you can about the company and about the job. What should you know about your potential employer? Appleby (1998b) suggests that you should know about the relative size and potential growth of the industry, the product line or services, information about management personnel and the headquarters, the competition, and recent items in the news. Also, you should know about training policies, relocation policies, price of stock (if applicable), typical career paths, and potential new markets, products, or services. Table 4.6 lists ideas on attending interviews suggested by the U.S. Department of Labor (1991b).

DeLuca (1997) suggests that before an interview, use this pre-interview checklist: (a) name and title of the person you are meeting, with correct spelling; (b) exact address and location of the organization, including accurate directions; (c) research notes regarding the organization and the position you are interested in; (d) a list of points that you want to make; (e) any questions remaining to be answered about the position; (f) your employment and educational history in case you are asked to complete an application on the spot; and (g) your business card and a recent copy of your resume. Being prepared for the interview helps to show your seriousness about the position you are applying for.

What type of questions might you be asked during an interview? Table 4.7 lists a sampling of the type of questions that interviewees have been asked. It's a good idea to do a mock interview with someone and think about your answers to these questions. Have your practice interviewer ask you some surprise questions. Often, the type of answers you can come up with "on the fly" impresses your potential employer as to how you can handle yourself in pressure situations, such as a job interview. Think about these questions when prepping for an interview (some of these questions come from CollegeGrad, 2001).

Also, you need to be ready with questions of your own (Table 4.8) Remember, although you are being interviewed by the organization, you are interviewing them as well! You need to determine if this position is a good match or fit for you. Having your own interview questions prepared in advance will indicate your level of interest to the employer and help promote a balanced interview.

BOISE STATE UNIVERSITY

College of Social Sciences and Public Affairs   1910 University Drive   Boise, Idaho 83725-1715

Department of
Pyschology

phone 208-426-1207
fax 208-426-4386

May 24, 2003

Tiffany Christensen, Director
Distance Education and Extended Studies
The University of Montana
32 Campus Drive
Missoula, MT 59812

Dear Tiffany,

I have been asked by Sean Adams to write a letter of recommendation in support of his application for your recently advertised position "Distance Education Coordinator." It is my pleasure to provide my support and this letter on Sean's behalf.

I have known Sean for a little over a year. Although he has not taken any courses from me, he served as one of my research assistants for the past year. He graduated with his bachelor's degree in psychology from Boise State earlier this month. Through these interactions I know Sean fairly well.

Quite frankly, I think he is a good match for the job requirements. As a research assistant, Sean often worked independently, balancing multiple tasks. His first project with me was to revise a previously rejected manuscript for publication in a scholarly journal. With Sean's assistance, we revised the manuscript and it has now been accepted for publication. His next project involved a major extension of the first one, involving working with adolescents to determine typical caffeine consumption along with their behavioral preferences while consuming caffeine. Sean diligently worked with multiple members of the community to establish a mechanism for collecting caffeine consumption data from high school students. When the approvals did not come in time to finish the project, Sean quickly shifted gears and studied college students. This quick thinking and ability to adapt allowed him to make a presentation at the Midwestern Psychological Association meeting in Chicago earlier this month. I have to say that it is unusual for an undergraduate to work hard enough to have both conference presentation and publication credits so early in an academic career. Even

FIGURE 4.2 Sample Letter of Recommendation

Letter of Recommendation for Sean Adams
May 24, 2003
Page 2

more impressively, he has also accomplished this while working with
another psychology professor as well!

I am confident that Sean has the analytical and problem-solving skills
necessary for this position. He has a bona fide passion for education, and he
will thrive with the opportunity to help distance education students achieve
their educational goals. I think that Sean currently possesses all of the skills
necessary to achieve in this job. His interpersonal skills are superb, and he
is pleasant to work with. He's just that good!

If I can provide any additional information about Sean, please contact me
directly. **I recommend Sean Adams for the Distance Education
Coordinator position with my highest recommendation and without
reservation.**

Sincerely,

R. Eric Landrum, Ph.D.
Professor
Department of Psychology

TABLE 4.6 Tips for Successful Interviewing

Dress for the interview and the job—don't overdress, don't look too informal.

Always go to the interview alone.

Find common ground with the employer, and if possible, with the interviewer.

Express your interest in the job and the company based on the homework you did prior to the interview.

Allow the interviewer to direct the conversation.

Answer questions in a clear and positive manner.

Speak positively of former employers or colleagues, no matter what.

Let the employer lead the conversation toward salary and benefits—try not to focus your interest on these issues (at least not during the initial interview).

When discussing salary, be flexible.

If the employer doesn't offer you a job or say when you'll hear about their decision, ask about when you can call to follow up.

Be sure to follow up at the appropriate time.

Thank the employer for the interview, and follow up with a thank-you note.

TABLE 4.7 Typical Questions You Might Be Asked in an Interview

What do you hope to be doing 5 or 10 years from now?

What made you apply for this particular job with us?

How would you describe yourself?

How has your education prepared you for your career?

What are your strengths and weaknesses?

What do you see that you can offer to us, and what can we offer to you?

What are the two or three accomplishments in your life that have given you the greatest satisfaction? Explain.

Tell me about yourself.

Do you work well under pressure and in stressful situations?

What did you learn as an undergraduate that you think will be helpful on this job?

Have you ever been in any supervisory or leadership roles?

What types of activities and extracurricular interests do you have? What do you like to do in your spare time?

Why should I hire you?

If you don't mind telling me, what other jobs are you applying for?

Tell me something I should know about you.

Is there anything else we should know about you?

First impressions on the interview are vitally important. Prickett, Gada-Jain, and Bernieri (2000) found that personnel directors can make accurate decisions about an applicant's employability in the first 20 seconds of the interview! To help with that first impression, DeLuca (1997) offered his top 10 rules for every interview: Be on time, Dress the part, Smile occasionally, Keep it conversational, Keep your purpose in mind, Accentuate the positive, Give details, Do not monopolize the conversation, Ask for the job, and follow up.

What if the interview does not pan out? In a recent survey, executives were asked what they think is the most common mistake applicants make during job interviews: little or no knowledge of the company (44%), unprepared to discuss career plans (23%), limited enthusiasm (16%), lack of eye contact (5%), and unprepared to discuss skills/experience (3%) (Lindgren,

TABLE 4.8 Typical Questions to Ask Potential Employers

How long has the organization been in existence?

How many employees?

Where are your other locations, if any?

What are your organization's current major challenges?

May I have a copy of a current organizational chart, employee handbook, or other relevant publications?

Was this job posted internally?

Do you feel I have the characteristics necessary to be hired and to advance in this organization?

What do you feel are the most important aspects of this position?

Who will make the final hiring decision?

When will you have to make a hiring decision?

How long have you worked here?

What do you like about this organization?

Would this position lead to other job openings?

Can I get a tour of the facility?

How does the organization regard its employees?

How many applicants have applied for this job?

How long do you think it will take until you make a decision?

Source: DeLuca, M. J. (1997). *Best answers to the 201 most frequently asked interview questions.* New York: McGraw-Hill.

2003). Think of each interview as a practice trial toward the next opportunity. If you can identify certain reasons why the interview did not go well, work on those problems—for example, do not ask during the initial interview "what about vacation time?" In some cases, you can contact the interviewer and ask for constructive feedback about the interview process: Was it the way that you handled yourself during the interview, or was it qualifications and experience? Appleby (1998b) expands on these potential explanations, by providing a list of 15 "knockout" factors (Table 4.9).

TABLE 4.9 Interview "Knockout" Factors

Lack of proper career planning—didn't match job applying for

Lack of knowledge in field—not qualified

Inability to express thoughts clearly and concisely—rambles along

Insufficient evidence of achievement or capacity to excite action in others

Not prepared for interview—no background research on company

No real interest in the organization or the industry

Narrow geographical location interest—not willing to relocate

Little interest and enthusiasm—indifferent, bland personality

Overbearing, too aggressive, conceited, cocky

Interested in only the best dollar offer

Asks no questions or poor questions about the job

Unwilling to start at the bottom—expects too much too soon

Makes excuses, is evasive

No confidence, lacks poise

Poor personal appearance, sloppy dress

TABLE 4.10 Tips for Dealing with Illegal Questions During an Interview

Interviewers should not ask illegal questions; you do not have to answer them.

You can control the amount of disclosure when faced with an illegal question. If the truth of the matter can help your application, consider providing the information.

Interviewers or organizations that insist on asking illegal questions or have a bias based on sex, race, color, national origin, religion, disability or perceived disability may be doing you a favor in revealing their motivations early in the interview process.

Even though it is disappointing and frustrating to be asked illegal and/or inappropriate questions, do not allow your professionalism to slip.

Questions are illegal whether asked orally or on the job application form if asked before you are offered the job. However, questions as to health, age, gender, and marital status may be appropriate after you are hired for insurance reasons and Equal Employment Opportunity (EEO) reports.

If the worst-case scenario occurs, follow up and make a claim of discrimination against the potential employer.

Source: DeLuca, M. J. (1997). *Best answers to the 201 most frequently asked interview questions.* New York: McGraw-Hill.

Occasionally you may also be asked questions that are inappropriate or illegal. Illegal questions are those that ask about personal characteristics protected by law and are not necessary to determine a person's eligibility for the job. Questions that concern a person's age, religion, national origin, gender, and disability can be illegal, although in limited cases this type of information about a person may be a bona fide occupational qualification. Also, note that the legality of questions changes after a person has been hired. If you think you might be in a situation where you will be asked an illegal question, Table 4.10 suggests some strategies for dealing with that situation.

WHAT IF YOU ARE NOT INITIALLY SUCCESSFUL IN YOUR JOB SEARCH?

This could happen. You could follow all of the advice in this chapter and throughout this book, and you might not get the job you want. Whose fault is that? It's not about fault, but it's about a host of factors. For instance, the success of the economy drives a large part of hiring decisions. If you happen to graduate with your bachelor's degree in psychology at a time when the economy is not doing so well, it might take some time to find the job that you want. In this type of situation, it might be best to take a job related to what you want and continue to build your skills and abilities, therefore building your resume. Also, it's hard sometimes for graduates to realize the size of the market and the competition. Although you might be competing with your classmates for some of the local jobs, the competition is even more fierce than that. Remember, there are over 70,000 graduates with bachelor's degrees in psychology every year. You are competing with many of them for the best jobs. You are also competing with some of last year's grads for those good jobs, and next year a new batch of graduates will be competing for your job. If you follow much of the advice offered throughout this book and by your faculty members, we sincerely believe that you will put yourself in an advantageous position to get the best jobs available.

If you have the opportunity, try to obtain feedback from employers about the status of your application. What was it that prevented you from getting the job you wanted? Was it poorly prepared materials? Was it nervousness at the interview? Was it a lack of match or fit with the organization? If you can obtain some feedback, it might give you some insight on how to proceed and how to minimize or eliminate any weaknesses. Whatever the feedback, try to assess its accuracy. Outside help would be good here. Discuss these issues with your faculty mentor or other trusted, respected individuals. The disappointment of rejection may cloud your objective evaluation of the critiques offered; an external opinion can help. After you have determined any actual weaknesses, then work to resolve them. It might mean taking a workshop or class.

It might mean consulting with a coach on how to better prepare and submit your materials. Be willing to invest in you—it will be the best investment you ever make.

It may be difficult to obtain this information from larger corporations; however, if you interviewed with someone, your interviewer would be a good first contact to receive feedback about your unsuccessful application. Additionally, pursuing this type of information, although not the most pleasant of tasks, will impress upon the company how serious you were about your job application and how serious you are about self-improvement. Inquiries such as yours might be remembered when future opportunities arise with that organization.

Finally, be persistent. Invest in yourself and expect to reap benefits. Be persistent in your acquisition of the type of position you want, and be persistent in self-improvement. It is important to be intelligent, personable, motivated, etc.—but if you are not persistent in pursuing your goals, all the rest may be for naught. Although we do not agree with every aspect of this quote (Combs, 2000), Calvin Coolidge, the 30th President of the United States, is attributed to have said the following: "Nothing takes the place of persistence. Talent will not. Nothing is more common than unsuccessful people with talent. Genius will not. Unrewarded genius is almost a proverb. Education will not. The world is full of educated derelicts. Persistence alone has solved and always will solve the problems of the human race." But just think about the possibility of this formula: talent + education + persistence = success!

"Looks like your fears of people, speaking, computers, and all forms of transportation might limit your career opportunities."

Exercise #4: Job Ads

In this exercise, look for jobs that are appropriate for those with a bachelor's degree in psychology. If possible, cut out newspaper ads and attach them to this page. You can also use Internet tools (such as www.monster.com or careerbuilder.com) to search for relevant jobs. We have included a sample that appeared in the *Idaho Statesman* published in Boise, Idaho.

216 – Management and Professional

PLANNING AND EVALUATION MANAGER
The Idaho Division of Vocational Rehabilitation is seeking qualified candidates for the position of Planning and Evaluation Manager. The position is full-time, non-classified and FLSA exempt with the State of Idaho. Incumbent is responsible for coordinating the Division's strategic plan, state plan and administrative reviews. Duties also include developing and coordinating customer satisfaction studies, marketing, public relations, program evaluation, research and grant writing. Outstanding interpersonal, time management and written/verbal communication skills are necessary. Minimum qualification: Bachelors degree or relevant substitute experience on a year for year basis; background in writing and statistical analysis; an understanding of research methods, statistics and strategic planning; use of SPSS computer software for statistical analysis preferred. Benefits include health insurance, vacation and sick leave, retirement and 401(k). Annual salary is $30,264-$48,443 DOE. To apply please mail resume to: IDVR-HRD, 650 W. State St, Rm 150, PO Box 83720, Boise, ID 83720-0096 or fax resume to 208-334-5305. No phone calls please. All inquiries must be received no later than 01/05/01. EOE/AA/ADA.

CHAPTER 5

Career Options With a Master's Degree or Doctoral Degree

You have decided that your interest in psychology is going to take you beyond the bachelor's degree in psychology. You have heard some of juniors and seniors in the psychology department talk about graduate school. You have heard some of your classmates complaining about all the time they spend studying for the GRE, and you do not even know what the GRE is. All you want to do is help people. Why do you need to go to graduate school to be able to do this? In this chapter we will tackle what your career options are with graduate training, and in the next chapter we will provide an overview on the process of applying and getting accepted into graduate school.

WHY GRADUATE TRAINING?

Psychology is one of those professions for which an additional professional degree is required to practice the craft. This requirement is similar to the additional training that you need to become a doctor (i.e., physician) or lawyer. You do not get your M.D. (medical doctor, physician) or J.D. (juris doctor, lawyer) after completing your bachelor's degree. This situation is unlike other undergraduate majors, such as teacher education or engineering, for which a bachelor's degree (and usually some type of licensing or certification, often included as part of the undergraduate instruction) is adequate preparation for employment. Here is what the Council of Graduate Schools (1989) says about graduate training in general: "If you enjoy reading, problem solving, discovering new facts, and exploring new ideas, you should consider going to graduate school. Your ideas become your major asset. A graduate degree can influence how fast and how far you can advance in your career. It can increase your earning power. It can also enhance your job satisfaction, the amount of responsibility you assume, and the freedom you have to make your own decisions rather than simply following someone else's directions. A graduate degree can also give you greater flexibility to change careers. By earning the degree, you demonstrate your ability to master complex topics and carry out projects on your own initiative" (p. 3).

Even before we discuss the occupational opportunities available and the entire graduate school admissions process, there is much to think about when considering the graduate school question. First, here is some background about who graduates. Table 5.1 presents the data for the latest academic year available, 2000–2001. Looking at graduate-school enrollments, there were 50,689 graduate students enrolled in psychology programs in 2000 (National Science Foundation, 2002). With regard to the diversity of ethnic backgrounds, here is the breakdown: 0.7% American Indian/Alaska Native, 4.4% Asian/Pacific Islander, 8.4% Black, non-Hispanic, 8.2% Hispanic, 7.2% Other or unknown, 66.7% White, non-Hispanic, and 4.4% students with temporary visas. In fact, there have been 50,000 students enrolled in psychology graduate education every year since 1992. Of those students attending graduate school, 52.9% attended public institutions whereas 47.1% attended private institutions.

TABLE 5.1 Psychology Degrees Conferred by Gender, 2000–2001

	Bachelor's Degree	Master's Degree	Doctoral Degree
Women	56,962 (77.5%)	11,581 (76.2%)	3,184 (68.3%)
Men	16,572 (22.5%)	3,615 (23.8%)	1,475 (31.7%)
Total	73,534	15,196	4,659

Note: Percentages apply to column totals.

Source: National Center for Education Statistics (2003).

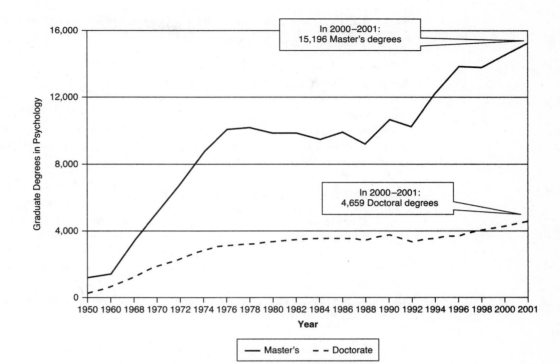

FIGURE 5.1 Number of Graduate Degrees Awarded in Psychology Since 1950

Note: For clarity in the figure, the odd-numbered years from 1967 to 1999 have been omitted.

Source: National Center for Education Statistics (2003).

It is also interesting to examine the historical trends in the awarding of graduate degrees in psychology. See Figure 5.1 for this data.

Examining the historical data confirms the continued popularity of psychology. Information from this chapter will inform you about what you can do with a graduate degree in psychology, and information from the next chapter will help you with information about the application and admissions process. As you think about your own decision about graduate school, consider the following questions in Table 5.2.

As you get more and more serious about pursuing a graduate degree in psychology, you may want to consult additional resources. There are a number of good books that can give you more insights into a degree in psychology. Although we recommend these books, they do not replace talking to your faculty members. Not only will faculty members be able to relate their own graduate school experiences, but discussions with them also give you an opportunity to build a relationship that might lead to later opportunities (such as serving as a research assistant or obtaining a letter of recommendation).

Opportunities in Psychology Careers (Super & Super, 1994) looks at the fields of psychology, the prospects, the rewards, and career-related issues. This book is oriented toward persons with an interest in a doctorate in psychology. *Great Jobs for Psychology Majors* (De-Galan & Lambert, 1995) addresses the interests of bachelor's-level graduates who are either pursuing jobs or graduate school. After covering topics such as self-assessment, resumes, networking, interviewing, job offers, and graduate school choices, this book presents five possible career paths. The career path theme is expanded in Sternberg's (1997) *Career Paths in Psychology*. This book contains chapters that are dedicated to tracing out potential career paths in psychology by presenting career paths of current psychologists. These career paths are organized into sections, such as academic careers; clinical, counseling, and community psychology; careers in organizations; and careers in diverse areas of psychology.

The emphasis on graduate training in psychology exists because of the skills and abilities required to function as a professional psychologist. Although some of these skills and

TABLE 5.2 Perspectives on Deciding if Graduate School is Right for Your

DeGalan and Lambert (1995)	Giordano (2004)
Is graduate school really an option for me?	Am I willing to go the extra mile to gain a wide range of skills now (as an undergraduate student) and as a graduate student?
Are you postponing some tough decisions by going to graduate school?	
Have you done some hands-on reality testing?	Am I willing to do that without being paid to do it?
	Am I intrinsically motivated?
Do you need an advanced degree to work in your desired field or would a bachelor's degree do?	Do I like being a student? Do I really, really like it?
	Am I able to work independently?
	Am I a good time and stress manager?
Have you compared your expectations of what graduate school will do for you compared to what it has done for alumni of the program you are considering?	How well do I take criticism?
	Can I live with the feeling that I may not be able to accomplish all that I am expected to accomplish?
Have you talked with people in your field to explore what you might be doing after graduate school?	Do I have some "street smarts" or practical intelligence?
Are you excited by the idea of studying the particular field you have in mind?	Am I willing to live without some of the luxuries of life for a while?

abilities are addressed in your undergraduate education, the idea is that you master these skills in the process of obtaining a higher degree (such as a master's degree or a doctorate). These skills include the following (APA, 1998a; Hayes, 1996):

General: Action oriented, take initiative, bright, energetic, learn quickly, understand and know how to deal with people, can work on several problems at once, good team player, dependable, can negotiate effectively

Literacy: Ability to write, can write in more than one literary format, accustomed to writing essays that allow the exploration of issues in detail, familiar with the techniques of concise writing in a particular format

Numeracy: Statistical reasoning and analysis skills, ability to draw appropriate inferences from numerical data, computer literacy and familiarity with statistical software, ability to present data to nontechnical audience, seeks to understand the issue through the examination of the data rather than avoiding the data

Information Finding, Measurement: Can conduct literature searches, structure conversations to obtain information, avoid bias and preconceptions in information searches, design experiments (e.g., surveys, questionnaires) to obtain information, use observational techniques, prepare and deliver oral and written reports, organize program evaluations

Planning: Identify steps in a project from beginning to end, identify potential problems ahead of time, identify needed resources, mobilize team members

Research, Computer Literacy: Ability to detect confound variables and design settings for appropriate comparisons and conclusions, able to conceptualize in terms of cause and effect, understand the limitations of particular methodological approaches to the conclusions that can be drawn, understand the design of experimental and quasi-experimental research studies, knowledge of survey and sampling techniques and qualitative analysis

Interpersonal Awareness: Knowledge of the capabilities/limitations of people from many viewpoints (cognitive, perceptual, physical, motivational, social, developmental, personality, emotional)

Problem Solving: Identify central issues and key questions, experience in identifying the most important problem(s) to be addressed from ambiguous information, can solve general problems and focus on details, understand that there may be more than one method for solving the problem, understand that there can be more than one right answer

Critical Evaluation, Higher-Order Analysis :Read critically, synthesize and summarize information from multiple sources, interpret qualitative and quantitative data, deal with inconsistent/uncertain information, extract key pieces from information in a rapid manner, impose structure on ambiguous, messy data, translate information into meaningful conclusions and recommendations

Perspectives: Understand that people trained in different disciplines may see the same problem differently, understand the advantage to understanding different perspectives; understand the perspectives of others (i.e., empathy), coordinate or facilitate action among people with different perspectives

These are the goals of a graduate education. These are not obtained easily, but slowly over time. As you can start to understand, graduate school is a major commitment not only to your own education but also to the discipline of psychology. Emanuel Donchin, Chair of the Psychology Department at the University of South Florida, summarizes the overall goals of graduate school quite well (cited in Murray, 2002a, p. 36): "What we're striving to produce in graduate education are well-rounded individuals with habits of thought and approaches and perceptions that allow them to change with the field and engage in lifelong learning, rather than ossify around a particular set of practice roles." When faculty members are asked about the most successful graduate school students, the descriptions presented in Table 5.3 emerge.

TYPES OF GRADUATE TRAINING AND GRADUATE DEGREES

In psychology, there are basically three broad career paths or models that most graduate school students pursue: the *scientist model*, the *practitioner model*, and the *scientist-practitioner model*. Under the scientist model (sometimes called the research model), graduate students receive training in a specific content area, as well as intense instruction in research methods statistics, and those methods of basic and applied research that further our understanding of human behavior. The trainee under the scientist model typically has a teaching or research emphasis, advancing our knowledge of human behavior. In the scientist model, the graduate receives a Ph.D. (doctor of philosophy).

In the scientist-practitioner model, the graduate student receives similar rigorous training in the creation and comprehension of scientific information but receives additional training in the helping professions. Thus, the student in the scientist-practitioner model typically has the goal of becoming a therapist (or a psychologist, in the strict licensing sense of the word). This person is trained in various therapeutic theories, conducts therapy under supervision, and completes an internship prior to receiving a Ph.D. This approach to training is called the Boulder model, named after a conference held in Boulder, Colorado, in 1949. This conference formalized the approach of equal weight given to the development of both research skills and clinical skills. Thus, clinical psychologists trained in the scientist-practitioner model are prepared for work in both academia and practice (Norcross & Castle, 2002).

The newest of these three career paths is the practitioner model. In the practitioner model, there is less emphasis on the science side of psychology, but there is additional training on the practitioner side. In this model, the person is trained to become a full-time practitioner. In this program, the graduate receives a Psy.D. (doctor of psychology). Training in a Psy.D. program is modeled after other professional degrees (M.D., J.D.) in that it is oriented toward being a practitioner in the field rather than the researcher (Keith-Spiegel, 1991). This approach to training is called the Vail model, named after a conference held in Vail, Colorado, in 1973. The general notion that emerged from this conference was that psychological knowledge had developed far enough that an explicitly professional degree was possible (similar to professional degrees in law, medicine, and dentistry). Also, it was proposed that different degrees be used to distinguish between the practitioner role (Psy.D.—doctor of psychology) and the scientist role (Ph.D.—doctor of philosophy). Clinical psychologists trained in this later approach focused primarily on clinical practice and less on scientific research. The Vail model also broadened where practitioner-modeled training could be delivered—those settings include a psychology department at a university, in a university-affiliated psychology school, and in an independent,

TABLE 5.3 Top Characteristics for Graduate School Success

Role Description	Mean Importance Rating
Working hard	5.60
Getting along with people	5.17
Writing ability	4.83
Clinical/counseling skills	4.81
Doing research	4.74
Handling stress	4.72
Discipline	4.64
Good grades	4.61
High intelligence	4.53
Empathy	4.48
Establishing a relationship with a mentor	4.39
Getting along with peers	4.00
Broad knowledge of psychology	4.00
Specialized knowledge in one or two areas of psychology	3.88
Reflecting program values	3.78
Being liked by faculty	3.69
Creativity	3.67
Obtaining master's degree as quickly as possible	3.60
Visibility in the department	3.45
Competitiveness	3.29
Relating to professors on a personal level	3.24
Teaching	2.81
Attractive physical appearance	2.53
Serving on student committees	1.95
Serving on department and university committees	1.62

Note: Items were rated on a scale from 1 = not important to 6 = very important.

Source: Descutner, C. J., & Thelen, M. H. (1989). Graduate school and faculty perspective about graduate school. *Teaching of Psychology, 16*, 58–61.

freestanding psychology school (not affiliated with a university) (Norcross & Castle, 2002). APA (1997a) provides this summary of degree options: "The Ph.D., then, is usually the degree granted by university-based psychology departments that train in the research or scientist-practitioner models, although some professional programs award the Ph.D. as well. The Psy.D. is usually granted by a university-based or freestanding professional school of psychology that trains with the professional model. The Ed.D. is a psychology Ph.D. that is granted by a university-based education department, as opposed to a psychology department, and, like the Ph.D., reflects either the research or the scientist-practitioner model" (p. 52). By the way, there continues to be varied opinions about the Psy.D. and the Vail model—see Peterson (2003) and the ensuing articles for more on this topic.

If you are confident that your future is in becoming a practitioner, then it is a safe bet to consider a Psy.D. program. The only disadvantage may be if you earn the Psy.D. and then apply for jobs in research or academic settings. For the helping professions, the Psy.D. appears to lead to successful training, and Scheirer (1983, as cited in Keith-Spiegel, 1991) suggests that the Psy.D. may offer a slight advantage in the service delivery job market. However, there are fewer Psy.D. training programs available, and they tend to be more expensive compared to Ph.D. training programs. Norcross and Castle (2002) succinctly summarize the difference between the two training approaches: "Boulder programs aspire to train producers of research; Vail programs train consumers of research" (p. 23).

It is important to note that the American Psychological Association (APA) accredits both Ph.D. and Psy.D. degrees. Accreditation asserts that a graduate program operates under certain practice and training principles that are believed to be beneficial to the training of future psychologists. Accreditation does not guarantee that you will have a good experience in the program, and many good graduate programs are not accredited. Accreditation is APA's seal of approval. APA does not accredit master's degree programs. The doctoral degree is recognized by APA as the credential for psychologists and the entry-level degree for the profession. Many jobs as well as licenses to practice require a doctorate (APA, 1997c).

Terminal programs are those intended to prepare a person for a specific occupation that requires only a master's degree for entry-level employment. Choosing between the master's degree and the doctorate? The master's option is less daunting because it requires a smaller investment of both time and money, and it affords the flexibility of part-time study in some cases. The master's degree offers a testing ground if a person is not completely sure that the doctoral degree is appropriate. If, as a master's degree student, you think you might eventually go on further for a doctorate, here are some suggestions that you can pursue while still earning your doctorate that should enhance your ability to gain admission into a doctoral program (APA, 1997a):

- Get as much research experience as possible.
- Establish good relationships with professors, who can later support your doctoral ambitions.
- Get the broadest training possible, and get a good foundation in core subjects.
- Maintain good grades.
- Obtain practical experiences in the areas on which you wish to concentrate.

SAMPLE JOB DESCRIPTIONS, WORK LOCATIONS OF GRADUATE DEGREE RECIPIENTS

Educational attainment of a graduate degree in psychology allows a great deal of flexibility for employment settings. Moreover, as careers change and evolve, the basic skills acquired through graduate education allow for adaptation to new work environments. To appreciate the diversity of potential work environments, see Table 5.4.

Due to the more specialized training at the graduate levels, there are actually fewer formal job descriptions available from O*NET (see Chapter 3 for more on this impressive resource). However, the skills and abilities attained through graduate training give these individuals a greater range of employment options. Some of the sample job titles and descriptions that are available on O*NET are presented in Table 5.5.

TABLE 5.4 Typical Work Settings for Psychology Graduates

Academic Settings

University	Two-year college
Academic department	University-affiliated professional school
Management or administrative office	Freestanding professional school
Professional school	Adult education program
Research center or institute	Elementary or secondary school
Four-year college	School system administrative office
Academic department	Special education or vocational school
Management or administrative office	
Research center or institute	

TABLE 5.4 (*Contd.*)

Human Service settings

Outpatient clinic	Independent practice
Community mental health center	Individual private practice
Health maintenance organization	Group psychological practice
Hospital	Medical/psychology group practice
Public general hospital	Other
Private general hospital	Health service for specific groups
Public psychiatric hospital	Nonuniversity counseling and guidance centers
Nonprofit private psychiatric hospital	University/college counseling and guidance
For-profit private psychiatric hospital	centers
Military hospital	Nursing home or other skilled-care facility
VA hospital	Training centers for people with mental retardation

Business settings

Business or industry

Consulting firm

Independent research organization or laboratory

Industrial/organizational psychology practice

Associations

Self-employed

Government and Military settings

Armed services

Civil service

Criminal justice system

Elected office

Federal, state, or local government agency

Government research organization

Source: American Psychological Association (1997c). *Getting in: A step-by-step guide for gaining admission to graduate school in psychology.* Washington, DC: American Psychological Association.

TABLE 5.5 Sample Job Descriptions with a Master's or Doctoral Degree (with O*NET-SOC codes)

Child, Family, and School Social Workers (21-1021.00). Provide social services and assistance to improve the social and psychological functioning of children and their families and to maximize the family well-being and the academic functioning of children. May assist single parents, arrange adoptions, and find foster homes for abandoned or abused children. In schools, they address such problems as teenage pregnancy, misbehavior, and truancy. May also advise teachers on how to deal with problem children.

Clinical Psychologists (19-3031.02). Diagnose or evaluate mental and emotional disorders of individuals through observation, interview, and psychological tests, and formulate and administer programs of treatment.

Counseling Psychologists (19-3031.03). Assess and evaluate individuals' problems through the use of case history, interview, and observation and provide individual or group counseling services to assist individuals in achieving more effective personal, social, educational, and vocational development and adjustment.

TABLE 5.5 (*Contd.*)

Educational Psychologists (19-3031.01). Investigate processes of learning and teaching and develop psychological principles and techniques applicable to educational problems.

Industrial-Organizational Psychologists (19-3032.00). Apply principles of psychology to personnel, administration, management, sales, and marketing problems. Activities may include policy planning; employee screening, training and development; and organizational development and analysis. May work with management to reorganize the work setting to improve worker productivity.

Mental Health and Substance Abuse Social Workers (21-1023.00). Assess and treat individuals with mental, emotional, or substance abuse problems, including abuse of alcohol, tobacco, and/or other drugs. Activities may include individual and group therapy, crisis intervention, case management, client advocacy, prevention, and education.

Mental Health Counselors (21-1014.00). Counsel with emphasis on prevention. Work with individuals and groups to promote optimum mental health. May help individuals deal with addictions and substance abuse; family, parenting, and marital problems; suicide; stress management; problems with self-esteem; and issues associated with aging and mental and emotional health.

Psychology Teachers, Postsecondary (25-1066.00). Teach courses in psychology, such as child, clinical, and developmental psychology, and psychological counseling.

Substance Abuse and Behavioral Disorder Counselors (21-1011.00). Counsel and advise individuals with alcohol, tobacco, drug, or other problems, such as gambling and eating disorders. May counsel individuals, families, or groups or engage in prevention programs.

Source: National O*NET™ Consortium. (2001, May). *O*NET occupational listings*. Raleigh, NC: National O*NET™ Consortium.

OCCUPATIONAL OPPORTUNITIES WITH THE MASTER'S DEGREE

In this section, we discuss the options and opportunities you will have with a master's degree (M.A. or M.S.). Some of the areas that we will cover include the outlook for the future of these positions, perceptions of the future, actual employment figures, different work settings, and relative salaries. The diversity of opportunities with a graduate degree is reflective of the diversity in psychology.

According to the Occupational Outlook Handbook (2004a), "overall employment of counselors is expected to grow faster than the average for all occupations through 2012, and job opportunities should be very good because there are usually more job openings than graduates of counseling programs. In addition, numerous job openings will occur as many counselors retire or leave the profession" (no page number). When master's degree recipients are asked about their perceptions of the job market, 36.0% percent report that it is fair, 32.4% report good, and 10.2% report excellent (APA, 2003). In the 2002 employment survey of master's specialist, and related degrees (Singleton, Tate, & Kohout, 2003), 67% of respondents were employed, 21% were enrolled in further graduate study, 9% were unemployed and seeking work, while 3% were employed and not seeking work.

Where are master's-level psychologists employed? According to the APA 2002 survey of master's degree recipients, full-time employment occurred in these proportions: 14.6% university and college settings, 23.6% in schools or other educational settings, 19.1% in hospitals and clinics, 3.0% in independent practice, 19.3% in other human services, and 20.4% in business, government, or other related settings (Singleton et al., 2003).

Unfortunately, the master's degree in psychology is widely misunderstood and undervalued. Actkinson (2000) provides an informative list of myths and misinformation about the master's degree. Remember, these are **myths** and **misinformation**: (a) Everyone should go directly for the doctorate. There is seldom, if ever, a good reason for getting a master's; (b) A good master's program will be APA-approved/accredited; (c) You cannot do counseling/psychotherapy with only a master's degree. Alternatively, you cannot get licensed with only a master's; (d) If you first get your master's, then decide to get a Ph.D., you will have to start over. None

Success Stories

Tony Mayo
Georgia Military College

When I was a senior in high school I became sick with an illness that damaged my optic nerves and left me legally blind. Although I did not plan to attend college, being legally blind changed my plans.

My part-time job in a grocery store became full-time, but only lasted for a few months. I worked 7 years in a garment factory, and less than a year as a hospital and police department dispatcher. For several years, I received social security disability because of my limited vision and lack of skills which prevented me from obtaining employment. It was during these years, I became frustrated and realized the importance of furthering my education. I was always encouraged by my family and friends to continue my education, but I had to experience some difficulty gaining employment before I acted on this advice. I taught myself to read Braille through a correspondence course and contacted a vocational rehabilitation counselor for information about Braille equipment. This conversation led to a discussion about school and 13 years after graduating from high school, I was a freshman in college.

Six years later, I had earned a B.S. degree in Psychology and Political Science, and an M.S. in Psychology. Within months after graduation, I became an adjunct instructor of Psychology in the department where I graduated. I also started teaching part-time at a community college. I taught at both schools for 5 years before becoming full-time at the community college. I have been teaching Psychology at this college for 7 years. Since graduation, I received the Outstanding Recent Alumnus Award from the college I attended, and was selected Outstanding Faculty Member at the college where I teach.

My college years were wonderful and opened doors I never thought possible. I tell my story to all my classes and encourage my students to continue their education.

of your work will transfer. An allied view is that getting your master's first will hurt your chances of getting into a Ph.D. program in the future; (e) Not many people get master's. Almost everyone goes directly to the Ph.D.; (f) You cannot get a good job with only the master's; and (g) People with the master's are not really psychotherapists/counselors. "Even plumbers can get the LPC" (p. 20). Many of these issues are directly addressed in this chapter. For more information about these myths, we encourage you to read the excellent article by Actkinson (2000).

The differences between a master's-level psychologist and a master's-level counselor are subtle. Master's-level psychologists probably received their education in a department of psychology, and although their degree is from a psychology department, they may call themselves a counselor depending on the state rules and regulations concerning the title. (For instance, in some states "psychologist" is a legally protected term, often reserved for persons with a Ph.D. or Psy.D. who have also passed a licensing examination.) Master's-level counselors may or may not have received their degree from a psychology department; they may have earned the degree in a counseling department, guidance department, educational psychology department, etc. In many states, the term "counselor" is not legally protected; hence in some situations almost anyone can advertise as a counselor.

How much do master's-level counselors and psychologists earn? The most recent data available are presented in Table 5.6. Remember, these are average starting salaries.

Master's-level counselors and psychologists help people in a number of ways, such as evaluating their interests, abilities, and disabilities, and dealing with personal, social, academic,

TABLE 5.6 Starting Salaries for Full-time Employment Positions Among 2001 and 2002 Master's, Specialist's, and Related Degree Recipients in Psychology

Master's Degree-Level Positions	Mean	Standard Deviation
Direct Human Service setting: Clinical Psychology (all settings)	31,623	7,230
Direct Human Service setting: Clinical Psychology (Community Mental Health Clinic)	29,711	3,784
Direct Human Service setting: Counseling Psychology (all settings)	33,854	8,162
Direct Human Service setting: Counseling Psychology (Secondary School)	35,890	5,351
Direct Human Service setting: Counseling Psychology (Elementary School)	33,813	10,392
Direct Human Service setting: Counseling Psychology (Outpatient Clinic)	36,600	8,504
Direct Human Service setting: Counseling Psychology (Community Mental Health Clinic)	31,286	4,804
Direct Human Service setting: Counseling Psychology (Other Human Services setting)	28,800	11,433
Direct Human Service setting: Counseling Psychology (Other Nonprofit Organization)	33,417	8,913
Direct Human Service setting: School Psychology (all settings)	40,980	9,765
Direct Human Service setting: School Psychology (Secondary School)	37,460	7,620
Direct Human Service setting: School Psychology (Elementary School)	41,462	9,978
Direct Human Service setting: School Psychology (Special Education)	45,500	7,159
Direct Human Service setting: Other, in Psychology (all settings)	32,335	3,943
Direct Human Service setting: Other, in Psychology (Community Social Service Agency)	30,250	1,605
Administration of Human Services (all settings)	35,741	10,595
Administration of Human Services (Other Human Service settings)	38,100	15,994
Applied Psychology (all settings)	50,121	21,703
Research (all settings)	36,065	10,348
Faculty Positions (all settings, 9- or 10-month calendar)	42,069	13,914
Faculty Positions (Secondary School, 9- or 10-month calendar)	31,739	5,636
Other Administration Positions (all settings)	36,701	15,502
Other Types of Positions (all settings)	43,633	19,177
Other Types of Positions (Business/Industry)	46,907	14,022
Overall (All Settings)	**34,080**	**8,320**

Source: Singleton, D., Tate, A. C., & Kohout, J. L. (2003). 2002 Master's, specialist's, and related degrees employment survey. Washington, DC: American Psychological Association.

and career problems. You should know that there are related disciplines that also address some of these similar issues—included in this category are professions such as college and student affairs workers, teachers, personnel workers and managers, human services workers, social workers, psychiatric nurses, clergy members, occupational therapists, and others (OOH, 1998a.) There are a variety of options available for helping those who need help; more on this topic is presented in the later chapters of this book.

Although not of concern now to undergraduates majoring in psychology, we thought you might be interested in what master's degree recipients report being the most effective means of a job search. We present these job search methods in Table 5.7, with their frequency of use. You will note that one of the items is advertisements in *APA Monitor*. Although not a highly

TABLE 5.7 Job Search Methods Most Commonly Used by Master's Degree Recipients

Frequency	Job Search Methods
25.0%	Informal channels (for example, colleagues or friends)
15.0%	Internet/electronic resources
15.0%	Newspaper advertisements
9.8%	Met employer through former job
9.3%	Other methods
8.8%	Faculty advisors
6.2%	Received an unsolicited offer
6.2%	Sent an unsolicited vita
1.4%	Filled out civil service application
1.0%	Regional convention placement service
0.7%	Advertisements in *Chronicle of Higher Education* or other professional newsletter
0.7%	National convention placement service
0.7%	Used employment agency
0.2%	Not specified
0.0%	Advertisements in *APA Monitor*
0.0%	Professional journals or periodicals

Source: Singleton, D., Tate, A. C., & Kohout, J. L. (2003). 2002 Master's, specialist's, and related degrees employment survey. Washington, DC: American Psychological Association.

used strategy for master's degree students, those newly minted Ph.D.'s with an interest in academia use this resource often in their job searchers. For additional exposure to *APA Monitor* ads, see the exercise at the end of this chapter.

OCCUPATIONAL OPPORTUNITIES WITH A DOCTORAL DEGREE

The doctoral degree in psychology (e.g., Ph.D. or Psy.D.) is generally required for employment as a licensed clinical or counseling psychologist. (Some states have limited licensure for master's-level psychologists. So you need to check the laws carefully.) Interestingly, over 25% of all psychologists are self-employed, nearly four times the average for all professional workers (OOH, 2004b). The employment outlook appears good. "Overall employment of psychologists is expected to grow faster than average for all occupations through 2012, due to increased demand for psychological services in schools, hospitals, social service agencies, mental health centers, substance abuse treatment clinics, consulting firms, and private companies. Clinical, counseling, and school psychologists will grow faster than average, while industrial-organizational psychologists will have average growth" (OOH, 2004b, no page number).

What degrees are being awarded? In a 1995 study of new doctorates conducted by the APA (1998b), Ph.D.'s accounted for 76% of the degrees awarded, Psy.D.'s accounted for 22%, and Ed.D.'s (doctor of education) accounted for 2% of the degrees awarded. In what fields were they awarded? Clinical psychology doctorates account for 40% of the total. In a different survey (Kohout & Wicherski, 2003), APA surveyed Ph.D. degree holders in 1999 and found that 67% were employed full-time, 10% were employed part-time, 17.3% were pursuing postdoctoral education, 2.7% were unemployed and seeking employment, and 2.6% were unemployed but not seeking employment. This type of result speaks to the diversity of employment opportunities and the value of the skills attained by the completion of the doctoral degree. Although the doctorate is more difficult to obtain, persons who obtain it provide themselves more opportunities for employment in a variety of settings.

Success Stories

G. Reynaga Abiko
Correctional Medical Facility—Vacaville, CA

I do not know when I decided to go to college, but I am quite certain it was directly related to life events during my early childhood. When I was 6 years old, my parents got divorced and gave my sister and me to our grandparents to live. Then, when I was 13, my father died of AIDS. I soon decided that I must become a doctor so that I could understand everything about my world. I convinced myself that if I read enough books and got good enough grades in school, I could fix all of the heartache in my family. College seemed the best way to gain access to more information, so I decided at a young age to pursue an advanced degree, even though many of my family members never even graduated high school!

I am a second generation Mexican American, born to a very poor family. More detrimental to my academic success than the material disadvantages of being poor was the mentality of my family that college was a luxury. Everyone was more concerned with paying the bills than reading books, even though everyone in my family was very intelligent. My mother told me when I was 15 that she could not help me pay for my education and that, if I wanted to go, I would have to figure out how to pay for it by myself. I had already determined that I was meant to be a doctor, so I learned about college admissions and financial aid, eventually securing sufficient student loans to finance my education. Even though it was hard to figure out, I navigated through these procedures on my own, since my family did not know anything about it.

The road from high school graduate to Psy.D. graduate was far more challenging than I ever imagined! Academic affairs always came easily to me, but financial concerns quickly became a predictable source of stress. I was forced to work at various part-time jobs throughout my education just to make ends meet. I worked hard, taking extra courses each semester, and graduated one year early with my B.A. in order to save money on living expenses. Even though it was often difficult to juggle working with a full-time schedule of classes, I was able to maintain high grades. I went straight into graduate school, because I wanted to get out into the work force as soon as possible. I completed my M.A. before moving on to a Psy.D. I ended up graduating from my doctoral studies with the highest GPA in the class!

Although I eventually accrued enough student loan obligation to buy a home, I feel extremely fortunate to be the first person in three generations of my family to have graduated college! I now watch as my younger cousins consider higher education as an option and enjoy helping them through the process. I also volunteer my time mentoring others, especially women and students of Color, because I do not want them to struggle through the process in the same ways I did. I have never regretted my decision to be a doctor (psychologist), though I learned long ago that I would never know everything! I enjoy helping people and am grateful to the strong work ethic I seemed to inherit from my immigrant family members. Although the process was incredibly challenging at times, my childhood goal of becoming a doctor was the best career choice for me!

What are some of the diverse employment settings? Table 5.8 presents the data on the primary employment setting for 1999 doctoral graduates.

What about the salaries for doctoral-level psychologists? The APA has completed the most recent surveys of doctoral employment and salaries in its 1999 doctorate employment survey (Kohout & Wicherski, 2003). Table 5.9 below presents median starting salaries for full-time employed doctorates in 1999—note the diversity of work settings and variations of job titles for doctoral-level psychologists.

TABLE 5.8 Primary Employment Setting for 1999 Doctoral Graduates

Frequency	Employment Setting
18.9%	Business, government, other
18.4%	University
13.9%	Other human service settings
12.5%	Hospitals
11.5%	Managed care
8.6%	Schools and other educational settings
6.1%	Independent practice
4.4%	Four-year college
3.4%	Medical schools
1.8%	Other academic settings
0.5%	Not specified

Source: Smith, D. (2002, June). Where are recent grads getting jobs? *Monitor on Psychology, 33* (6), 28–29.

TABLE 5.9 Starting Salaries for Full-Time Employment Positions, 1999 Doctorate Recipients in Psychology

Position Type and Employment Setting	Mean Starting Salary	Standard Deviation
Assistant Professor (all settings)*	41,959	10,918
Assistant Professor: University psychology department*	40,678	6,478
Assistant Professor: University education department*	41,671	5,286
Assistant Professor: University other academic department*	42,198	8,007
Assistant Professor: Four-year college psychology department*	36,545	5,634
Adjunct/Visiting Faculty (all settings)*	35,023	6,550
Adjunct/Visiting Faculty: University psychology department*	34,845	3,536
Lecturer/Instructor (all settings)*	36,636	5,767
Other Faculty Position (all settings)*	36,535	12,454
Other Faculty Position: University settings*	31,165	8,879
Educational Administration (all settings)	59,374	23,363
Research Positions (all settings)	49,946	13,017
Research Positions: University research center or institution	48,455	10,737
Research Positions: Private research organization or laboratory	54,214	11,267
Research Positions: Business, government	56,696	15,654
Research Positions: Other	53,586	10,245
Research Administration (all settings)	54,148	18,606
Direct Human Services, Clinical Psychology (all settings)	44,708	10,923
Direct Human Services, Clinical Psychology: University/college counseling center*	31,855	3,361
Direct Human Services, Clinical Psychology: Elementary/secondary school*	47,851	14,044
Direct Human Services, Clinical Psychology: Public general hospital	49,474	12,460
Direct Human Services, Clinical Psychology: Private general hospital	49,714	13,005
Direct Human Services, Clinical Psychology: Public psychiatric hospital	50,269	8,441

TABLE 5.9 (Contd.)

Direct Human Services, Clinical Psychology: VA hospital	47,500	5,462
Direct Human Services, Clinical Psychology: Individual private practice	44,659	19,758
Direct Human Services, Clinical Psychology: Group psychological practice	44,991	13,352
Direct Human Services, Clinical Psychology: Medical/psychological group practice	44,500	9,360
Direct Human Services, Clinical Psychology: Outpatient clinic	43,194	10,193
Direct Human Services, Clinical Psychology: Community mental health center	40,311	7,001
Direct Human Services, Clinical Psychology: Other human service setting	43,155	9,641
Direct Human Services, Clinical Psychology: Criminal justice system	46,964	9,167
Direct Human Services, Clinical Psychology: Business, government	46,324	9,519
Direct Human Services, Counseling Psychology (all settings)	44,714	11,599
Direct Human Services, Counseling Psychology: University/college counseling center*	31,660	3,510
Direct Human Services, Counseling Psychology: Community mental health center	39,063	8,152
Direct Human Services, Counseling Psychology: Independent practice settings	52,504	17,110
Direct Human Services, Counseling Psychology: Hospital	50,077	11,572
Direct Human Services, Counseling Psychology: Other human service settings	38,931	5,189
Direct Human Services, School Psychology (all settings)	53,994	14,407
Direct Human Services, School Psychology: Elementary/secondary school*	48,210	13,213
Administration of Human Services (all settings)	51,075	11,416
Administration of Human Services: Community mental health center	47,200	9,858
Administration of Human Services: Hospital	50,200	6,680
Administration of Human Services: Other human service settings	52,678	12,624
Applied Psychology (all settings)	67,093	21,162
Applied Psychology: Consulting firm	75,350	23,466
Applied Psychology: Business/industry	75,077	16,454
Applied Psychology: Other	70,852	21,952
Administration of Applied Psychology (all settings)	72,000	23,997
Other Administrative Position (all settings)	59,188	28,261
Other Type of Position (all settings)	65,395	28,391
Other Type of Position: Business, government	63,214	24,195

Note: *These salaries are typically based on a 9- or 10-month contract—the data here have not been corrected for a 12-month salary.

Source: Kohout, J., & Wicherski, M. (2003). 1999 Doctorate employment survey. Washington, DC: American Psychological Association.

WHAT IS A POSTDOC?

You might think that after having completed your doctorate, you are done with your formal education. For some, that is not the case. The term "postdoc" is short for post-doctorate or postdoctoral study. Technically, it means just what it implies—additional education post (after) receiving the doctorate. Postdoctoral study is fairly common for clinical psychology students, but students from other areas of psychology also pursue the postdoctorate. By the way, no degree is associated with the postdoc (thus, no "Ph.D." or other letters attached to this additional education).

Clinical psychology students typically need a year of postdoctoral supervised clinical experience before they can be licensed in states. However, most third-party payers will not reimburse fees for unlicensed psychologists (Clay, 2000). Walfish (2001) reported that significant percentages of interns were not aware of the details of postdoctoral requirements for licensure within the state where they intended to become a licensed psychologist. This is an essential detail that cannot be overlooked. What is the point of doing additional postdoctoral study? Clay (2000) provides this background: "the requirement for supervised postdoctoral experience was originally put in place because of the limited clinical experience many psychology students received in graduate school. It was believed that an additional year of supervised experience after graduation would enhance their readiness for independent practice and protect the public. But with the tremendous growth of predoctoral training and the rise of the professional school movement, many psychologists are convinced that the extra year has become outdated" (p. 2). However, some, such as Walfish (2001), recognize the potential long-term benefits of postdoctoral study: "in clinical areas, postdoctoral fellowships allow the new doctorate to specialize in one particular area of work. Although predoctoral internships tend to be generalized (inpatient and outpatient, child and adult, assessment and therapy), postdoctoral fellowships tend to be extremely focused. The fellowships tend not to pay much and are very intensive. However, the intensity of the learning experience can lead to the development of specialized and marketable skills, which may pay rich dividends for a long time to come" (p. 390).

Are postdocs just for clinical psychology students? Not at all. Walfish nicely summarizes the benefits for those interested in a research career: "for those seeking a career in research, doing a postdoctoral internship can be an important stepping-stone to developing a specific area of future study. These positions are usually grant-funded opportunities with faculty members who already have an established research project. The new doctorate typically joins the research team and collaborates with team members, while being mentored by the senior faculty member" (p. 390). In APA's study of 1999 doctorate recipients (Kohout & Wicherski, 2003), those with full-time postdoctoral appointments identified a list of reasons for postdoctoral study (in no particular order), presented in Table 5.10.

At this point in your undergraduate career, you do not need to worry about a postdoc. We just wanted you to know what it is and why it exists. The bottom line is this—to become a psychologist, you will need additional training beyond the bachelor's degree. How much additional training may depend on the area of psychology you want to specialize in and the type of employment settings in which you may be placed. You do not need to think about all the combinations and permutations available right now—that will all work itself out. For now, try to follow the suggestions in this book for what you can do *as an undergraduate* to maximize your opportunities for success. It's OK to think about the future and plan accordingly, but do not lose sight of the present and succeeding in the here and now, else that future planning may be for naught.

TABLE 5.10 Reasons for Postdoctoral Study, 1999 Doctorate Recipients with Full-time Postdoctoral Appointments

To complement research knowledge and skills in same subfield as doctorate

To obtain research knowledge or training in another field

To work with a particular scientist or research group

To obtain specialized clinical training

To obtain supervised postdoctoral hours to take the licensing exam

To switch from research to practice

To become more employable

Employment not available

Source: Kohout, J. & Wicherski, M. (2003). 1999 Doctorate employment survey. Washington, DC: American Psychological Association.

Exercise #5: Reading *APA Monitor* Ads

In this exercise, carefully examine the ads re-created from the *APA Monitor on Psychology*. Note that there are standard parts of the ads, and search committees can require various types of documents from the applicant. Some positions are more research oriented, while others focus more on teaching. Some are for postdocs, and others are for temporary positions. These are actual job ads taken from APA job/career website, www.psyccareers.com on July 10, 2004. Look at the diversity of positions available, and this is just a nonrandom sample. Read these ads carefully, and determine (a) what sounds good to you, and (b) what parts of the ads you do not understand. Every discipline has its own jargon, including psychology. Asking a potential faculty member or professor about the peculiarities of these job ads might be a nice conversation starter.

Department of Psychology at the University of Vermont seeks to fill a tenure-track position at the Assistant Professor level in Adult Psychopathology to begin August 2005. Candidates will teach courses that may include graduate Adult Psychopathology, graduate Adult Behavior Therapy, undergraduate Abnormal Psychology, and an advanced undergraduate course in clinical psychology. Applicants must have a doctorate in clinical psychology, a strong record of publication, demonstrated excellence in teaching, and the ability to develop a funded research program in adult psychopathology. Applicants with additional skills in health psychology or family psychology are welcomed. Candidate should be able to provide clinical and research supervision, and be license eligible. Review of applications will begin on October 1, 2004. Submit vitae, representative publications, statements of research and teaching interests, and three letters of recommendation to: Professor Esther Rothblum, Psychology/Dewey Hall, University of Vermont, 2 Colchester Avenue, Burlington, VT 05405-0134. The University of Vermont is an Affirmative Action/Equal Opportunity Employer. The Department is committed to increasing faculty diversity and welcomes applications from women and underrepresented ethnic, racial, and cultural groups, and from people with disabilities.

One-year visiting Assistant Professor beginning August 31, 2004. Primary responsibilities include: teaching Introduction to Psychology, upper-level courses in cognitive and experimental psychology, and directing undergraduate research and practica. Applicant must have a Ph.D. (ABD considered), demonstrate a strong commitment to undergraduate teaching at both the introductory and advanced levels and research ability. All relevant documents must be received by July 15, 2004 for full consideration. Applications will be received until the position is filled. Applicants should send a curriculum vitae, transcripts, teaching evaluations, and three letters of recommendation to: Ellen S. Wilson, Division of Social Sciences, Ohio Northern University, Ada, OH 45810; e-wilson@onu.edu; (419) 772-2094. This position will be advertised Fall 2004 as "tenure-track, nine-month appointments at the rank of Assistant Professor" for the Fall of 2005.

Argosy University, Atlanta, has two full-time faculty position openings at the rank of Assistant/ Associate Professor. One position begins in September, 2004 and involves coordination responsibilities in the MA Clinical Psychology Program as well as teaching in both the MA and PsyD programs. The second position begins January, 2005 with preference given to individuals with expertise in child and adolescent assessment and intervention. Duties include teaching, clinical supervision, dissertation supervision, student advisement, faculty governance, and contributions to clinical psychology as a science and a profession. The positions require a doctorate in clinical psychology from an APA-accredited program and license or license-eligibility in the State of Georgia. GSPP is an APA-accredited program in Clinical Psychology representing a practitioner-scholar training model. Administration and faculty are dedicated to maintaining an environment that supports effective teaching and learning. GSPP at Argosy University/Atlanta is an equal opportunity employer. Review of applications will continue until the positions are filled. Applicants should submit a letter of interest, curriculum vitae, and three letters of recommendation to: Virginia L. Goetsch, Ph.D., Chair, Search Committee, Georgia School of Professional Psychology at Argosy University/Atlanta, 990 Hammond Drive, Atlanta, GA 30328.

Sheppard Pratt Health System–Towson, Maryland Inpatient Adolescent Neuropsychiatry Unit: Sheppard Pratt is seeking a full-time doctoral level psychologist with a behavioral background and experience in IQ testing, to provide individualized behavioral assessment and treatment of complex patients with a psychiatric diagnosis, developmental disability, and/or genetic condition and oversee a unit wide behavior management program as part of the Neuropsychiatry Program at Sheppard Pratt. Qualified candidates must have three plus years of relevant experience in behavior therapy, current license to practice in Maryland, and be eligible for listing in the National Register of Health Service Providers in Psychology To explore this opportunity, contact and send curriculum vitae in confidence to: Sheppard Pratt Health System, Attn: Ms. Krista Keehn, Unit Manager A-7, 6501 North Charles Street, Baltimore, Maryland 21204. Phone: 410/938-4734; Fax: 410/938-4431. E-mail: kkeehn@sheppardpratt.org. An Equal Opportunity Employer. Sheppard Pratt a not-for-profit behavioral health system.

A postdoctoral research fellowship position is available for competitive applicants in the Compulsive, Impulsive and Anxiety Disorders Program at the Mount Sinai School of Medicine, under the direction of Eric Hollander, M.D. This research-training grant prepares psychologists for careers in psychopharmacology and outcomes research. The research facilities and faculty of the Department of Psychiatry at the Mount Sinai School of Medicine serves as the site and resource for this training program. The program consists of three primary components: 1) mentored research, 2) didactic curriculum, and 3) basic science and clinical research electives. Research populations include individuals with OCD, binge-eating disorder, body dysmorphic disorder, compulsive gambling, and other impulse control disorders). Collaborations are available with associated researchers in neuroimaging, molecular neuropharmacology, and neurobehavioral genetics. Applicants must have completed their Ph.D. and must have research experience. Salaries are competitive with excellent benefits. Positions are available starting June 30, 2004 and will remain open until filled. Send curriculum vitae and three letters of recommendation to: Eric Hollander, M.D. Director, Compulsive, Impulsive and Anxiety Disorders Program Department of Psychiatry, Box 1230 Mount Sinai School of Medicine One Gustave L. Levy Place New York, N.Y. 10029, Fax: (212) 987-4031, Phone: (212) 241-3623, E-mail: eric.hollander@mssm.edu

The Research and Development Department at PAR is continuing to expand to meet excellent customer response to our rapidly growing product base. This expansion includes the addition of a Project Director position. The successful applicant will be a dynamic, entrepreneurial Psychologist and will have the following qualifications: Ph.D. degree in clinical, school, or educational psychology, or a closely related field, with experience and interest in psychometrics, measurement, and test development; a minimum of two years post-doctorate work experience; an excellent work ethic; very strong writing and editing skills; and meticulous attention to detail. PAR is a major psychological test developer/publisher located in Tampa, Florida. We have experienced consistent growth since our inception, and we are pursuing additional expansion of existing areas, as well as establishing new test development markets. We offer Project Directors the opportunity to work in a stimulating, business-oriented environment that supports professional growth and development. Specifically, Project Directors review submitted proposals and work with authors of accepted projects to ensure their reliability, validity, quality, and utility. Project Directors coordinate a multidisciplinary development team, guide product design, formulate and manage project budgets and schedules, develop assessment items and forms in accordance with APA and PAR standards, direct ongoing test development projects, plan and conduct statistical and psychometric analyses, prepare and edit test manuals for publication, and provide input on software design and testing. Established skills in tests and measurement, statistics, writing, and editing are a necessity. Experience in project management is a plus. PAR offers a highly competitive salary and benefits, a generous relocation package, and an attractive work/residential setting in the Tampa Bay metropolitan area. To apply, mail, fax, or e-mail your vitae to: Travis White, Ph.D., Director of Product Development, Psychological Assessment Resources, Inc., 16204 N. Florida Ave., Lutz, FL 33549; Phone: (813) 968-3003; Fax: (813) 968-4684; E-mail: twhite@parinc.com.

The I/O Psychology program at George Mason University invites applications for two tenure-track faculty positions beginning Fall 2005. Candidates are expected to have a record of quality research with potential for external funding; more senior candidates should have a demonstrated record of external funding. Area of research interest is open, although we have a special interest in applicants who have expertise in statistics, measurement, selection and/or cross-cultural psychology. The Industrial and Organizational Psychology program at George Mason University is a nationally ranked program. The doctoral program has a strong research focus and currently has 25 Ph.D. students and 25 MA students. More information on the program can be obtained at http://www.gmu.edu/org/iopsa. For a description of the department, see http://www.gmu.edu/departments/psychology. Review of applications will begin October 1, 2004 and continue until positions are filled. A letter of application, curriculum vitae, and statement of research and teaching interests should be sent electronically to: Dr. Lois Tetrick, Director, Industrial and Organizational Psychology Program at ltetrick@gmu.edu. In addition, mail hardcopies of these materials with selected reprints and three letters of recommendation to: Lois Tetrick, George Mason University, Department of Psychology MSN 3F5, 4400 University Drive, Fairfax, VA 22030. George Mason University is an Equal Opportunity/Affirmative Action Employer.

The Department of Psychology at California State University, Bakersfield (CSUB) seeks to fill multiple positions to teach in degree programs at the main campus of the university. One position is at the assistant professor level in quantitative psychology with primary teaching emphasis in undergraduate and graduate statistics, research methods, psychometrics, and the candidate's expertise area. A second position, also at the assistant professor level, is in personality psychology with additional background in clinical/ counseling a plus. The start date for both tenure-track positions is September 1, 2005. A third position is a one-year non-tenure-track lectureship in personality with expertise that would allow the offering of a lab in personality. Other courses for the lectureship would include, test and measurements and introductory psychology. The position start date for the lectureship is September 1, 2004. For details about all positions, see the webpages at: www.csub.edu/psychology/PsycJobs. CSUB is an Equal Opportunity/Affirmative Action/Title IX Employer. CSUB fosters and appreciates ethnic and cultural diversity among its faculty, students, and administrative staff. Applications from women, ethnic minorities, veterans, and individuals with disabilities are welcome.

CHAPTER 6

The Graduate Admissions Process

The message is clear about the benefits of receiving a master's degree or a doctorate. These advanced degrees prepare you for a career as a professional—they afford you greater job opportunities and flexibility, as well as salary benefits. So you want to earn your master's or doctorate in psychology—how do you get started? This chapter is dedicated to providing an overview of the details of the graduate school application process. You will need to have some clear ideas about your short-term and long-term goals before you can start the graduate school search process in any meaningful manner.

Before you start down this long and winding road, we encourage you to seek out information from a variety of sources about your graduate education options. Like any other career, it would be helpful if you enjoy and like what you end up doing. Lord (2004) echoes this sentiment: "If you find yourself not loving research and less than thrilled about designing, conducting, and writing up research studies, one of the saddest decisions you could make is to go through the motions just to get a Ph.D. You might grudgingly continue in a Ph.D. program just to get those magic letters after your name, but you have also boxed yourself into one of life's least pleasant corners. You have spent valuable years establishing credentials that qualify you to do one thing—a thing you do not enjoy" (p. 7). Not everyone agrees with this sentiment, but the more you can understand about your own goals and desires for your future, the better choices you can make down to follow a path toward those goals.

THE POPULARITY AND COMPETITIVENESS OF GRADUATE ADMISSIONS

In general, psychology is a popular choice at the undergraduate level. As you already know, each year over 70,000 students in the United States graduate with a bachelor's degree in psychology. Graduate education is quite popular, with continued increases in both master's degrees and doctorates awarded, and there are over 50,000 students enrolled in graduate programs of psychology at any given time. Whereas these statistics should not dissuade you from applying to graduate school, you do need to know the ropes. What is popular right now? How many applications are received in specialty areas of psychology? What about the Ph.D. vs. Psy.D. doctoral applications?

Table 6.1 presents the most up-to-date information we have on answering the above questions (Landrum, 2004a). The data presented in Table 6.1 were compiled by the American Psychological Association (APA) Research Office. The data come from APA's (2003) *Graduate Study in Psychology*, a compendium of American Departments of Psychology offering graduate education. The number of applications, number of applicants accepted, and number of newly enrolled are reported verbatim from the APA Research Office; the column "Percentage of Applicants Accepted" has been added.

It is important to understand the nature of these data and its limitations. First, the data reflect the Departments of Psychology that are represented in the *Graduate Study in Psychology* (2003) volume. If a particular department does not participate, then its data are not included. Second, we have only presented three degrees: Ph.D., Psy.D., and master's degree. The actual data from APA are more detailed, and include other degree options. Given those limitations, these are the best data available (to our knowledge) on the relative competitiveness and popularity of subspecialties in psychology. It is important, however, not to overreact to with this data. For instance, in 2001–2002 there were 18,392 applications to Ph.D. clinical programs. This fact does not mean 18,392 separate students. Many students apply to many schools, sometimes at both doctoral (Ph.D., Psy.D.) and master's levels.

The data in this table provide indirect measures for competitiveness and popularity. Look again at the clinical specialty area under Ph.D. With 18,392 applications, 1,928 were accepted for an acceptance rate of 10.5%. This figure can be considered an index of competitiveness; only

TABLE 6.1 Graduate School Admissions in Departments of Psychology by Subfields, 2001–2002

Specialty Area	Ph.D.				Psy.D.				M.A./M.S.			
	Number Applications	Number Applicants Accepted	Percentage Applicants Accepted	Number Newly Enrolled	Number Applications	Number Applicants Accepted	Percentage Applicants Accepted	Number Newly Enrolled	Number Applications	Number Applicants Accepted	Percentage Applicants Accepted	Number Newly Enrolled
Clinical	18,392	1928	10.5	1230	4982	2031	40.8	1218	4218	2085	49.4	1413
Clinical Neuropsychology	807	137	17.0	83	240	106	44.2	70	72	27	37.5	11
Community	302	71	23.5	52	80	31	38.8	19	761	444	58.3	338
Counseling	4800	704	14.7	412	85	12	14.1	12	5314	3228	60.7	2370
Health	605	251	41.5	135					45	28	62.2	23
School	1031	295	28.6	190	617	191	31.0	106	1281	596	46.5	579
Other Health Service Provider Subfields	3049	350	11.5	269	365	76	20.8	85	2254	1164	51.6	851
Cognitive	1994	559	28.0	288					99	48	48.8	21
Comparative	49	8	16.3	6								
Developmental	2204	546	24.8	343					462	243	52.3	150
Educational	410	153	37.3	128	4	4	100.0	4	156	112	71.8	78
Environmental	33	12	36.4	9					21	10	47.6	9
Experimental	959	207	21.6	140					715	388	54.2	261
Industrial/Organizational	2631	399	15.2	218	46	20	43.4	13	2133	963	45.1	580
General	24	14	58.3	9					2314	1343	58.0	749
Neuroscience	735	169	23.0	114					122	14	11.4	11
Personality	475	81	17.1	35					61	5	8.1	4
Physiological	24	10	41.7	2								
Psychobiology	386	103	26.7	57								
Psycholinguistics	0	0	0.0	0								
Quantitative	113	53	46.9	26					30	19	63.3	8
Social	2496	450	18.0	221					222	84	37.8	45
Other Research Subfields	1930	422	21.9	266	33	24	72.7	14	1366	751	55.0	497
Other Fields	471	41	8.7	25					9	16	100.0	2
TOTAL	43,920	6963	15.8	4258	6452	2495	38.7	1541	21,655	11,568	53.4	8000
Number of Departments	962				74				659			

Note: The data in this table were compiled by the American Psychological Association (APA) Research Office, based on the 2003 volume of *Graduate Study in Psychology.* Blank boxes indicate no Departments of Psychology offering degrees in those specialty areas in 2001–2002.

Source: American Psychological Association (2003). Applications, acceptances, and new enrollments in Graduate Departments of Psychology, by degree area and subfield area, 2001–2002 [Table]. *Graduate study in psychology 2003.* Washington, DC: American Psychological Association.

10.5% of applicants to Ph.D. clinical programs get accepted. However, of those acceptances, 1,230 actually enrolled. Of course, some students receive multiple acceptances as well, so 1,930 acceptances evolve into 1,230 students actually enrolling in 2001–2002.

The data in the "Number Newly Enrolled" column is an index of the popularity of a specialty area. Ph.D. clinical tends to be both competitive and popular, but not all specialty areas share those characteristics. For instance, a developmental Ph.D. program is somewhat popular (343 newly enrolled), but not as competitive (24.8% accepted). These comparisons become more meaningful when looked at across degree programs. For instance, the master's degree in counseling ($N = 2,370$) is much more popular than the Ph.D. in counseling ($N = 412$), but the Ph.D. counseling programs are more competitive (14.7% accepted) than the master's degree in counseling programs (60.7% accepted). Use the data in this table wisely—don't let it drive your decisions about applying to graduate school, but at the same time use the data to keep informed and make reasoned decisions about your options for graduate school.

OVERVIEW: THE APPLICATION PROCESS

Before we jump into the details of the process, an overview is in order. Buskist (2002) provides a thoughtful overview of the graduate application process in his seven tips for preparing a successful graduate school application (pp. 32–34): (a) be planful; (b) develop competencies as an undergraduate; (c) settle on a specialty area; (d) involve yourself in undergraduate research; (e) do homework on potential graduate schools; (f) identify possible major professors; and (g) write an outstanding letter of intent. APA (1997a) suggests that the three keys to getting into graduate school are (a) preparation, (b) application know-how, and (c) patience. Moreover, they indicate that you will need to:

- Determine your chances for getting admitted to a graduate program. This chapter should be helpful in starting to determine those chances.
- Take the Graduate Record Examination (GRE); plan to take the exam during the fall semester prior to your expected admission to a graduate program.
- When you have narrowed your program list and have taken your GRE, you are ready to apply.

Narrowing Your Program List. An excellent guide to finding information about graduate programs in psychology in the United States is the annual *Graduate Study in Psychology* published by the American Psychological Association. The 2000 edition of this book contained the following suggestions:

- Apply to a range of programs, with most offering you a reasonable chance at acceptance. It takes too much time, effort, and money to apply to programs at which you have no reasonable chance of acceptance.
- When possible, apply to programs that offer the degree that you ultimately want to obtain.
- Apply to programs that offer the specialty in which you would like to eventually gain employment. It is difficult to change your major emphasis or area "midstream" in your graduate education.
- Apply to programs that match your interests and your experience. Know who the faculty members are, do your homework, and apply to programs where you believe you will be a good "fit."
- Be informed about the issues related to career opportunities of your chosen area of psychology. Although your graduate program is responsible for your educational opportunities, *you* are responsible for your employment opportunities.

Understanding the Application Process. The second area of expertise that you will have to develop in this endeavor is a good working knowledge of the application process (APA, 1997a). Some concerns and activities in this area include the following:

- Contact programs to request an application, departmental information, and financial aid information (if necessary).

- Prepare the materials required by most applications (in addition to the application fee): (a) letter of intent/autobiographical statement/personal statement; (b) letters of recommendation and transcripts/grades; (c) GRE scores forwarded directly from the Educational Testing Service (ETS); (d) curriculum vita or resume (see more below), and a cover letter; and (e) personal interview (in some cases for some programs).

What is the difference between a curriculum vita (commonly called a vita) and a resume? A vita is an academic document that chronicles your accomplishments and achievements related to the discipline. A resume is more of a work history and advertisement of your skills and abilities. In general, a resume needs to be short, one to two pages, whereas a long vita means a long list of accomplishments. More on these two documents can be found later in this chapter. A guide to vita preparation and sample vitae of undergraduate students is also presented later.

Diehl and Sullivan (1998) also offer additional suggestions to make this process result in a desired outcome. Several of their suggestions cover a timetable of activities for an ideal process; we will present a slightly different version of the timetable in a moment. They suggest that when you are applying, send more than what is asked. Send more than the required number of letters of recommendation. If the application materials do not request a vita, send one anyway (unless you believe your vita hurts your application). Send copies of your written work, such as an impressive term paper from an upper division psychology course, or a copy of some work from a senior thesis, internship, independent study, or directed research project. After you have sent off your packet of application materials, make sure that the department received *everything*. It is *your* responsibility to make sure that letters of recommendation and transcripts are received. Appropriately timed telephone calls can save an application. An incomplete application package is an easy excuse for a graduate admissions committee to *not* review your materials. Note that sometimes a graduate application might not even make it past the secretary's desk. Many graduate programs are serious about minimum GPAs and GRE scores; the remainder of the packet may be for naught if these initial hurdles are not adequately completed.

Also, when filling out applications, *type everything*. Be sure to fill out all forms completely, including those forms that you must give to the people who write your letter of recommendation. You usually have to sign a waiver of your rights to inspect your documents—be sure to fill out all the information; your faculty member cannot fill this out for you, and often the document is sent directly from the faculty member to the graduate institution. Watch for more tips about the application process throughout this chapter.

Patience. The third component in this overview of the process is patience. Sometimes patience is the hardest part. The process typically works like this: (a) You will usually be notified of your acceptance or rejection before April 15; sometimes earlier, and sometimes later (if you are on a wait list); however, you should receive some feedback by April 15. (b) Accept or reject an offer, in writing, by or on April 15; if you decide to attend, it's good to have that decision over with; if you decide not to attend, the school can go to the next person on the wait list and make that person an offer; although you may need some time to make your decision, it is not appropriate to delay this decision after April 15.

In the remainder of this chapter, we will look at the details of navigating through this process and finish up with some of the keys to being a successful applicant and a successful graduate student. An excellent resource that you may want to consult is *The Complete Guide to Graduate School Admission: Psychology, Counseling, and Related Professions* (2nd ed.) by Keith-Spiegel and Wiederman (2000). Reading this book and following the advice will probably improve your performance in the entire admissions process.

PRIMARY AND SECONDARY SELECTION CRITERIA, WITH CAVEATS

What can you do to make your application more competitive? What do graduate admissions committees look for? How do they make these decisions about whom to admit into their program or reject? The primary selection criteria are your GPA, your GRE scores, and your letters of recommendation (Keith-Spiegel & Wiederman, 2000)—sometimes called the "big three." Landrum, Jeglum, and Cashin (1994) examined the decision-making processes of graduate admissions committee members and found that in addition to the big three, two more factors have emerged—research experience and the autobiographical statement/letter of intent. The importance of these latter two factors is also seen in Table 6.2, which presents Keith-Spiegel and Wiederman's (2000) secondary selection criteria. Interestingly, work by Cashin and Landrum (1991) found that undergraduates understand the importance of factors such as GPA but tend to *underestimate* the importance of GRE scores and letters of recommendation, and they *overestimate* the importance of extracurricular activities.

TABLE 6.2 Secondary Selection Criteria in Rank Order of Importance

Items Rated as "Very Important"

- Research experience, resulting in a publication credit in a scholarly journal
- Degree to which applicant's skills and interests match those of the program
- Research experience, resulting in a paper presented at a professional meeting
- Degree of interest expressed by one or more of the members of the selection committee in working with particular applicants
- Clarity and focus of applicant's statement of purpose

Items Rated as "Generally Important"

- Research assistant experience
- Writing skills as revealed in the applicant's statement of purpose
- Status and reputation of applicant's referees
- Strong, supportive mentor actively involved in advocating applicant's candidacy
- Degree to which applicant possesses a knowledge of and interest in the program
- Underrepresented ethnic minority membership of applicant
- Number of statistics/research methodology courses taken as an undergraduate
- Number of hard science courses taken as an undergraduate
- Prestige and status of psychology faculty in applicant's undergraduate department
- Prestige of applicant's undergraduate institution
- Potential for success as judged by preselection interviews or some other form of personal contact
- Honors or merit scholarships awarded to applicant by undergraduate institution

Items Rated as "Somewhat Important"

- Area of undergraduate major
- Relevant field/volunteer experience in placement relevant to your program
- Social/personality style as revealed through preselection interview or some other form of personal contact
- Relevant paid work experience related to program
- Neatness and "professional look" of the application materials
- Teaching assistant experience
- Level of applicant's active participation in department activities

Items Rated as "Minimally Important" or "Not Important"

- Student affiliate status in a relevant professional organization
- Gender balance in the program applied to
- Psi Chi membership
- Multilingual capabilities
- Contribution to geographical diversity

Source: Keith-Spiegel, P. (1991). *The complete guide to graduate school admission: Psychology and related fields.* Hillsdale, NJ: Erlbaum.

These conclusions are further supported by Keith-Spiegel and Wiederman's (2000) secondary selection criteria. Imagine this scenario—a top graduate program attracts many qualified applicants, who meet the standards set with respect to GRE scores and GPA, and all applicants have excellent letters of recommendation. How does the committee distinguish among applicants in this group—that is, after qualifying on the primary selection criteria (GRE, GPA, letters of recommendation), what information does the committee now use to make its decisions (in essence, what are the tie-breakers among a group of well-qualified students where not enough graduate student slots exist to admit all applicants who qualify on the primary selection criteria)? Keith-Spiegel and Wiederman (2000) compiled a detailed list of these factors, empirically based, presented by rank of importance (ranked in Table 6.2 from highest to lowest).

If you are not careful, it is easy to misunderstand some of the items in this table. For example, the information about Psi Chi membership does not mean that participation in Psi Chi is not important—it means that Psi Chi membership is an unlikely factor to make or break an application—it is not a tie-breaker. However, the contacts that you make in Psi Chi, the opportunities to go to conferences, gain leadership ability, and work with faculty members one on one (that may lead to the very important letters of recommendation) are all good things that come out of Psi Chi participation. Membership itself may not be an application tie-breaker, but that does not mean that the activity is unimportant.

Landrum and Clark (2004) analyzed departmental ratings of graduate school admissions criteria. Overall, the criteria receiving the highest percentages of "high importance" ratings were letters of recommendation, statement of goals and objectives, and grade point average. However, the importance ratings varied depending on the type of degree a department offers (master's only, doctorate only, master's and doctoral degrees). Instead of GPA, GRE, and letters of recommendation (the "big three"), the overall pattern of highest importance ratings (percentage of departments rating a criterion of high importance) was: letters of recommendation (79.3%), statement of goals and objectives (75.0%), GPA (71.0%), and the interview (61.7%). This grouping was followed by research experience (52.2%) and GRE scores (48.2%). Do these data mean that GRE scores are no longer important—no, it does not. It does mean, however, that only 48.2% of all departments rate the GRE with the highest important rating; students need to remember to find the best fit or match between what they have to offer and what graduate departments are looking for.

Your graduate school application package is bound to be a very complex series of documents. Unfortunately, there is no uniform method of applying to graduate schools, and each school wants each bit of information in its own format—as an applicant, you have very little power in this situation, so you need to play the game exactly by the rules set by each school. The graduate school application is not the place to ad lib and do it your own way—that strategy almost always backfires. What might be in your application package? Keith-Spiegel and Wiederman (2000) generated a fairly comprehensive list (see Table 6.3).

In the rest of this chapter, we will address some of the key components of this application process, by examining (a) grades, transcripts, and the GRE, (b) letters of recommendation with faculty examples, (c) the personal statement with student examples, (d) a student's version of a vita, (e) the importance of research experience, and (f) the importance of match or fit with

---

TABLE 6.3 Potential Components of a Graduate School Application Package

Curriculum vita or resume

Biographical statement (sometimes called personal statement, autobiographical statement, letter of intent), including a statement of your interests and career goals

Overall grade point average (GPA), GPA in psychology, verified by an official copy of your transcripts

List of relevant courses you have completed in the major, and a timetable for those courses not yet completed but planned for the future

GRE scores

Letters of recommendation, sent by you or directly to the school by the referees as directed
Application fee (if applicable)

Cover letter, if necessary

your graduate programs of interest. Remember these words of wisdom from Arnold and Horrigan (2002): "You can amplify your chances of gaining admission into graduate school by developing good relationships with professors and work managers (this is significant for establishing good recommendations), actively and continuously working on a research project, obtaining and expansive background in psychology and related fields (e.g., math and statistics), receiving good grades (especially in upper division classes), and achieving a high score on the GRE. Maintaining a high GPA and testing well on the GRE will provide you with an advantage over the competition, but as a serious applicant you should have a combination of all these educational areas" (p. 31).

GRADES, TRANSCRIPTS, AND THE GRE

Your grades in college serve as one of the big three admissions factors. Although programs vary, as a general rule most graduate programs are going to have a minimum GPA cutoff of 3.0; many programs have higher minimum requirements. The best sources of information about these requirements come from the APA's *Graduate Study in Psychology* published annually, and from materials received directly from your institutions of interest. Although exceptions are occasionally made about the minimum cutoff, they must be accompanied by an explanation about why an exception to the rule is warranted. Given that more students want to attend graduate school than graduate school slots are available, universities can be (and must be) selective in choosing those students who have the best potential to be successful graduates of their program. A low GPA, without any accompanying information, is a predictor of your future performance. C or average work is not acceptable in most graduate programs. If you are striving for admission into a graduate program, and a 3.0 is probably the minimum requirement, think about this—*every C that you earn as an undergraduate hurts your chances for admission to graduate school* because every C (and of course, even lower grades) lowers your GPA below 3.0.

If you are serious about graduate school and have modest grades (a GPA of 2.7 to 3.2 on a 4-point scale), you may want to consider the following additional strategies as suggested by Keith-Spiegel and Wiederman (2000):

Delay graduation. Take extra time to get better grades in the classes that you have left to take. If you do this, however, make sure that you earn mostly A's in these remaining classes—low grades at a slower pace will not look good at all in your quest for graduate school.

Take selected courses over again. Check the policies at your school—does the last grade replace the first, or are the grades averaged together? What happens if the second grade is lower? Repeat courses not to hide a problem grade, but to prove that you can do better work.

Become a post-baccalaureate student at your undergraduate school. Go ahead and graduate, but stay at your school another semester or year, taking selected classes, working with faculty on research and other projects, etc., doing all the things you can to strengthen your application.

Perform exceptionally well on the GRE. Very high GRE test scores may be able to compensate somewhat for a modest GPA. Sometimes a strong GRE score can make up for a weak GPA; the reverse is *rarely* true.

Take classes at your desired graduate institution. You can probably enroll as an unclassified graduate student (like having an undeclared major as an undergraduate), and, space permitting and as long as you meet the prerequisites and requirements, you may be able to take some of the classes with the first-year (admitted) graduate students. This approach can be a high-risk tactic because there is no guarantee of eventual admittance into the program; you've got to get into the classes and do well; you may have to relocate to take these classes, etc.

Settle for programs with lower academic requirements. With modest grades, you may not be able to gain admission to your top-tier or dream schools. You may have to go to a lesser-known school in a part of the country you do not know much about. Some schools may admit you provisionally, a type of probationary status that gives you a chance to demonstrate your competency.

Earn a master's degree before applying to a doctoral program. Your grades may not get you into a doctoral program, but they might get you into a master's degree program. This program becomes your proving ground, and when you apply for doctoral programs, more emphasis is placed on your graduate work and less emphasis is placed on your undergraduate work. *Great* grades are important, but the bottom line is research, research, research!

Earn the master's degree instead of the doctoral degree. As you have seen in earlier sections of this chapter, there are a number of excellent opportunities for employment with a master's degree. You may be able to have a satisfying career without the Ph.D. or Psy.D.

Your transcript is an important record of your academic accomplishments, and as Appleby (2003) suggests, it speaks volumes about your potential as a future graduate student. Landrum (2003) examined the effect of student withdrawals (W's) on the transcript and its effect on graduate admissions. Based on the responses of 139 graduate admissions directors, this study found (a) graduate admissions committees carefully examine transcripts; this is typically done by two faculty members; (b) graduate admissions committees highly value transcripts, and either a low GPA or low GRE score may trigger a closer examination of transcripts; and (c) one withdrawal on the transcript does not seem to be a problem. Two withdrawals is probably not a problem, except for a small number of schools. For some schools, withdrawals in particular courses (such as Statistics or Research Methods) are more detrimental than withdrawals in other courses. Your transcript is one of your credentials that you will need for future opportunities—be sure your transcripts tell the story you want. We encourage you to consult with faculty mentors and academic advisors when considering the effects of withdrawals on future prospects.

Another significant component of the big three is the GRE, a series of tests administered nationally by the Educational Testing Service. The GRE is administered via computer, and you take the GRE in authorized test centers located throughout the nation (and literally the world). This test is administered continuously October through January, from February to September you can take the test the first 3 weeks of each month. You schedule the computer-based test at your convenience; another benefit is that you know your unofficial test scores prior to leaving the test center. What does the GRE test measure? According to ETS (1998b), "the verbal measure tests the ability to analyze and evaluate written material and synthesize information obtained from it, to analyze relationships among component parts of sentences, and to recognize relations between words and concepts. The quantitative measure tests basic mathematical skills and understanding of elementary mathematical concepts, as well as the ability to reason quantitatively and to solve problems in a quantitative setting" (p. 5). Graduate admissions committees often care about verbal and quantitative GRE scores because they are useful predictors of performance of some of the key tasks of graduate school, namely writing and statistical ability. In addition, a subject test is available in psychology, and some graduate schools may require psychology subject test scores. It is important to know that the GRE test has changed. See Table 6.4 for examples of the types of analytical writing tasks used.

The range of the two traditional measures (verbal, quantitative) is from 200 points to 800 points. Each graduate school you are interested in may have different preferences in your scores. Some may want at least a 450 in both verbal and quantitative. Some schools may just look at your total score (V+Q; your verbal score + your quantitative score). Hence, the minimum cutoff may be a V+Q of 1200, meaning any combination of V+Q to reach 1200 points, not necessarily 600 verbal and 600 quantitative. The psychology subject test has a range of 200 to 990 (ETS, 1998). It should be noted that many disciplines require potential graduate students to take the GRE general test, not just psychology; other disciplines also have specialized subject area tests.

When examining all GRE general test takers from October 1994 to September 1997 (a total of approximately 1.14 million examinees), the average verbal ability score was 474, and the average quantitative score was 558 (ETS, 1998). When looking at just psychology students taking the general test during that same time frame (over 55,000 students), the average verbal score was 472, and the average quantitative score was 514.

TABLE 6.4 Sample Questions from the GRE Analytical Writing Section

Sample Issue Task: Present Your Perspective on an Issue

Directions: Present your perspective on the issue below, using relevant reasons and/or examples to support your views.	Sample: "In our time, specialists of all kinds are highly overrated. We need more generalists—people who can provide broad perspectives."

Sample Argument Task: Discuss How Well Reasoned You Find This Argument

Directions: Discuss how well reasoned you find this argument.	Sample: "Six months ago the region of Forestville increased the speed limit for vehicles traveling on the region's highways by ten miles per hour. Since that change took effect, the number of automobile accidents in that region has increased by 15 percent. But the speed limit in Elmsford, a region neighboring Forestville, remained unchanged, and automobile accidents declined slightly during the same six-month period. Therefore, if the citizens of Forestville want to reduce the number of automobile accidents on the region's highways, they should campaign to reduce Forestville's speed limit to what it was before the increase."

Source: Educational Testing Service (2001). *Coming in October 2002: A new GRE General Test.* Princeton, NJ: Educational Testing Service.

LETTERS OF RECOMMENDATION, WITH FACULTY EXAMPLES

Your letters of recommendation serve as a key component of the big three. Letters of recommendation are interesting and somewhat different from the GPA or your GRE scores. Although other people certainly have some degree of influence over GRE and GPA, your professors and supervisors have direct influence over the letters of recommendation given. You are going to need to choose people who know your professional development, skills, and abilities and know them *well*. For a faculty member to get to know you this well, you are going to have to get involved outside of the classroom. It takes more than being a good book student to get superb letters of recommendation. In fact, Table 6.5 presents a listing of items that your letter writers might be asked to write about you. By inspecting this list carefully, you will realize that you have to *interact personally* with faculty members for them to recognize your talents to the degree that it benefits you in a letter of recommendation.

That's quite a list! If you are a student in one class with a faculty member, do the bare minimum work, never speak up in class, and never have a conversation with the faculty member outside of class, then that faculty member will have a difficult time with almost all of the ideas presented in Table 6.5. Whom should you ask? Keith-Spiegel and Wiederman (2000) found that the best sources for letters are from (a) a mentor with whom the applicant has done considerable work, (b) an applicant's professor who is also well known and highly respected, (c) an employer on a job related to the applicant's professional goals, and (d) the department chair.

In a survey of writers of letters of recommendation, Keith-Spiegel and Wiederman (2000) asked faculty to rate particular behaviors or attitudes that letter writers want to write about most. Examine this list carefully (see Table 6.6), and think about what your letter writer is going to write about you. The left column presents the best options, whereas the right column presents the worst options.

Letters of recommendation are sometimes stressful for both the student and the letter-writer. For more tips on how to solicit strong letters of recommendation, see the exercise at the end of this chapter. Students often wonder about their letters of recommendation. When applying to graduate school, one of the forms will ask the student if they want to waive their access to their application file (including letters of recommendation). However, if you do not waive your right, you will get to see your application file if you are accepted into that graduate program.

Faculty members differ on their practices of releasing letters to students. For very good students with very good letters, faculty may be inclined to give the student a copy of the letter.

TABLE 6.5 Possible Characteristics To-Be-Described in Letters of Recommendation

- Academic achievement
- Research ability, experience, or potential
- Teaching potential or experience
- Verbal skills, public speaking ability
- Writing skills, level of writing proficiency
- Industriousness, motivation, perseverance, energy level, drive
- Quantitative abilities
- Creativity, originality, imagination
- Analytical ability
- Leadership skills, level of respect accorded by others
- Sociability, social skills, ability to get along with peers
- Emotional stability, level of emotional adjustment
- Judgment, ability to make sound decisions, ability to reason
- Flexibility, adaptiveness
- Ability to work independently
- Knowledge of the field
- General knowledge base
- Desire to achieve, seriousness of purpose, initiative
- Professionalism, maturity
- Social awareness, level of concern for others
- Physical grooming, personal appearance
- Character, honesty, integrity, ethical and moral standards
- Ability to work with others, teamwork potential, cooperativeness
- Dependability, level of responsibility
- Potential as a teacher
- Potential as a practitioner

Source: Keith-Spiegel, P., & Wiederman, M. W. (2000). *The complete guide to graduate school admission: Psychology, counseling, and related professions* (2nd ed.). Mahwah, NJ: Erlbaum.

TABLE 6.6 What Letter Writers Want and Do Not Want to Write About

Student Behavior in the Classroom

Best	*Worst*
Seems very interested in the course	Cheats on an exam
Usually has good answer to questions in class	Plagiarizes a written assignment
Very attentive during lecture	Sleeps during lectures
Disagrees with opinions but in a respectful way	Talks to neighbors during lectures
Asks lots of questions in class	Sneers/rolls eyes during your lecture

Student Behavior Outside of Class

Best	*Worst*
Drops by office occasionally to comment on topic that has sparked some interest	Is openly hostile toward you
Comes to office during office hours for assistance	Is very complementary but manipulative
Always smiles and says hi in the hallways	Is flirtatious and seductive
	Is openly critical of you

Personal Characteristics

Best	*Worst*
Highly motivated to achieve	Arrogant
Responsible and dependable	Always depressed
Professional and mature manner and attitude	Silly
Very likable	Requires considerable, structured direction

TABLE 6.6   (Contd.)

Miscellaneous Behaviors and Characteristics

Best	Worst
Top student in the class	Caught cheating on one exam, appeared genuinely contrite and promised to change
Puts extra effort into term paper, class assignment	
Top 5% (GPA) in graduating class Shows up frequently to departmental colloquia	Dresses and grooms very unconventionally

Source: Keith-Spiegel, P. (1991). *The complete guide to graduate school admission: Psychology and related fields.* Hillsdale, NJ: Erlbaum.

Other faculty members never release letters to students, no matter how good the letter (or the student). A direct conversation with the faculty member can resolve any of these concerns. Also, do not assume that the lack of access means a bad letter—faculty may be following their own personal policy, or even a departmental or university policy. To take some mystery out of the process, we include a sample letter of recommendation for a student applying to graduate school (see Figure 6.1). Think about the types of things YOU need to do to garner strong letters of recommendation.

THE PERSONAL STATEMENT, WITH STUDENT EXAMPLES

Although the letters of recommendation communicate the faculty members' perspectives about you, you also have the opportunity to present yourself. Most graduate programs require applicants to submit something called a personal statement (or statement of intent, or autobiographical statement, or letter of intent). This activity is becoming more and more important in the admissions process (Landrum et al., 1994). It allows you to provide valuable background information about yourself, and it also provides the graduate admissions committee with a writing sample. The requirements for completing this task are about as varied as most graduate programs—there is not a uniform method or procedure to follow. Hence, you need to make sure that you completely satisfy the requirements of *each* school when you are preparing your personal statement. For a nonrandom sample of personal statement instructions, see Table 6.7. If you note the variability, you will see that the same statement could not possibly satisfy the different instructions.

There are a growing number of sources for advice on preparing a personal statement. For instance, Bottoms and Nysse (1999) suggest that the major sections of your personal statement should be previous research experience, current research interests, other relevant experience, and career goals. Additional tips for preparing your personal statement are presented in Table 6.8, coming from both Osborne (1996) and APA (1997c).

Keith-Spiegel and Wiederman (2000) found that in the personal statement instructions that they examined, 13 themes emerged. One point to be stressed—*do not write a single one-size-fits-all letter for all schools.* Do your homework, and give the committee the answers it wants, not a generic statement that vaguely addresses the school's information needs. To help personalize your responses, you may wish to closely examine the 13 themes listed on p. 91. Also, addressing these issues should help you focus on why you want to go to graduate school, what you want to accomplish with your degree, and how best to get from here to there.

College of Social Sciences and Public Affairs   1910 University Drive   Boise, Idaho 83725-1715

Department of   phone 208-426-1207
Psychology   fax 208-426-4386

February 28, 2003

Graduate Admissions Committee
Department of Psychology
Idaho State University
Pocatello, ID 83209-8112

Dear Colleagues,

I have been asked by Kevin Howardlock to write a letter of recommendation
in support of his application to your graduate program in psychology. It is
my pleasure to provide this letter and my support for Kevin.

I have known Kevin for almost one year. He was my student in PSYC 295
Statistical Methods, PSYC 120 Introduction to the Psychology Major
course, and PSYC 321 Research Methods course. In addition, I invited him
to serve as a teaching assistant for my PSYC 295 Statistical Methods course
for Spring 2003. Through these interactions in and out of class, I feel that I
know Kevin very well. I think this is remarkable in itself, because I don't
usually get to know my students that well in that short a time frame. That
begins to tell you Kevin's story.

I think Kevin is probably one of the most motivated, talented, and self-
directed students I have encountered in many years. I have enjoyed getting
to know Kevin because he has a mature attitude about his education. He
takes every opportunity seriously, and maximizes every possible moment.
On many occasions I have had the chance to talk to Kevin about his graduate
school plans and career aspirations. Not only will he be successful in
graduate school, but he will thrive in whatever program is lucky enough to
get him. He is very personable, and easy to talk to. I have enjoyed my
numerous conversations with him.

I have seen his class performance and his work ethic firsthand in the courses
that he has taken from me. For instance, after completing Research
Methods, Kevin took his manuscript and modified it for submission to the
2003 Rocky Mountain Psychological Association meeting in Denver (we

Figure 6.1 Sample Letters of Recommendation for Graduate School Applicants

Letter of Recommendation for Kevin Howardlock
February 28, 2003
Page 2

just heard earlier this week that it was accepted!). Although I make that
opportunity available to all my Methods students, very few are willing to go
the extra mile and see the opportunity available to them. With some careful
planning on his part, he used his project in my class as a pilot project for a
senior thesis that he plans to complete with a colleague of mine in the spring.
Kevin thinks about everything. He plans in advance. He sees the
relationship between the classroom and his future; he recognizes the
opportunities available to him as an undergraduate, and he maximizes those
opportunities to full potential. When Kevin approached me about being a
teaching assistant for Statistics, I jumped at the chance because I knew it
would be a good experience for him, and that he would be a great teaching
assistant for our students. I wish that Kevin had a bit more time at Boise
State; I would have invited him to serve as a Research Assistant with me,
and I am confident that our collaborations would have been extremely
fruitful. He knows how to get things done, and done well.

The skills and abilities that I have observed in Kevin will serve him well in
graduate school. His persistence, strong self-motivation, clear career goals,
and pure talent will help him to succeed in graduate school and beyond. He
is the type of student that will instantly emerge as a natural leader, even
among the talented graduate students he will be joining. He will be a credit
to our profession, and I look forward to having him as a professional
colleague. He's simply that good.

If you think I can be of any additional assistance, please contact me directly.
**I recommend Kevin Howardlock to you with my highest
recommendation and without reservation.**

Sincerely,

R. Eric Landrum, Ph.D.
Professor
Department of Psychology

Phone: (208) 426-1993   Fax: (208) 426-4386   Email: elandru@boisestate.edu

TABLE 6.7 Sample Instructions for a Personal Statement

Include a one- to two-page statement describing your plans for graduate study and professional career in psychology.—University of Wyoming

The statement of purpose should be 500–600 words (clinical: 900 words) in length and should contain a description of relevant work/research/volunteer activities, outline future professional goals, and state your expectations of the graduate school experience.—Arizona State University

A letter of intent describing your clinical and research interests, educational and professional goals, faculty whom you might be interested in working with, factors that you would want the admissions committee to consider in evaluating your application that are not evident from other materials, and some background information describing how you became interested in these areas.—University of Nevada–Las Vegas

On this or a separate page(s), please provide a clear, concise one- to two-page essay summarizing your background in psychology (or related field), career objectives, research experience, research interests, and why you are applying to Montana State University's M.S. program in Applied Psychology. Please be sure to read and sign the signature page at the end of this document.—Montana State University

Clinical program: Your autobiographical sketch should answer the following questions:

What is the source of your interest in psychology?

Why do you want to pursue graduate studies in clinical rather than another area of psychology?

Why do you want a clinical Ph.D. rather than a Psy.D. degree?

Why are you applying to the University of Colorado?

Which two (2) research mentors have you selected at the University of Colorado and why?

What has been your previous research experience? Provide letter(s) of recommendation from your research supervisor(s) with their phone number(s).

What has been your previous practical experience, paid or volunteer? Provide a letter of recommendation from your clinical supervisor.

All other programs: Your autobiographical sketch should address the following items, numbering your answers as listed below:

Describe your previous research experience.

Why do you wish to pursue graduate studies in your chosen area of specialization?

Why are you applying to the University of Colorado?

Which two (2) research mentors have you selected at the UC and why?—University of Colorado

Please prepare approximately two to three pages of typewritten, double-spaced autobiographical material which will be considered confidential. If available include a copy of your vita and e-mail address. (Please be aware that the review committees may contain graduate student representatives.)

Indicate the source of your interest in psychology and the reasons why you wish to pursue graduate studies in your chosen area of specialization. If you have had practical experience (work or volunteer) in psychology, please describe it. If you have been in another areas of academic study or employment, discuss your change. When and how was your attention directed to our graduate program? Indicate how the specific features of our training program would facilitate your professional goals, and indicate which faculty's research interests represent a match with your own training goals. What are your career plans? What would you ultimately like to do?—University of Denver

Source: Landrum, R. E. (2004b, April). *Building blocks of a personal statement.* Presented at the Rocky Mountain Psychological Association meeting, Reno, NV.

TABLE 6.8 Tips for Preparing Your Personal Statement

Allow yourself ample time to write, revise, edit, and proofread.

Be willing to write as many drafts as are necessary to produce a unified, coherent essay.

Attend to the instructions carefully and discover what the program is most interested in knowing about you.

Personal details included in the statement seem relevant to my ability to be a successful graduate student.

Follow the instructions to the letter, adhere to length limitations, and answer everything that is asked.

Do not repeat information that is already in your application, such as your GRE scores or your GPA.

Use the essay as an opportunity to highlight your uniqueness and your strengths.

Describe yourself honestly and realistically, acknowledging your weak points (if requested) and stress your good points without exaggerating. Try to connect these good points to your aspirations in psychology.

Demonstrate that you have taken the time to familiarize yourself with the program. Emphasize the match between your goals and those of the program.

Reveal characteristics of my "self" that reflect maturity, adaptability, and motivation.

Use formal language and a serious tone; avoid slang, clichés, and colloquialisms. Pay attention to spelling and grammar. Mistakes here seriously detract from your overall statement.

Avoid jargon. It is more important to use the right word than the complex word.

Be careful in using superlative language, such as all, every, always, and never.

Read your essay out loud to help find trouble spots.

Have someone else help edit and proofread your work.

Convey a convincing portrayal of my abilities to succeed in this school's graduate program.

Sources: American Psychological Association (1997). *Getting in: A step-by-step guide for gaining admission to graduate school in psychology.* Washington, DC: American Psychological Association. Osborne, R.E. (1996, Fall). The "personal" side of graduate school personal statements. *Eye on Psi Chi, 1* (1), 14–15.

Career plans (Tell us about your plans. What do you see yourself doing five to ten years from now?)

General interest areas (What are your academic interests?)

Research experiences (Have you had any research experiences? What did you do as a research assistant?)

Academic objectives (Why are you interested in graduate study? What can our graduate program do for you?)

Clinical or other field experience/practicum/internship (Tell us about any these experiences.)

Academic background and achievements (What should we know about your academic work? Are your GRE scores and GPA representative of your ability?)

What do you see in us (Why did you choose us? What can you do for our graduate program?)

Motivation (Why did you choose graduate study? What events shaped your current career aspirations?)

Personal material (Tell us about yourself. What do you think we should know about you?)

Autobiography (Provide a brief biographical sketch. Tell us a bit about your background.)

Specific graduate faculty of interest (Cite two faculty members who most closely represent your own interests in psychology. Whom would you like to work with in our graduate program?)

Anything else we should know? (This can be a dangerous question—do not offer too much!)

Special skills (Languages known, mathematics, or computer skills)

One final note on this topic—be sure to answer the questions exactly. Graduate admissions committee members will actually read your personal statement, so make sure that you answer the questions that you are asked. Answer completely and concisely. To help visualize this process, see Figure 6.2 below that contains a sample personal statement from a former student who successfully entered graduate school.

The field of psychology has always been very interesting to me. It all began with an Introduction of Psychology class when I was a junior in high school. In that class, I was introduced to human development, human assessment, and psychological disorders. I recall thinking that psychology can serve a purpose, especially in the aspect of counseling people and helping them with their problems and concerns. It turned out to be one of my favorite classes of high school.

Unfortunately, I re-entered college late starting up again when I was 27 years old. When I had decided to go back to college, I chose the field of psychology as my major. This choice was influenced by my previous experiences that I had while I was a junior in high school. Also, many people had told me that I had a talent for listening to them, and helping them solve their issues and concerns. I thought that becoming a psychologist would be an excellent way to help others, and was something that I could be happy with as a career.

My interest and knowledge of psychology really grew as I continued my studies as an undergraduate. I was amazed at all the fields of study that psychology had to offer. Even though there were so many to choose from, I always knew that I wanted to become a therapist so I would be able to help others with their needs. Also, research has become a large part of my life. Part of my research was to develop and distribute a survey in the community where I currently live. Through this research I was able to see the benefits of statistics in telling my group what people liked and disliked about their community. As it turns out, the local government used the results of the study to see what was needed for improvements in the community. Another research project that I was involved in was an analysis of what graduate schools valued as important for graduate admissions. What I learned from that experience was what schools I would like to attend, and what they required for admission. This research is in review now for publishing, and it is my hope that others may benefit from my work on the project. Through it all, I have come to love psychology, and I want to be able to use research and the skills learned from psychology to create a better world for others and myself.

To continue on with my studies, I have chosen to pursue a Ph.D. in Counseling Psychology. I really feel that a Ph.D. in Counseling Psychology will give me the skills and the knowledge to become a source of help for many people. With the research experience that I will gain, it is my great desire to publish my research through textbooks and novels that can be available to the public. I am also interested in the ability to teach at the university level. I feel that the Ph.D. program offered by the New Mexico State University can provide all of these.

I can see that the program at New Mexico State University can provide many opportunities for me. I am especially interested in the focus of cultural diversity in our society. I lived in Spain for two years, and am fluent in Spanish. Therefore I am very interested in working with Dr. Luis A. Vázquez in his bilingual counseling. I feel that I could be a great service to my community if I had bilingual skills in counseling. It is my concern that there are many Spanish-American people that does not receive the help they need due to a language barrier. Along the same lines, I am interested in working with Dr. Rod J. Merta due to his expertise in addictions and multicultural counseling. Some of the research conducted by Dr. Charles H. Huber on family and marriage holds great interest for me. The family is the cornerstone of society. I am very interested in working with younger people. Therefore, I would be interested in working with Dr. Peggy Kaczmarek in her study of child and adolescent therapy. Any and all of these professors would be great mentors for my goals as a professional.

It is easy to see that New Mexico State University has much to offer for a Ph.D. in Counseling Psychology. I am very impressed with the focus of research that the professors are conducting. I feel that the university holds the goals that I am looking for. My favorite is rule #13 which states, "Students will be expected to integrate the roles of psychologist, counselor, and researcher, to assess their own strengths and weaknesses, and to remain open and committed to both personal and professional growth." I strongly feel that this says it all. I know that I can be a great asset to New Mexico State University. Thank you.

FIGURE 6.2 Sample Personal Statement

A STUDENT'S GUIDE TO THE CURRICULUM VITA (CV), WITH EXAMPLES

Another component of this arduous graduate school application process involves the preparation of a *curriculum vita*, which literally means "academic life." Although related to the resume, the vita chronicles your accomplishments, whereas the resume is a brief introduction to your skills, abilities, and employment history. A goal in resume writing is keeping the resume short, one or two pages. A CV is usually a longer document that tracks your entire history of academic performance, not just a summary of employment positions. In a bit, we offer some sample student CVs—first, here are some ideas on how to organize your CV. (See also Table 6.9.) Some general suggestions come from Hayes and Hayes (1989, no page number): (a) "Write up your vita now. No matter how puny. From acorns giant oaks grow, and you might as well begin. It will also get you thinking about your career development; (b) Keep a vita development file. (If you aren't keeping any kind of files yet, start). Throw notes into this file regarding the kinds of things you are doing on your assistantships, special talks you gave, activities you performed that were noteworthy, committee assignments, papers presented, associations joined, everything you need to update your vita; (c) Set goals for your career and work toward them. Design a reasonable strategy to reach those goals. Use the periodic updates of your vita as an opportunity to assess the development of your career; (d) Revise your vita at least once a year or more often if the need arises; and (e) Have your advisor and others go over your vita before you send it out."

There is much good advice about preparing a vita, including what do to and what not to do (however, much of the available advice is aimed at faculty members and their CVs). Lord (2004) suggests using a beginning CV as an inspirational document: "At first, you might find it depressing to construct an academic vita, because many of the headings will be followed by blank lines. Do not worry about it. Everyone starts that way. One reason for constructing an academic vita is to remind you that it is empty. Write in your appointment book a time once a month when you will print your vita and think about how you could improve it" (p. 10). Roddy Roediger, former President of the American Psychological Society, offered this advice concerning vita preparation (2004, no page number): "You should put your educational and occupational history on the first page of your vita and try to make it complete enough to explain any gaps. If you worked in industry for 4 years between the bachelor's degree and your graduate education, list your work experiences here, along with other experiences, in chronological order. Do not let the reader guess what you might have been doing, as readers might assume the worst (were those the drug rehab years?)." Table 6.10 lists some additional tips offered by Plous (1998b) for creating your CV.

In Figure 6.3, you will find two sample student vitae. These vitae represent years of work by these students to build their credentials. *If you are just starting out in psychology, your vita will not look like these samples.* It takes time to gain experience, so start as early in your career as you can. If you wait to do things like serving as a research assistant or teaching assistant

---

TABLE 6.9 Suggestions for Organizing Your Curriculum Vita

Personal information (address, phone number, email)

Educational history (degrees earned, when and where)

Honors and awards (list each, who awarded, and date awarded)

Association memberships (relevant clubs and societies, student affiliate status)

Professional experience (beginning with college, list jobs relevant to the major)

Research interests (if applicable and appropriate)

Current research and teaching experience (if applicable and appropriate)

Professional presentations (titles, organizations, in APA format if possible)

Publications (use APA format, be careful with "in press," "under review")

References (list names, titles, and addresses of three to four people whom you have asked)

Sources: Hayes, L. J., & Hayes, S. C. (1989, September). How to apply to graduate school. Retrieved September 28, 1998, at http://psych.hanover.edu/handbook/applic2.html. Plous, S. (1998c). Sample template for creating a vita. Retrieved September 28, 1998, at http://www.weslyan.edu/spn/vitasamp.htm.

TABLE 6.10 Tips for Preparing Your Curriculum Vita

Your vita should be a clear and concise summary of your professional qualifications. Take care in every word used.

Try to obtain copies of vitae from people who are at your stage or slightly ahead of you; although a faculty member's vita might give you some organizational ideas, some sections will be inappropriate due to your entry-level status in the discipline.

Create an inviting and elegant format. Take the time to add some style, and include white space (but, don't overdo it).

Make *absolutely sure* that there are *no* errors in your vita. Have more than one person proofread it for you—show it to your professors to review. It must be completely error-free.

Avoid padding your vita because you feel you don't have much to list. Do not list high school accomplishments or excessive details about activities you have completed en route to your bachelor's degree.

Do not list irrelevant personal information, such as height, weight, or general health. List hobbies only if you think they make you look like a more well-rounded individual.

Try not to list categories on your vita if you have only one accomplishment in that category (like the outlining rule, you need a B for every A.). The exception to this rule would be if you have only one publication—it is so worthy of note, the category will draw the attention to this accomplishment. Remember, publication credit is the number one secondary selection criterion for graduate admissions committees.

When using category headings and subheadings, don't get too ambitious. This is where copying the format of a faculty member may be a bad idea; don't have a "Grants and Contracts" section if you have neither grants nor contracts.

Success Stories

Dr. Randall E. Osborne
Texas State University—San Marcos

I was teaching at a small university in Oklahoma and had a top-notch student. She had a 4.0 GPA, had won a research award, had presented at conferences, worked for a clinician, and had stellar reference letters. I encouraged her to work hard on her personal statement but she kept putting it off. She finally sent it in just before the deadline but I never got to read it. Months went by and we did not hear from the school. I finally called the school to inquire about her status. They said, "we haven't rejected her, we just cannot decide if she really wants to be in our program."

What she had done was ramble on and on about her wide interests in psychology, yet she was applying for a very specialized program. They wanted to accept her but were unsure she would be happy.

In the end, I encouraged them to call her, called her myself and told her she was about to receive the most important phone call of her life. She called me 30 minutes later with the news they had decided to accept her and offer her a teaching assistantship.

The moral of the story, listen to your advisor and DO NOT take any aspect of the application lightly. You never know what one thing will make the difference either in getting you in—or keeping you out.

Andrea Webb
12345 Main Street
Boise, ID 83705
208-555-1212
email@me.com

Education

Boise State University
BS Psychology (expected May 2002)
Current GPA 3.941/4.0

Research and Teaching Experience

January 2001-present	Research Coordinator, Idaho Neurological Institute, Saint Alphonsus Regional Medical Center.
May 2000-January 2001	Research Assistant, Idaho Neurological Institute, Saint Alphonsus Regional Medical Center.
Fall 2001	Psychology of Health, Teaching Assistant
Spring 2001-present	General Psychology, Teaching Assistant Coordinator
Spring 2001	Research Methods, Teaching Assistant
Spring 2000	Statistical Methods, Teaching Assistant

Presentations

Henbest, M. L., Seibert, P. S., Jutzy, R. E., Ward, J. A., Webb, A., & Zimmerman, C. G. (2001, September-October). *Developments in the treatment of Chiari malformation.* Poster session presented at the annual meeting of the Congress of Neurological Surgeons, San Diego, CA.

Seibert, P. S., Reedy, D. P., Webb, A., & Zimmerman, C. G. (2001, September-October). *Post TBI gender disagreement in perceptions of social support and quality of life.* Poster session presented at the annual meeting of the Congress of Neurological Surgeons, San Diego, CA.

Zimmerman, C. G., Seibert, P. S., Owen, T. O., Webb, A., & Brieske, C. (2001, September-October). *Intraoperative use of electrically stimulated responses ensures accurate pedicle and transfacet screw placement.* Poster session presented at the annual meeting of the Congress of Neurological Surgeons, San Diego. CA.

FIGURE 6.3 Sample Student CVs

Webb, A. (2001, April). *Effects of age, gender, religion, and religious strength on obedience to authority.* Poster session presented at the College of Social Sciences and Public Affairs Undergraduate Research Conference, Boise State University, Boise, ID.

Seibert, P. S., Stridh-Igo, P., Hash, J., Unione, A., Webb, A., Atwood, C., Nakagawa, H., Nudson, O., Owen, T., Barnes, J., Basom, J., & Zimmerman, C. G. (2001, April). *Undergraduate teaching and research roles are constrained only by imagination.* Symposium conducted at the meeting of the Rocky Mountain Psychological Association, Reno, NV.

Webb, A. (2001, April). *Effects of age, gender, religion, and religious strength on obedience to authority.* Poster session presented at the meeting of the Rocky Mountain Psychological Association, Reno, NV.

Publications

Seibert, P. S., Leal, S. T., Webb, A., Holder, T., Stridh-Igo, P., Hash, J., Basom, J., Nakagawa, H., & Zimmerman, C. G. (in press). A checklist to facilitate cultural awareness and sensitivity. *Journal of Medical Ethics.*

Seibert, P. S., Reedy, D. P., Hash, J., Webb, A., Stridh-Igo, P., Basom, J., Zimmerman, C. G. (in press). Brain injury: Quality of life's greatest challenge. *Brain Injury.*

Papers Currently Under Submission

Seibert, P. S., Stridh-Igo, P. M., Webb, A., & Zimmerman, C. G. (2001). *Challenging the stigma of stroke.* Manuscript submitted for publication.

Honors and Scholarships

1998-present	Brown Honors Scholarship
1998-present	Member of the Honors Program
1998-2001	Dean's List
2001	Psychology Department Scholarship, Boise State University
2001	Member of Phi Kappa Phi, National Honor Society
1998-2000	Frank and Ruth Hunt Scholarship

Professional Memberships

2000-present	Rocky Mountain Psychological Association (student member)

Megan I. Sorvaag
5678 Main Street
Boise, ID 83706 / (208) 555-1212

EDUCATION

BS Psychology (May 2002, expected)   Cumulative GPA 4.0/4.0
Boise State University
Boise, Idaho

RELEVANT EXPERIENCE

2001-present   Applied Cognition Research Institute, Webmaster/Webdesigner:
2001-present   Advisory Board Member: Family Studies Research Initiative Psychology
               Department
2000-2001   Committee member: Dean Search Committee Panel for the College of Social
               Science and Public Affairs
1999-present   Software Designer: Academic Advising Software for College Students,
               (developed/provisionally patented)
1999-present   Webmaster: Developed and maintain the Boise State University Psychology
               Department Website

SCIENTIFIC PUBLICATIONS: *PAPERS AND PRESENTATIONS*

Sorvaag, M., Landrum, R.E., & Agras, P. (2001). A new method of technology to assisted in academic planning. Poster presented at the National Academic Advising Conference, Ottawa, Canada.

Sorvaag, M. (2001). Informational academic advising vs. counseling academic advising: Is there a difference? Poster presented at the National Academic Advising Conference, Ottawa, Canada.

Sorvaag, M. & Landrum, R.E. (2001). The response to assisting academic advising with software: Could this be the needed link to improving the system? Poster presented at the Midwestern Psychology Association, Chicago, IL.

Sorvaag, M., Clary, L., Landrum, R.E. (2000). Relationship between students' need for achievement and academic performance. Poster presented at the Rocky Mountain Psychology Association, Tucson, AZ.

Clary, L., Sorvaag, M., & Landrum, R.E. (2000) Academic performance in college students: What's love got to do with it? Poster presented at the Rocky Mountain Psychology Association, Tucson, AZ.

TEACHING & RESEARCH ASSISTANTSHIPS

Spring 2002   Advanced Statistical Methods, Teaching Assistant
Fall 2002   Psychological Measurement, Teaching Assistant
Spring 2000   Statistical Methods, Paid Tutor

Fall 1999   General Psychology, Teaching Assistant
2001-present   Research Assistant: Dr. Keli Braitman, Body Image Issues in Woman
2001-present   Research Assistant: Dr. Rob Turrisi, Family Studies Research Initiative
1999-present   Research Assistant: Dr. Eric Landrum, Technological Academic Advising
                       Support for College Students

PROFESSIONAL MEMBERSHIPS AND LEADERSHIP POSITIONS

2001-present   Student Member of Division 7 of American Psychological Association
                       (Developmental)
2001-present   Student Member of the American Psychological Association
2000-present   Student Member of the National Academic Advising Association
2000-2001   Student Member of the Rocky Mountain Psychological Association
2000-2001   President: Boise State University Association of Psychology Students
2000-2001   Secretary: Psi Chi Chapter Boise State University, Psychology Honors Society
1999-2000   Vice President: Boise State University Association of Psychology Students

HONORS

1998-2001   Dean's List with Highest Honors
2000-2001   Undergraduate Research Award, College of Social Science and Public Affairs
2000-2001   Homecoming Queen Boise State University
2000-2001   Women Making History in Idaho, Recognition Award of Female Achievement
2001-present   Member of Phi Kappa Phi, National Honors Society
2000-present   Member of Psi Chi, Psychology National Honors Society
2000-present   Member of The National Society of Collegiate Scholars

SCHOLARSHIP AWARDS

1998-2002   Gem State Scholarship, Out-of-State Tuition Waiver
1999-2002   Psychology Department Scholarship, Boise State University
2001-2002   Ford Motor Undergraduate Scholarship
1999-2000   Arguinchona Honors Scholarship

SPECIAL TRAINING

SPSS, FrontPage Editor, Microsoft Word, Excel, Power Point

REFERENCES

Dr. Eric Landrum, Professor, Department of Psychology, Boise State University
Dr. Daryl Jones, Provost and Vice President of Academic Affairs, Boise State University
Dr. Rob Turrisi, Professor, Department of Psychology, Boise State University
Dr. Keli Braitman, Assistant Professor, Department of Psychology, Boise State University

until your last semester of college, those experiences will not be as valuable as they could have been had they occurred earlier. Also, we recommend NOT using faculty CVs as examples for preparing your own CV. A faculty vita is likely to have many more categories that do not apply to undergraduate students. Also, if you compare your student CV to a faculty members' CV, you may become disappointed because it looks as if you have done so little. Remember, you are just getting started, and it has been that faculty member job to be a psychologist; they have years and years head start on building a vita. Thus, if you want to look at a faculty member's vita, do so after you have created yours. By the way, this social comparison and dejection occurs for faculty members too—Roediger (2004) alludes to this in his interesting article.

RESEARCH EXPERIENCE, AND MATCH & FIT WITH YOUR PROGRAM OF INTEREST

As alluded to earlier, research experience is important in the admissions process. It is at the top of the secondary selection criteria, and by serving as a research assistant you will gain valuable knowledge, skills, and abilities, and you will likely have enough meaningful interactions with a faculty member through the research process that he or she will be able to write you a strong letter of recommendation. Plus, psychology is an empirical science—we investigate and test our theories and hypotheses about the nature of human behavior—research skills lay at the core of this discipline. Much of the next chapter is devoted to demonstrating the importance and benefits of participating in research.

Additionally, you need to carefully consider your own personal goals (answering the 13 themes above will help you) with respect to the goals and orientation of the graduate schools to which you are applying. The "match" or "fit" between you and the school is not to be underestimated. Landrum et al. (1994) asked graduate admissions committee members to describe the exact procedures and decision-making rules they followed in the selection process. Content analysis of these decision protocols indicated that the most frequent strategy used in selection was the match between the applicant and the school and faculty. On another level, although the prospects of gaining admission may be daunting at this point, you do not want to go to any school just for the sake of going to graduate school. You might be admitted, but if the program is not a good match or good fit, you may be miserable and drop out (this chapter started with the acceptance rates into graduate school). A disastrous first experience may impact everything you attempt to do later in psychology. We would encourage you not to underestimate the importance of the match or fit between you and the schools you are applying to. Thus, if you mention in your personal statement that you want to work with a particular faculty member—mean it—because it might happen. In fact, some graduate programs take an additional step to ensure match or fit—they invite applicants for an on-campus interview. If at all possible, attend, even if it costs you money out of your own pocket. Some programs, like clinical and counseling psychology programs, rely on interviews more than other specialty areas. Just like a job interview, although the program is interviewing you, you are also interviewing the program. Table 6.11 presents some possible interview questions for you to use when on-campus.

According to Appleby (1990), there may be two general types of students in graduate school: students who find the experience unpleasant, to be endured, survived, and eventually forgotten, and students who thrive in the system, are respected by the faculty, and end up with the best employment prospects. If you would rather be in the latter group, here are some of the characteristics (Bloom & Bell, 1979) of those individuals who became graduate school superstars:

Visibility—highly motivated, seem to always be in the department at all hours

Willingness to work hard—seen by faculty as hard-working, persevering

Reflection of program values—seen by faculty as having professional values that lead to research and scholarly success

True interest in research—engaged in research projects in addition to the master's thesis and dissertation; curious enough about a problem and wanted to see data on it

Development of a relationship with a mentor—listen, learn, grow, and are productive through a close working relationship with one or two faculty members

As Appleby (1990) alluded to, none of these characteristics mention intellect, GPA, or writing ability. Perhaps those qualities are constants that the faculty member expect to see in all graduate school students. The above list constitutes qualities *over and above* those needed for

---

TABLE 6.11 Questions Prospective Graduate Students Might Ask on an Interview

---

How is the training in this program organized? What is the typical program of study?

What training model is emphasized (ask only if this is not clear in the materials provided)?

What kind of practicum opportunities would I have?

Are there opportunities to work with specific populations, such as (fill in here)?

What is the typical success rate for finding jobs for individuals in this program?

Would I be likely to get financial aid my first year?

What kinds of teaching and research assistantships or traineeships are available? Can first-year students receive them?

What is this program's retention rate? How long does it typically take to get through?

I understand that I will get a master's degree on my way to the doctorate. What are the master's and doctoral requirement?

When are comprehensive (or preliminary) exams typically taken?

Are faculty members supportive with regard to original ideas for research?

Is it possible to talk to a few graduate students in this program?

Note. Not all questions may apply both Ph.D. and Psy.D. applications.

Source: Adapted from APA (1997a).

entrance into the graduate program. Lord (2004) specifically addresses the undergraduate to graduate school transition: "The transition from undergraduate to graduate study involves a transition from student to scholar and researcher. Many of the skills that guarantee success as an undergraduate (e.g., strong test-taking skills and good grades) can be unrelated to success as a graduate student, where the ability to conduct research—both effectively and prolifically—is the strongest measure of success. For some students, this transition is difficult, and successful graduate students are those who are able to discover research areas they truly enjoy and who are able to translate this interest into publications, the holy grail of graduate work" (p. 15). Lord's conclusion is probably more applicable to those seeking the Ph.D. than the Psy.D., however. Concerning this transition from college to graduate school, one of the reviewers of this book mentioned that the transition "is difficult because the pond is smaller and the fish are bigger!"

STRATEGIES TO CONSIDER IF YOU DO NOT GET IN

It is quite a process, but that is what it takes to become a psychologist. If it were easy, many people would do it, and the value of the skills and abilities learned would be lessened. It is difficult for undergraduate students to step back and get the "big picture" when you are in the process of applying to graduate schools and planning for your future. When students are unsuccessful in graduate school admission, they often forget about context. Said another way, you are competing with the best and brightest students from around the nation, and often the world. Some students think that because they consistently get the top grades in their classes that they will be the top applicants. Adding to the complexity, the pool of applicants changes every year, so one year you might be quite competitive and the next year you might not make the next cut. If you are not accepted on your first attempt, what are your options?

We suggest that you seek out honest appraisals of your credentials. The first step might be able to consult with your faculty mentor or other psychology department faculty about your application package. With a high GPA, were your GRE scores a bit low? Because you transferred your senior year, were your letters of recommendation not very strong? What types of experiences did your letter writers write about? Did you attend any conferences to present your research? Seek an honest and blunt appraisal of your credentials. If weaknesses can be identified, then try to correct them. It might mean retaking courses to raise your GPA, retaking the GRE to increase scores, or adding an extra year of your undergraduate education so that you can acquire additional experiences, such as serving as a research assistant or completing an internship.

Another strategy to consider is to contact the graduate schools that you applied to. Write to the director of graduate admissions, and ask for a sincere appraisal of your application. Try to obtain a personalized response—this may take a bit of work and persistence. However, your persistence may pay off the next year that you apply—especially if someone on the graduate admissions committee takes time to point out the weaknesses in your application and you take the next year turning those weaknesses into strengths. Be reasonable with yourself, and don't beat up on yourself concerning your weaknesses. But if multiple opinions emerge (faculty advisor, multiple graduate program faculty) concerning areas of concern, then you should consider what you can do to improve in those areas. Be sure to tap into the experiences and expertise of your mentors, faculty members, and academic advisors. Persistence can pay off!

Exercise #6: Letter of Recommendation Request Worksheet

In this exercise, use this form to organize the letter of recommendation process. This form can be used for employers as well as graduate school applications. There are lots of details to attend to, so use the checklist to make sure you don't forget everything and that your letter writer has everything he or she needs to write you the strongest letter they can. The checklist has been derived in part from Bates College (2000) and Rewey (2000). Remember, paying attention to details is important; if you can't follow the instructions for applying to graduate school, many graduate schools will figure that you couldn't follow the instructions once you were admitted to graduate school (so why bother?).

Category	Check ✔	Details
Initial Contact	_____	Discuss the letter of recommendation with each faculty member/letter writer face-to-face.
	_____	Ask "would you be willing to write me a strong letter of recommendation?"
	_____	Make this contact as soon as possible; no later than 1 month before the first letter is due.
Demographic Information	_____	Provide the letter writer with your name, campus and permanent address, email address, and phone numbers (including cell phone)
Academic Information	_____	List your major, minor, GPAs, test scores, academic awards, honor society memberships
	_____	State the nature of the relationship, the length of time they have known you
Experiences	_____	Describe internships, independent study, directed research, senior thesis, work experiences, extracurricular activities (e.g., Psi Chi, Psychology Club)
Accomplishments	_____	Give some details about your skills, talents, abilities, personal qualities, and relevant accomplishments
	_____	List relevant accomplishments with details, dates, etc.
	_____	List relevant scholarships, recognitions (e.g., Dean's List)
Personal Characteristics	_____	Describe academic strengths and weaknesses, why you are qualified for graduate school
	_____	Provide concrete examples of skills, such as dependability, intellect, drive and motivation, written and oral communication skills, interpersonal skills
Wrap Up	_____	State how you can be reached by the letter writer if he or she needs more information
	_____	Clearly tell the letter writer if the letter is mailed directly or returned to you (sign on the flap?)
	_____	Thank the letter writer formally with a hand-written card
	_____	Keep the letter writer informed about the progress of your efforts

CHAPTER 7

Research and Teaching Assistantships

If you have carefully read the first few chapters of this book, one theme is that you should get involved outside the classroom to obtain the full range of skills and abilities you need to be successful in psychology. These experiences are invaluable whether you are going to graduate school or not. This chapter directly addresses opportunities such as research assistantships, a senior thesis project, and teaching assistantships.

These extracurricular activities give you an opportunity to increase your skills in applying the psychological principles you are learning in the classroom. Also, reading about research results and being involved in collecting data and actually doing research are two very different things. Furthermore, by being involved, you give your psychology faculty more opportunities to get to know you and become familiar with your professional abilities and potential. Moreover, these faculty–student collaborations can often lead to strong letters of recommendation. If you are a student in my class, I have a relatively limited exposure to your skills and abilities. If you are a student in my class and also did research with me for a year, did an off-campus internship, and served as a teaching assistant for another professor, I will be able to write a stronger letter because you are a more well-rounded student (and because you worked with more than one faculty member, you will have additional sources of letters of recommendation). Whether you are looking for a job with your bachelor's degree or looking for admission into graduate school, you need to make yourself a competitive applicant. If you can take advantage of some of the opportunities presented in this chapter, you will be well on your way to achieving a competitive edge.

WHAT IS A RESEARCH ASSISTANTSHIP?

In an article by Clay (1998), Eugene Zechmeister, the director of the undergraduate program at Loyola University (in Illinois), said, "I know this will sound sacrilegious, but skills are actually more important than course content" (p. 2). He is right. Courses lay the foundation for information and knowledge about psychology, but that information and knowledge will do little good without the skills needed to utilize that knowledge. Since its inception in 1879, psychology has been an empirical, research-based discipline. Teaching and research focus on the heart of the matter—we expand our knowledge about psychology through research, and it is this research that gives us the subject matter that we teach. For the discipline of psychology to succeed and thrive, we need a balance between teaching and research.

What is a research assistantship? It is an opportunity for undergraduate students to assist faculty members in a program of research. When you serve as a research assistant (RA), you will actually be involved in *doing* the research rather than reading about it in your textbook or journal article. There are multiple advantages to serving as a research assistant: (a) acquisition of skills and knowledge not easily gained in the classroom; (b) opportunity to work one on one with a faculty member; (c) opportunity to contribute to the advancements of the science of psychology; (d) exposure to general research techniques helpful for pursuing later graduate work; (e) opportunity to practice written and oral communication skills by preparing for and attending professional conferences and preparing and submitting manuscripts for publication; and (f) cultivation of a mentoring relationship with a faculty member that will be helpful for acquiring letters of recommendation.

What do you do as a research assistant? This is best answered by asking the faculty member directly. Although the answer will vary from research topic to research topic, the list presented in Table 7.1 describes some of the general tasks and duties that you may be asked to perform.

Your commitment to serve as a research assistant is a weighty one—you have some responsibility to see that several aspects of the research process get done. It is a serious commitment that you should not take lightly. The faculty member you are working with will be

---

TABLE 7.1 Typical Tasks Performed by Research Assistants (RAs)

Administer research sessions with student participants (this procedure is called data collection, or "running subjects").

Score and/or code the collected data, and enter them into a spreadsheet or statistical analysis program (such as SPSS).

Conduct literature searches using resources like *PsycINFO* and Social Sciences Citation Index; search your local library database for books and periodicals; make copies of articles available; order unavailable resources through interlibrary loan; general library research.

Work with the faculty member to develop new research ideas; often these ideas are developed from research just completed, the need that arises from a particular situation, or reviews of the existing literature.

Attend lab meetings with other undergraduate research assistants, discuss research ideas, collaborate on projects.

Use word processing, spreadsheet, scheduling, and statistical analysis programs to complete the research project.

Work on project outcomes so they can be submitted for presentations at local or regional conferences, prepare abstracts; if accepted, work on poster or oral presentations of the research materials for presentation at professional conferences.

Collaborate with faculty member to submit work to an appropriate journal to share the results with the broad scientific community.

---

counting on you to get things done, and done right; here is the place you want to shine. By watching you complete tasks and by observing you take on more and more responsibility, your faculty mentor will have plenty of good things to write about in those letters of recommendation. However, the reverse is true. If you don't take the commitment seriously, if you make repeated mistakes on important tasks, then the recommendations of the faculty member will be weakened. If you choose to take on this commitment, know what you are getting into. At many schools, research assistants can also earn course credit—with a title such as directed research, independent study, or supervised research—and these credits are often senior-level upper-division psychology credits. Take advantage of this opportunity; these credits make a positive impression on your transcripts. When asked about why they became involved in research, Slattery and Park (2002) found that students' most common responses were to increase probability of graduate school admission and interested in research.

Other researchers have approached this issue from another perspective. For instance, Vittengl, Bosley, Brescia, Eckardt, Neidig, Shelver, and Sapenoff (2004) found that when predicting those students who will have higher interest in research, the key predictors are (a) viewing research as relevant to plans after receiving the bachelor's degree, (b) a personality with high openness to experience, and (c) score higher on the ACT mathematics subscale. Said another way, ". . . undergraduates with relatively low interest in research might be described as (a) less sophisticated, more conventional thinkers with lower intellectual curiosity than their peers; (b) students who struggle with the concepts and application of high-school-level mathematics, which is commonly used in statistical analyses; and (c) students who, accurately or inaccurately, consider research knowledge and skills to be largely irrelevant to their anticipated postundergraduate activities" (p. 94). You must remember that these are not cause-and-effect relations, however. We encourage all psychology undergraduates, regardless of their career plans, to pursue opportunities such as research and teaching assistantships. The benefits of such participation are highlighted throughout this chapter. Table 7.2 offers some suggestions on how to go about securing an RA position.

In a national survey, Landrum and Nelsen (2002) systematically studied the benefits of serving as an RA from the faculty member perspective. Out of a 40-item survey, faculty members ranked these benefits as most important: (a) an opportunity to enhance critical thinking skills, (b) preparation for graduate school, (c) gains enthusiasm for the research process, (d) participates in the data collection process, and (e) improved writing ability. Although the research assistant–faculty collaboration is often a positive experience, there are times when

Success Stories

Dr. Kenneth A. Weaver
Department of Psychology
Emporia State University

First appeared in *Psiowa*, the newsletter of the Department of Psychology
at the University of Iowa, 2000–2001

Featured alumnus: **Patty Deldin**

Patricia Deldin was an undergraduate psychology major at Iowa from 1981–1985, and has become one of our more distinguished alumni. But it didn't always seem as if it was going to turn out that way.

Patty grew up in a small town in Illinois in a blue-collar family. In high school, she was a cheerleader and ran track but gave relatively little thought to academics. In her first year at the University, her grades were mediocre at best. The turning point for her came when she met with her advisor to discuss the future. When she told him she planned to go to graduate school in clinical psychology, he told her that with her grades that goal was unrealistic. She cried for a day or two, but then she pulled herself together and resolved to study much harder and improve her grades.

Patty's grades did, indeed, improve. By the time she was a senior, she was making mostly A's and was conducting an Honor's thesis with Professor Irwin Levin as well as doing research with Professors Don Fowles and Milton Rosenbaum. But when she graduated, she decided to delay applying to graduate school for a couple of years to look for relevant experience that would boost her credentials.

At about that time, Professor Fowles received an announcement for a position as a research assistant in a clinical psychophysiology laboratory at the National Institute of Mental Health. Patty applied for the job and was hired. What followed were two years of extraordinary experience in the nationally prominent clinical psychophysiology lab of Connie Duncan, during which Patty distinguished herself and became a mainstay of the lab.

TABLE 7.2 Suggestions for Securing a Research Assistant Position

Review the listing of the faculty in your psychology department and their research interests. You might find this information available in a pamphlet in the department, as part of advising materials, or perhaps on the department's Web site. If there is no such list available, encourage your Psi Chi chapter or local psychology club to create one.

Then, make appointments with faculty members, preferably during their posted office hours, to discuss research possibilities.

If you want to impress this faculty member, do your homework. Do a PsycINFO search beforehand and be ready to talk about topics that this faculty member has already studied.

When you meet with the faculty members, be yourself. Let them know that you are willing to work hard on their program of research. Ask them about the specific requirements that they expect from their research assistants. You'll want to know about the duration of the project, what your responsibilities will be, grading practices, weekly time commitment, etc. Also, what length of commitment is the faculty member looking for? Some faculty may want RA help only for a semester, whereas other faculty will ask for a 1-year or longer commitment.

If you come to an agreement with a faculty member to serve as an RA, there may be additional forms that you have to fill out to register for credit.

problems arise. Slattery and Park (2002) described some of the most strategies to avoid problems in research collaboration: (a) meet students regularly, (b) mentor student researchers in whatever way possible, (c) train students carefully for tasks given to them, (d) involve them in faculty research, and (e) choose student researchers carefully. As stated previously, research is a serious commitment by both student and faculty—care should be taken to properly nurture this relationship and monitor progress toward common goals.

PRESENTING RESEARCH AT CONFERENCES

By becoming involved in research, you will give yourself a number of additional opportunities as well. For instance, you may be able to make a presentation at a local or regional professional conference, or at a more student-centered research conference. Two types of "presentations" are typically made at conferences—papers and posters. A paper presentation is usually a 12- to 15-minute talk given to an audience about your research project. You may have handouts for your audience, or use audiovisual aids (such as overhead transparencies, slides, or a PowerPoint presentation), or do both. Table 7.3 offers suggestions for oral paper presentations.

A poster presentation is substantially different from a paper presentation. In the paper presentation, you present your findings to a large audience in a relatively short time period. The method is somewhat impersonal, but it is an efficient method to present the materials to a large number of people. In a poster presentation, you present your research work in a poster format for a longer period of time ($1\frac{1}{2}$–2 hours). You are available to speak personally with "audience members" who are interested in your work. In the poster session, you will probably reach fewer people, but you'll have more personal conversations with people who are genuinely interested in your work. Your poster is displayed on a freestanding bulletin board in a session with other posters, in a room large enough to hold the posters, the presenters, and the people who wander through the session. The audience picks and chooses what posters to read; they can acquire more detailed information from the poster authors in this one-on-one conversation format. Table 7.4 presents tips for preparing and making poster presentations.

TABLE 7.3 Making an Oral Presentation at a Conference

Consider the big picture. What are the main ideas and findings of your study?

Decide on a limited number of significant ideas that you want your audience to comprehend and remember.

Minimize the nitty-gritty details (like procedure, data analysis strategies, etc.) and highlight the main points.

State clearly, without jargon, the point of your research, what you found, and what it means—try to tell a good story.

Write out your presentation as a mini-lecture, with a clear outline. You may use these as cues while you make your presentation.

Practice your presentation out loud, making sure it fits into the time restraints, and have a small audience listen to you to give you constructive feedback.

Prepare overheads or PowerPoint slides to keep your audience engaged in your presentation.

Do not read your paper. Talk to your audience about what you did to complete the work. At a professional conference, it is very irritating to be read to—everyone there can already read.

Try to speak loudly and clearly enough to hold the attention of your audience. There will be distractions—people coming in, others getting up and leaving. Don't be offended. Try to be enthusiastic enough to sustain interest over these distractions.

State your final conclusions and end on time. Be prepared to answer audience questions if time permits.

If you have handouts, be sure to include contact information on them—name, conference, and date of presentation.

Bring copies of your paper to the conference, or provide a sign-up sheet for persons who may want copies to be sent to them.

Source: Karlin, N. J. (2000). Creating an effective conference presentation. *Eye on Psi Chi, 4* (2), 26–27.

TABLE 7.4 Presenting a Poster at a Conference

Construct the poster to include the title, authors, affiliations, and a description of the research.

Minimize the detail that is presented, and try to use jargon-free statements.

Pictures, tables, and figures are especially useful and helpful in poster presentations.

If possible, use color in your poster panels.

Make sure the lettering is neatly done and large enough to be read from a distance—poster session attendees will quickly scan the content before stopping to inquire further—use fonts no smaller than 18 points; try to use 24 points or larger if possible.

During your poster presentation, have your name badge on and placed where conference attendees can see it.

Do not overwhelm the viewer with excessive amounts of information; try to construct a poster display that encourages and enhances conversation.

Be ready to pin up and take down your poster at the specified times (you may want to bring your own thumbtacks or pushpins); often poster sessions are scheduled back to back, so you want to be on time so the next session can also be on time.

Bring 30–50 copies of your handouts to provide more information about your study and your contact information.

Sources: Karlin, N. J. (2000). Creating an effective conference presentation. *Eye on Psi Chi, 4* (2), 26–27.

Carmody (1998) surveyed graduates of psychology programs who were Psi Chi members as undergraduates about their views and perceptions of value about undergraduate presentations. One of the questions addressed who inspired the student to become a research assistant. Carmody found that the motivators to get involved were (a) course instructors (56%), (b) self-motivation (55%), (c) mentors (33%), and (d) fellow students (14%). Why did students choose to do research? Students mentioned personal challenge (89%), for graduate school purposes (76%), encouragement from a professor (59%), and for career aspirations (34%). "All groups strongly agreed that presentations helped to advance one's career and increase one's skills. Presenters agreed more strongly than nonpresenters that going beyond coursework was fun and promoted personal growth" (Carmody, 1998, p. 13).

If you have the opportunity, try to get involved as a research assistant. If you do not have the opportunity, try to create it. When you work with a faculty member on a research project, it is a mutually beneficial relationship. What does the faculty member get out of this relationship? He or she gets a hard-working, eager student to do some of the labor-intensive portions of any research project. Many faculty members, especially those at institutions that do not have a graduate program in psychology, depend on undergraduate students to help further their own research agenda. If this research culture does not exist at your school, try to develop it. Find that student-friendly faculty member who realizes how important the research opportunity is to you, and chances are you will find a way to collaborate on some sort of research project. Many faculty members have ideas for studies that they would like to do but don't have the time nor the assistance. A talented undergraduate student assisting that faculty member can make that project happen. Davis (1995) clearly articulated the advantages faculty members receive from conducting collaborative research with undergraduate students (see Table 7.5).

TABLE 7.5 Benefits to Faculty in Working with Undergraduate Research Assistants

Witnessing student professional growth and development—perhaps the best reward

Facilitating reviews of the current literature in a particular research area, keeping current

Keeping analytic skills fine-tuned and active through the design and the completion of research

Generating useful and meaningful empirical data

Maintaining and expanding professional networks through attending conventions, especially for students

Enhancing effectiveness as a teacher through active involvement in research

WHAT IS A SENIOR THESIS?

At many colleges and universities, undergraduate students have the opportunity to complete a senior thesis project (at some schools, a senior thesis project is required). What is the difference between a research assistant position and a senior thesis? Generally speaking, when you agree to become a research assistant, you are going to help the faculty member with his or her research. Although you might make some suggestions and eventually put your own "spin" on the research program, this research essentially "belongs" to the faculty member, and you are truly "assisting." For a senior thesis project, the student is the principal investigator, the student "owns" the research, and the faculty member plays an advisory or consulting role. Often, in a senior thesis project the student gets to test his or her own research ideas, under the supervision and guidance of a faculty member. Note that you will have to find a faculty member willing to supervise your work—so you might be limited to the specialty areas of your faculty. The only way to find out is to consult with faculty members individually.

The senior thesis typically requires much more responsibility and independence compared to the research assistantship. Faculty members have an inherent self-interest in seeing their own research succeed, for multiple reasons (including promotion and tenure). Note, however, that many faculty members supervise senior thesis projects with little or no compensation—so be sure to be appreciative, keep appointments, and value the opportunity that the faculty member is providing. Of course, faculty members want to see students succeed in their own senior thesis research, but the stakes are lower for faculty members. Unfortunately, there is essentially no research available on the benefits of completing a senior thesis project, and the senior thesis is barely mentioned in the literature. One exception—Wood and Palm (2000) utilized students enrolled in a psychology senior thesis course and examined if anxiety scores would be elevated prior to a required oral presentation; they were. This does not tell us much about the benefits of a senior thesis project, though.

We would assume that the benefits of a senior thesis project would be similar to those experienced by students serving as an RA. When the time comes, talk to faculty members at your school to see if a senior thesis option is available—and note that it could be called something else at your institution (e.g., independent study). In general, you will want to have completed your courses in statistics and experimental design/research methods prior to embarking on such an independent project. With careful planning and the right supervision, you can make this project into something that will help you stand out from the crowd, engage in original research, perhaps lead to a conference presentation, and help build rapport with a faculty member. The potential is huge!

BECOMING A TEACHING ASSISTANT

What about being a **teaching assistant**? Serving as a teaching assistant is usually much less involved and time-consuming than being a research assistant. Usually, a teaching assistant helps a faculty member for one semester (or term) in the administration of a specific course, such as Introduction to Psychology or Statistical Methods. You might have a number of different responsibilities as a teaching assistant, depending on the instructor, the course, the history of the institution in utilizing teaching assistants, etc. Table 7.6 presents some of the tasks you might complete.

The teaching assistantship is an excellent way to build a mentoring relationship with a faculty member. Also, serving as a TA is a low-risk activity. Being a TA is not nearly as demanding as being an RA, and the typical time commitment for TAs is one semester only. Thus, if you really don't "bond" with that faculty member, there is no harm done (and you earned credits toward graduation).

But the benefits can be substantial. Almost certainly during the course of the semester, a situation will occur where you can step in and provide some real assistance to a faculty member teaching a course. These are the types of events that faculty members will be thankful for and may write about in a letter of recommendation. Also, many of our students tell us that sitting in on the general psychology course is a great study strategy when they prepare for the GRE Advanced Test in Psychology. You should know, however, that not all schools offer the opportunity for students to serve as undergraduate teaching assistants. If being a teaching assistant is not an opportunity at your school, you may have to be creative in finding

TABLE 7.6 Potential Tasks of a Teaching Assistant (TA)

Attend class and take notes so that students have a resource available to get notes when they miss class

Hold office hours where you may conduct tutoring sessions, review notes with students, review class assignments before they are due, and answer class-related questions

Help to proctor exams, help to grade exams and/or term papers, and help to enter these scores in the instructor's gradebook

Hold general review sessions prior to tests where groups of students can receive supplemental instruction over course-related topics

Help the instructor in the general administration and completion of the course to provide the best experience possible for enrolled students

this opportunity—perhaps seeking out an instructor who "wants help" in administering his or her course and is willing to give you independent study or internship credit. If the formal opportunity does not exist, there are creative ways of gaining the beneficial experience anyway! If you are faced with a choice of serving as a research assistant or as a teaching assistant, try to do both. You will be busy, but you will gain valuable skills, abilities, and knowledge for your future.

Exercise #7: Outside-of-Class Activities Plan

Use this planning sheet below to map out your strategy for completing out-of-class activities while finishing your undergraduate degree. Try to be as specific as possible in whom you are planning to work with, making contact, duration of work, and outcomes. The shaded regions are examples of how you might use this planning tool.

Teaching					
Specific Type of Activity	**When Do I Make Initial Contact?**	**Who Do I Contact?**	**Duration of Time Spent on Activity**	**Outcomes**	**Notes to Myself**
Teaching Assistant, General Psychology	November 2005 (prior to Spring 2006 semester)	Dr. Smith	I semester	-Make connection with faculty member - Review general psychology info	If this works out, maybe I'll ask Dr.Smith about being an RA

Research					
Specific Type of Activity	**When Do I Make Initial Contact?**	**Who Do I Contact?**	**Duration of Time Spent on Activity**	**Outcomes**	**Notes to Myself**
Research Assistant	May 2006 (at the end of Research Methods)	Dr. Davis	2 semesters	- Gain research experience -Conference presentation	Let Dr. Davis know I'll be asking him for a letter of recommendation

Service					
Specific Type of Activity	**When Do I Make Initial Contact?**	**Who Do I Contact?**	**Duration of Time Spent on Activity**	**Outcomes**	**Notes to Myself**
Volunter at Psychiatric Ward at Hospital	After completing Abnormal Psychology (Fall 2006)	Dr. Jones, VA Hospital	2 semesters	- Make a professional connection - Gain valuable out-of-class experience	This might turn into an internship next summer

CHAPTER 8

Getting Involved: Internships and Organizations

In the preceding chapter we began the discussion of vital, outside-of-class activities that students need to engage in to make themselves more rounded and give themselves the opportunities for experience that help them stand out from the crowd. Becoming a research assistant or teaching assistant is certainly a way to achieve those goals, but they are not the only ways. In this chapter we will discuss the ins and outs of internships, as well as apprise you of the opportunities to get involved in psychology via organizations. These organizations range in scope from national to regional, and range in focus from professionals to students.

FIELD EXPERIENCES AND INTERNSHIPS

Field experiences and internships are opportunities to learn about and apply psychological principles out of the classroom and in the field. These placements are in agencies that relate to some aspects of human behavior—hence, you can imagine that many places are possible internship sites. They also differ from teaching and research assistantships in that a nonfaculty member at the placement site typically supervises field experiences. A faculty member usually serves as the campus coordinator of the field experience or internship program.

If you do an internship in your community, what might you do? You might be an intern at a social service agency, assisting in intake interviews, psychological testing, report writing, and behavior modification. You might be an intern in a human resources department, where you learn to administer structured interviews, write performance appraisals, and coordinate special projects and programs. The opportunities are endless. In some instances, if an internship opportunity is not available to meet your needs, you may be able to arrange your own specialized internship.

Blanton (2001) developed an internship model for undergraduates based on the Chickering and Reisser (1993) model of college student development. The Chickering and Reisser model generates four primary tasks for undergraduate students: (a) increasing self-awareness, (b) managing emotions, (c) increasing integrity, and (d) developing purpose. In this model, increasing self-awareness is achieved by achieving the latter three tasks. How does this apply to internships? Blanton (2001) uses this framework and applies it to the internship environment. For instance, "managing emotions relates to interns' ability to notice, identify, accept, and control the feelings they have toward their internship site, people at their site, and themselves. Increasing integrity refers to students' ability to clarify personal values and then align these values with their behavior. Students who are developing purpose are examining their personal interests, making plans for the future, and deciding on the next step as graduation nears" (Blanton, 2001, p. 218).

What are the benefits of participating in an internship? Table 8.1 was compiled from Jessen (1988), Mount Saint Vincent University (1998), and the University of Michigan at Dearborn (1998).

How do you find out about field experiences and internships? There is probably a key faculty member in your department who makes sure that internship sites are suitable, establishes the policies and procedures for working with agencies, ensures that grades are submitted on time, handles inquiries from internship supervisors, etc. Find that person. Most departments have some well-established connections with agencies in and around your community; if you want to do something where the relation is not established, you may have to do more of the groundwork yourself. This latter approach gives you the chance to show some initiative and really demonstrate to your internship site your willingness to work hard and persevere at the task.

TABLE 8.1 Potential Benefits from Completing an Internship

Practical, on-the-job experience

Development of professional and personal confidence, responsibility, and maturity

Understanding of the realities of the work world and acquire human relations skills

Opportunity to examine a career choice closely and make professional contacts

Opportunity to test the ideas learned in the classroom out in the field

Opportunity to make contacts with potential employers

Enhancement of classroom experiences

Learning what careers *not* to pursue

Development of skills that are difficult to learn and practice in the classroom

College credit in some but not all circumstances

Possible earnings to help offset college expenses

WHAT INTERNS DO

What will you do as an intern? Ideally, you will get a realistic glimpse of the types of tasks necessary for success in a particular office or agency. Where appropriate, you will have the opportunity to acquire new skills and hone those that you already have. Internships are not designed to provide agencies with extra office staff or gophers, although you may occasionally be asked to help pitch in when agencies are under time and budget constraints. Although you might not be running a group therapy session, you might sit in on such a session and help facilitate that session under the supervision of appropriately trained and licensed personnel. In addition to these tasks, there may be group supervisory sessions if your site has multiple interns, and your on-campus faculty internship coordinator will probably require that you keep a weekly journal of your intern experiences (Jessen, 1988). Grayson (n.d.) offers advice for those who administer internship programs—see Table 8.2

Although most students have an invigorating internship experience, we have known some students who come back from an internship with the conclusion "I definitely do *not* want to do that for my entire career." This decision is a very valuable outcome of the internship process. Although it is unfortunate that the student did not enjoy the internship process, it is better to have an unsatisfying 16-week internship experience than to go to a graduate program to get a degree to enter a job that leads to a lifetime of misery. Knouse, Tanner, and Harris (1999) evaluated an internship program for business majors, and found that students with internships had higher GPAs, were a bit younger, and were more apt to be employed after graduation compared to students without internships. Thus, internships were positively related to both college performance and receiving a job offer postgraduation. Kampfe, Mitchell, Boyless,

---

TABLE 8.2 Suggested Principles for Administering Internships

Principles for Internship Supervision	Goals of Internship Supervisors to Achieve
Start small, stay small	To develop professionalism
The supervisor is more important than the site	To develop critical thinking skills
Negotiate placement early	To assist in the narrowing and clarifying of
Be accessible	career goals
Work all year round	To communicate love of your work
Train and assist supervisors	To increase students' self-confidence
Supervise students very closely	To help students transition into employment
Have alternatives for additional students	To serve the community
Be prepared for anything	To advertise the program

Success Stories

Dr. Jeanne M. Slattery
Clarion University

One of our students had the "Internship from Hell." She had chosen a site in her home county, so it wasn't a site that we knew a lot of specifics about. Several weeks into the term she discovered that the staff was not respectful of their clients nor of each other, confidentiality was poorly maintained, and treatment goals were very rarely strength-based. Another student in her class worked in a setting where the patients seemed to be "set off" by staff, probably unintentionally, then forcibly restrained. We spent a significant amount of our class time talking about these ethical problems and what they could reasonably do there and in their future careers to make things better.

Although I no longer see many of these students on a continuing basis, I do see some. Three from this class stand out for me: these two students and a third who practices in my community. Each of these students has developed into fine clinicians who are strong individuals and also very respectful of their clients. While I cannot prove that their negative internship experiences caused their positive outcomes, I do think that their success is, in part, due to our focus on the problems as something other than the normal and status quo. The whole class profited from seeing both the successful internships and the unsuccessful ones. Seeing the unsuccessful ones helped them define what they did not want to be after they graduated. Seeing the successes helped them imagine and realize a better alternative.

In the best of all possible worlds, my students would only have successful internship experiences. However, developing a professional self-image depends, in part, on identifying both who you are and who you don't want to be. I'm very proud that these students did this so well.

and Sauers (1999) concluded that students perceived their internships as important, relatively nondisruptive, and that they had control over the circumstances of their internship. Close to half perceived their internship as stressful, however, and about 25% perceived very little control over the internship situation. Blanton (2001) bases the evaluation of a successful internship experience on these three criteria: (a) perceiving the supervisor as understanding, (b) feeling supported in the growth process, and (c) satisfaction with the level of supervision.

OTHER INTERNSHIP OPPORTUNITIES

Related to these field experiences and internships are some other options to gain practical, hands-on experiences. You might not have all these opportunities available on your campus, or they might exist under different names, so look carefully. These other methods of getting involved include service learning, peer advising, and paraprofessional programs. Service learning (in some cases, called the fourth credit option) involves adding one credit to a three-credit class and involves providing volunteer services to the community. Supervised by the course instructor, students receive an additional one credit for completing the volunteer service.

Some psychology departments have a peer-advising program that provides academic advising services to undergraduate majors. This program is an opportunity for undergraduates to become involved in interviewing and conversational skills, and gain professional and personal confidence in dealing with the issues related to undergraduate education. Additionally, some psychology departments that have a counseling center affiliated with them also have a paraprofessional program. In a paraprofessional program, undergraduates receive training in some therapeutic approaches and, under the supervision of counseling faculty, practice these skills by providing workshops to other students. Check with your department to see if any of

Success Stories

Dr. Eliot J. Butter
University of Dayton

In the last several years, the University of Dayton Psychology Department has been contacted by many families who have children that were recently diagnosed with autism. In this time period, over 60 students have taken advantage of our elective internship in psychology course where they have received credit for working with these families. This has turned out to be a win–win–win situation. Our students have tremendously benefited from the experience of learning and applying skills that were taught by the family's consultant and the extension of their classroom learning. The children have benefited by showing significant improvement in their behaviors; and the families have tremendously benefited as well.

One touching story is that of a male student who was working with a 4-year-old child who had never said a word. During a session, about 4 months into the student's therapy training, the child said his first word; it was the name of the student therapist. One can only imagine the feelings and thoughts that were going through the minds of the child and the student!

What is additionally relevant is that the internship experiences that the students have participated in have led them to make career-changing decisions. Most of the students who participated in this type of internship experience had no knowledge of autism and had never worked with autistic children. As a result of their experiences, many of the students have reconsidered their career goals—and have either applied to graduate programs where autism is one aspect of the training, or have found employment at clinics for autism. One of the recent students was accepted into a Ph.D. program where she is working with researchers on autism. Several others have applied to or graduated from masters programs in applied behavior analysis. Others have worked with B.A. degrees at centers for autism. One current student, as a result of her experience of taking a child to occupational therapy, has decided to apply to occupational therapy graduate programs.

The important lesson is that exposure to internship experiences allows one to "test the waters" and explore potential careers. For all of our students, these internship experiences have been personally rewarding, and for many, have opened new doors and assisted the students in solidifying career decisions.

these types of outside-of-class opportunities are available for you. The bottom line is that internships are a great chance to expand upon your skills outside of the classroom and begin to make valuable connections in the field. Many undergraduate internship opportunities turn into job offers postgraduation. We highly recommend that you inquire about the possibility of an internship at your school.

ORGANIZATIONAL INVOLVEMENT

The opportunities discussed in this and the preceding chapter focus on skill and ability development. Organizational involvement also provides the chance to enhance knowledge about the discipline and to find opportunities to network within it. On a regional or national level you can become involved in organizations designed for students, or join organizations (as a student affiliate) designed for psychology professionals. In addition, you may have some opportunities on your own campus to get involved and gain valuable information and skills.

THE AMERICAN PSYCHOLOGICAL ASSOCIATION

On the national level, the flagship organization for psychologists is the American Psychological Association (APA). APA was founded in 1892. APA provides an impressive Web site that we both recommend, www.apa.org. "Based in Washington, DC, the American Psychological Association (APA) is a scientific and professional organization that represents psychology in the United States. With more than 150,000 members, APA is the largest association of psychologists worldwide" (APA, 2004a, ¶ 1). What are the goals of APA? According to APA (2004a), "the objects of the American Psychological Association shall be to advance psychology as a science and profession and as a means of promoting health, education, and human welfare by

- the encouragement of psychology in all its branches in the broadest and most liberal manner
- the promotion of research in psychology and the improvement of research methods and conditions
- the improvement of the qualifications and usefulness of psychologists through high standards of ethics, conduct, education, and achievement
- the establishment and maintenance of the highest standards of professional ethics and conduct of the members of the Association
- the increase and diffusion of psychological knowledge through meetings, professional contacts, reports, papers, discussions, and publications.

thereby to advance scientific interests and inquiry, and the application of research findings to the promotion of health, education, and the public welfare" (¶ 2).

In addition to using its Web site, one of the best ways to find out about APA is to talk with your faculty. Some of them may be current members of APA. Although undergraduate students cannot be full members, undergraduates can become student affiliates. Any undergraduate taking courses in psychology can apply to become an undergraduate student affiliate of the American Psychological Association (APA). Currently, annual dues are $27 for undergraduates; this includes an annual subscription to *American Psychologist* and *Monitor on Psychology*. For an additional $14, undergraduates can become a member of the American Psychological Association for Graduate Students (APAGS), which includes a subscription to the gradPSYCH magazine. Additional benefits, as described by APA (APA, 2004b), include (a) networking opportunities with other students and established psychologists, (b) access to career information, (c) a Web site tailored to the needs of students in psychology, (d) APA journals and other online products at up to 60% off nonmember rates, (e) discounts up to 30% on APA books and videos, (f) online access to any journal subscriptions, and (g) low APA convention registration fees.

THE AMERICAN PSYCHOLOGICAL SOCIETY

Although much younger than APA, the American Psychological Society (APS) has also become an important source of information for psychologists (www.psychologicalscience.org). According to APS (2004a), "The American Psychological Society (APS) is a nonprofit organization dedicated to the advancement of scientific psychology and its representation at the national level. The Society's mission is to promote, protect, and advance the interests of scientifically oriented psychology in research, application, teaching, and the improvement of human welfare. The American Psychological Society was founded in 1988 by a group of scientifically oriented psychologists interested in advancing scientific psychology and its representation as a science at the national level" (¶'s 1–3). As of 2003, there were 13,500 members in APS.

APS also offers an undergraduate student affiliate program. An undergraduate student affiliate membership is open to any student who is currently enrolled as a psychology major at an accredited institution. Student members receive the same benefits as regular members. For a $35 annual fee, members receive an annual subscription to the APS journals *Psychological Science*, *Current Directions in Psychological Science*, and *Psychological Science in the Public Interest*, as well as the *Observer*. Other benefits include a discount on registration rates for the annual convention, award and grant opportunities for students, a student caucus, access to an online membership directory, and discounted subscriptions to psychological journals (APS, 2004b).

PSI CHI

The best-known organization explicitly designed for students is Psi Chi, the National Honor Society in Psychology (www.psichi.org). Psi Chi was founded in 1929 for the purpose of encouraging, stimulating, and maintaining excellence in scholarship, and for the advancement of psychology. Psi Chi membership is conferred on students who have met minimum qualifications at institutions where there is a chapter (there is an application process, and not all students can be members). If you are a student at a community or junior college (and if there is a chapter), you can become a member of Psi Beta (psibeta.org), Psi Chi's sister honor society.

According to Psi Chi (2004b), the organization "serves two major goals. The first of these is the Society's obligation to provide academic recognition to its inductees by the mere fact of membership. The second goal is the obligation of each of the Society's local chapters to nurture the spark of that accomplishment by offering a climate congenial to its creative development. The Society publishes a quarterly magazine, *Eye on Psi Chi*, which helps to unite the members, inform them and recognize their contributions and accomplishments. The quarterly *Psi Chi Journal of Undergraduate Research* fosters and rewards the scholarly efforts of undergraduate psychology students and provides a valuable learning experience by introducing them to the publishing and review process. Students become members by joining the chapter at the school where they are enrolled. Psi Chi chapters are operated by student officers and faculty advisors. Together they select and induct the members and carry out the goals of the Society. All chapters register their inductees at the National Office, where the membership records are preserved for reference purposes. The total number of memberships preserved at the national office during the first 73 years is over 422,000" (no page number).

Psi Chi has grown into an impressive organization benefiting students on many levels. Involvement in your local chapter can lead to opportunities to develop leadership skills, and Psi Chi members are often the most involved and well-connected psychology students around. Note however, like other campus organizations, that your Psi Chi chapter (and/or a psychology club) will only be as strong as the student leaders. On the regional and national levels, Psi Chi has various offerings. At major regional and national conferences held each year, Psi Chi has an important presence in promoting the scholarly achievements of undergraduate psychology students. Psi Chi has a long tradition of providing student-friendly programming at these conferences. Both of your authors were Psi Chi members as undergraduate psychology students! If your school does not have a Psi Chi chapter, consult with a faculty member about starting a chapter. The benefits of becoming a member (as described by Psi Chi, 2004a) are presented in Table 8.3.

Even if your institution does not have a Psi Chi chapter, there may be a psychology club on campus. Usually, these clubs are open to anyone with an interest in psychology, and members do not have to be psychology majors. Often, students who are unable to join Psi Chi (perhaps due to GPA problems) can be active and involved as members of the local psychology club. On campuses where both groups exist, they often coordinate activities and opportunities for the benefit of all students interested in psychology. It is important to note that not everyone can join Psi Chi. The eligibility requirements include: (a) completion of 3 semesters or 5 quarters of the college course, (b) completion of 9 semester hours or 14 quarter hours of psychology courses, (c) ranking in the top 35% of their class in general scholarship, and (d) having a minimum GPA of 3.0 (on a 4.0 scale) in both psychology classes and cumulative grades (Psi Chi, 2004a). We believe that the benefits of Psi Chi are substantial, and worth your time and investment. Others have come to the same conclusion. In a study of 20-year worth of psychology alumni, Tarsi and Jalbert (1998) compared Psi Chi alumni with non–Psi Chi alumni on a number of measures. For instance, Psi Chi members were significantly more positive about their education than non–Psi Chi members; this may be due to the higher Psi Chi standards leading to a greater self-investment by students. Among Psi Chi members only, Tarsi and Jalbert (1998) found that the more active students were, the more worthwhile they reported their Psi Chi experience. We encourage you to continue this tradition of involvement and contribution.

TABLE 8.3 Advantages of Becoming a Psi Chi Member

Psi Chi provides national recognition for academic excellence in psychology, an honor that can be noted on employment applications, vitae, and résumés.

Through membership in Psi Chi, students gain a sense of community with others in psychology and an identification with the discipline.

Psi Chi provides a local, regional, and national forum for obtaining information and developing perspectives about the field of psychology, learning about educational and career opportunities, and forming meaningful professional networks.

On the local level, chapter membership facilitates leadership development, interaction with other students who have similar interests, and service to the department and institution sponsoring Psi Chi.

Members receive a membership card and certificate and, through chapter mailings, copies of *Eye on Psi Chi*. (Following graduation, members may subscribe to *Eye on Psi Chi*.)

Psi Chi chapter activities provide students with valuable opportunities to develop one-on-one relationships with professors who can stimulate their interest in psychology, involve them in research projects, and write meaningful letters of recommendation for them.

Psi Chi encourages student research at the regional and national as well as local levels through undergraduate and graduate research award competitions and provides opportunities for students to present research and receive certificates recognizing their accomplishments at regional and national psychological association meetings.

Psi Chi provides over $225,000 annually in awards and grants to its student members, faculty advisors, and chapters.

Psi Chi sponsors outstanding programs at regional and national psychological association meetings. Members benefit not only from the programs, but also from the opportunity to meet leading psychologists and students from other chapters.

Membership in Psi Chi meets one of the requirements for entrance at the GS-7 level in numerous professional and technical occupations in the United States government.

Membership is for life. The national registration fee of $35 is the only payment ever made to the national organization, which does not charge dues.

Source: Psi Chi (2004b). *Benefits of membership*. Retrieved July 18, 2004, from http://www.psichi.org/about/benefits.asp

REGIONAL ASSOCIATIONS

In addition to the national organizations described previously, there are a host of regional psychological associations that host annual conferences in psychology. Whereas APA and APS hold national conventions, regional associations also host an annual convention. Oftentimes, this regional convention is more convenient and accessible for faculty members and students to attend. Each regional convention also encourages student involvement. Students can present oral papers and posters of their research—in fact, Psi Chi often hosts student-centered events at regional conventions. We encourage you to discuss with your faculty members the possibility of attending a regional convention. Even if you are not presenting research, attending a convention can have numerous benefits. In addition to exposing you to a wide variety of psychological topics and psychologists, conventions allow students to network with other students and faculty members. If you are interested in graduate school, you might be able to meet directly with faculty members from your school of interest who are attending the convention. Making paper or poster presentations also helps build your vita and helps to acculturate you to the way scientists exchange information and present diverging viewpoints. Attending a regional (or national) convention does involve a small financial investment, but if you are serious about psychology and your future, it is money well spent.

TABLE 8.4 Regional Psychological Associations and Web Sites

New England Psychological Association (NEPA)
www.nepa-info.org

Eastern Psychological Association (EPA)
www.easternpsychological.org

Midwestern Psychological Association (MPA)
www.midwesternpsych.org

Rocky Mountain Psychological Association (RMPA)
www.rockymountainpsych.org

Southeastern Psychological Association (SEPA)
www.cas.ucf.edu/sepa

Southwestern Psychological Association (SWPA)
www.swpsych.org

Western Psychological Association (WPA)
www.westernpsych.org

There are seven loosely organized "psychological" regions in the United States. We say loosely for a couple of reasons. First, sometimes a state is claimed by more than one region. Second, even though these regions are by definition "regional," many are more national in scope. You do not have to be from a particular region to attend that conference's regional convention. Thus, attendees at the Midwestern Psychological Association meeting (held in Chicago each year) are from all over the country. The seven regions and their associated Web sites are presented in Table 8.4. Note that these regions are not exactly the same regional designations as Psi Chi—Psi Chi divides the country into six regions, not seven.

One last recommendation is that you get involved in activities in your own department! Often during the academic year your department may sponsor guest speakers, or faculty members may participate in some sort of colloquium series (sometimes held over the lunchtime, these are called "brown bags"). As a student, you want your faculty to be supportive of your efforts—you also need to be supportive of the faculty. Attending such presentations also gives you a chance to hear about faculty research, which might interest you and lead to an opportunity to serve as a research assistant. Perhaps hearing about research being conducted at a homeless shelter in your community might inspire you to think about an internship. Attending these departmental events shows your commitment to psychology and your general interest in the happenings of the department.

Taking advantage of the opportunities highlighted in this chapter should lead to a better education and give you the skills, abilities, and knowledge to make you more marketable with your bachelor's degree or better qualified as a candidate for graduate school. It's up to you to seize the opportunity—now make it happen!

Exercise #8: Time Management

As you are beginning to see, success after college means that you must be actively involved. Going to class and earning good grades are not enough to give you a competitive advantage. We have described a number of opportunities available to you at the undergraduate level. However, it is difficult to "do it all," and that may not be the best goal for you. However, most students can benefit from better time management. Using the checklist below, see if you can discover new ways to use your time more efficiently.

Use a checkmark (✔) to indicate that you already use this technique. Use a plus sign (+) to indicate an idea that you need to try out or use more.

Status: ✔ or +	Time Management Suggestion
_____	Study difficult (or "boring") subjects first.
_____	Be aware of your best time of day.
_____	Use waiting time. Go through flashcards or review notes.
_____	Use a regular study area.
_____	Study where you will be alert.
_____	Use a library. The situation is often optimum for studying.
_____	Pay attention to your attention.
_____	Agree with living mates about study time.
_____	Get off the phone/Internet.
_____	Learn to say no.
_____	Hang a "do not disturb" sign on your door.
_____	Get ready the night before. Plan the tasks of the next day.
_____	Call ahead. You can minimize closed stores and missed directions by calling ahead.
_____	Avoid noise distractions.
_____	Notice how others misuse your time.
_____	Ask: What is the one task I can accomplish toward my goal?
_____	Ask: Am I being too hard on myself?
_____	Ask: Is this a piano? (Does this have to be absolutely perfect?)
_____	Ask: What would I pay myself for what I'm doing right now?
_____	Ask: Can I do just one more thing?
_____	Ask: Am I making time for things that are important but not urgent?
_____	Ask: Can I delegate this?
_____	Ask: How did I just waste time?
_____	Ask: Could I find the time if I really wanted to?
_____	Ask: Am I willing to promise it?

Source: Ellis, D. (1997). *Becoming a master student* (8th ed.). Boston: Houghton Mifflin.

CHAPTER 9

Sharpening Library and Research Skills

Beginning with this chapter and continuing throughout the rest of this book, we will focus on the skills and abilities needed to navigate the psychology major and be a successful college student. In this chapter, we focus on how to find research that has already been conducted and generate ideas for research; in the next chapter we address how to write about research. Before we cover how to find research that is already completed, you will need to know what you are looking for. Sometimes, this task might be a paper or study idea that your instructor assigns, but you may also be asked to generate your own ideas for research projects (such as in an independent study, senior thesis, or perhaps even in a research methods/experimental design course).

GENERATING RESEARCH IDEAS

Students are sometimes stumped when faculty ask them about their own ideas for research. How do you get these ideas? How do experimental psychologists get ideas for doing research? The following guidelines, based in part on Martin (1991), should give you some starting points in thinking about topics to study:

Observation. Just look at the world around you and feel free to tap into your own interests. If you enjoy people-watching, go watch and be willing to wonder about their behavior and why people behave the way they do. Remember that better questions to be asked in a research-type format are (a) repeatable, (b) observable, and (c) testable.

Vicarious observation. Vicarious observation is a sophisticated way of saying observe through the observations of others. Simply put, read about research that has already been done and then think about follow-up studies that are needed. Find a psychological journal in the library with articles in your favorite subject area, and look for ideas and issues to explore.

Expand on your own previous ideas. Perhaps in other courses you have written a paper, done a project, studied a topic, or heard a lecture that you found especially interesting. Why not pursue that avenue of interest through a research project?

Focus on a practical problem. Many students select topics that are of practical, everyday concern as opposed to theoretical, basic research. Select a facet of real life that interests you, and study it systematically as your research project.

When you work with a faculty member on a research project, you may not be able to select what you want to study. In fact, that faculty member might want you to generate research ideas specific to his or her research domain. In that case, much of the work is already focused for you—what will be important here (and with every project) is that you have a firm understanding of the literature. Hence, the literature review is a critical component of the research project.

Success Stories

Dr. James H. Korn
Saint Louis University

Daria (not her real name) was a student in my General Psychology class, a freshman in her first semester of college. It may have been as early as the second week in the semester when she said, "How can I get involved in research?" Most freshman want to know about the psychology major and about possible careers, but rarely about doing research, which is the key to getting into graduate school.

When I spoke with Daria, she clearly knew that research meant working in a lab, not just doing surveys. I told her about several faculty members who welcomed undergraduates into their labs, and she then spoke to two of them. She chose to work in a lab that was studying the behavioral effects of a genetically transmitted nerve disease, a very sophisticated problem. "I really don't like rats," she said, "but I can learn a lot about doing research." What a great attitude! About 6 months later she presented her data on four rats at an undergraduate research conference. It was only her second semester in college.

She now is working in a cognitive lab that is studying effects of aging on memory, and is well on her way to another presentation, a publication, and an excellent graduate program somewhere.

THE LITERATURE REVIEW

Each manuscript published in a scholarly journal reviews (to some extent) prior, relevant studies and develops a background to the problem of interest. This introductory portion of the journal article is called the literature review. By reviewing previous research, you set the theoretical foundation for your topic. The author also discusses why the present study is valuable and states the hypotheses that the research will test. This section organizes the articles you have identified as important.

Sometimes new researchers are so excited about the prospects of doing their own original research that they minimize or overlook the importance of the literature search. If you try to skip this step, it could be very costly in terms of your investment of time and energy to complete a research project. Also, if you have long-term goals of presenting the outcomes of your research at a professional conference or submitting a manuscript for publication, it will be necessary for you to have "done your homework," that is, review the literature and place your current work in the context of your particular area in psychology. There are a number of benefits that accrue from reviewing the literature:

- Maybe someone has already done something very similar. Why reinvent the wheel? Although there are a number of areas in psychology that are not well understood (hence ripe for new research), other areas in the field are fairly well understood. You won't know which is which unless you review the literature.

- Other investigators might have already identified some of the key challenges to doing research in a particular area. Learn from their efforts and avoid their mistakes. Many publications end with a discussion of where future research should go—you might get an idea for your own research project just by reading and understanding what has already been done.

- New ideas in psychology (actually, in any science) must fit within the framework of existing ideas and theories. New theories can put forward new information, but those theories also must explain why former theories were wrong, inaccurate, or inappropriate. To be able to do the latter, you must be familiar with those former theories—hence the importance of the literature review. By the way, completely new, original ideas are fairly rare.

THE SPECIAL ROLE OF REFERENCES

The references listed at the conclusion of a research report make the cited literature accessible to the reader. This documentation enables other scientists to locate and explore firsthand the prior research or theoretical sources that constitute the framework for the current research. The reference section is critically important because it is a demonstration of the scholarly nature of your work. The scientist and the critical thinker examine and use evidence to support ideas and contentions; you provide your evidence in the reference section (as well as in the

TABLE 9.1 Tips for Selecting a Research Topic

Try not to choose a topic that is too broad.

Choose a topic that is of interest to you—choose an additional backup topic.

Choose a topic that will enable you to read and understand the literature.

Choose a topic that has resources available.

Make sure that the resources are available in time for you to meet your deadlines.

Read through the background information.

If there is not enough information available, you may want to go to your backup topic.

State your topic idea as a question—this will help you outline and frame your paper.

Start making a list of key words to use in later searches.

results section). When you cite a source, be sure you are familiar with the article. It can be a dangerous practice to cite references that you have never seen or actually read. This type of citation is called a reference from a secondary source and there are specific ways to list such references. Be careful: Your instructor just might be familiar with that reference. You should note that reference lists are *not* bibliographies. Bibliographies refer the interested reader to additional sources for further reading that were not necessarily cited in the manuscript through paraphrasing or direct quotation, and are not used in APA-style manuscripts. Remember that the reference section contains *only* the articles directly cited in the text of the paper, and all articles cited in the text of the paper should be in the reference list.

LIBRARY RESEARCH STRATEGIES

At some level you have to choose or select a research topic. Again, your faculty supervisor may dictate this choice, or it could be an assigned class project. Nevertheless, you will probably have some range of topics to select from within your specific areas of interest. The list in Table 9.1 (from University of California–Santa Cruz 1998; Vanderbilt University, 1996) should help in your choice of a topic. Inevitably, this choice also involves the next step, which is finding the background information.

There are numerous library research strategies that you can use to find useful information. In the remainder of this section we will cover how to (a) make the best use of books, (b) find journal articles, (c) use the Web, and (d) use other strategies with which savvy researchers are familiar. Perhaps one of the best tips we can offer is to be sure to utilize the reference librarians who are available to you. Not only can they help you determine the library's holdings, but they can also offer additional, specific search strategies for your particular library. We should also note that the Internet has become a powerful source of information, but using this resource requires caution. Later in this chapter we will offer some guidelines from Kirk (1996) concerning the evaluation of Internet information.

BOOKS

With respect to *books*, there are at least two avenues to pursue. First, there are general reference books that can lead you to other sources, and then there are specific books in psychology that may be written about your topic. To find books in the latter category, you can use the search methods for finding journal articles that we discuss in the next section.

In addition to these resources, your university library has an electronic card catalog/computer database that contains the inventory of the library. Terminals for access to this database are probably located in the library and around campus, and are probably available off-campus through an Internet/Web connection. In courses where research is time-dependent, you may want to get a jump-start on your library literature search because some of the books and journal articles that you need will probably not be available in your library. You can usually obtain these materials through *interlibrary loan*, but depending on where this information has to come from, your request will probably take between 2 and 6 weeks to fill. Also, do not overlook other libraries in your community, such as the public library, other college and university libraries in your region, or perhaps even a hospital library. Note that if you attend a state school, you may have borrowing privileges at other state colleges and universities. Most college and university libraries are organized using the Library of Congress Cataloging System. Table 9.2 presents some of the psychology-related categories for finding books in this system.

TABLE 9.2 Library of Congress Classification Codes of Topics Related to Psychology

BF 1	Psychology
BF 173	Psychoanalysis
BF 180	Experimental psychology
BF 231	Sensation
BF 309	Cognition, Perception
BF 501	Motivation
BF 511	Emotion
BF 608	Will, Choice
BF 636	Applied psychology
BF 660	Comparative psychology
BF 698	Personality
BF 699	Genetic psychology
BF 712	Developmental psychology
BF 721	Child psychology
BF 795	Temperament, Character
BF 840	Physiognomy
BF 866	Phrenology
BF 889	Graphology
BF 908	The Hand, Palmistry
BF 1001	Parapsychology
BF 1404	Occult sciences
HM 251	Social psychology
LB 5	Theory and practice of education
LB 51	Systems of individual educators and writers
LB 1025	Teaching, principles and practices
LB 1050.9	Educational psychology
LB 1101	Child study
LB 1131	Psychical development
LB 1140	Preschool education
LB 1141	Kindergarten
LB 1501	Primary education
LB 1555	Elementary or public school education
LB 1603	Secondary education, high schools
LB 1705	Education and training of teachers
LB 2300	Higher education
LB 2801	School administration and organization
LB 3201	School architecture and equipment
LB 3401	School hygiene
LB 3525	Special days, school life, student manners, and customs

Source: Library of Congress (1990). *LC classification outline.* Washington, DC: Author.

JOURNAL ARTICLES

Although books are an important resource for information and leads to additional information, perhaps the most important communication mode of the results of psychological research comes in the form of journal articles. Journals have a more timely publication frequency, can reach large numbers of people, have a rigorous acceptance and publication process, and are a well-established means of information distribution. There are hundreds of journals in psychology that publish 4, 6, or 12 issues per year (i.e., per volume).

As a psychology major, if you haven't started reading psychology journal articles on a regular basis yet, you will soon. When you read your first journal article, you immediately notice some important differences in relation to regular magazine articles; it may seem as if a journal article follows a quirky set of rules. The rules that dictate how articles are to be written in psychology are found 5th edition of the *Publication Manual of the American Psychological Association* (APA, 2001). Knowledge of the APA format rules aids you in reading psychological research and is essential for success in writing your own research papers in psychology— more on this topic in Chapter 10.

How is a journal article different from a magazine article? Perhaps the fundamental difference between a magazine and a journal is how the article is published. Journals in psychology operate under a *peer review system* where several professionals review article submissions before an acceptance decision is made. Let's say that you wanted to publish the results of your research. After selecting a journal to send your manuscript to (not always an easy task), you would send multiple copies to the journal editor. You may submit a manuscript to only one journal at a time. The editor sends copies of your manuscript out for review. Here is where the process begins. The editor asks your peers in the field (other psychologists) to review your manuscript and decide if it is suitable for publication. The peers are also called referees, and sometimes you hear the phrase "refereed journal" (which means the journal follows this peer review process).

How does an individual reviewer evaluate a manuscript? (To be clear about terminology, authors submit a manuscript in hopes that it will be accepted; this accepted manuscript becomes a journal article.) The answer to this question varies across journals and individuals, but in general, scholarship is the key. For the manuscript to be considered scholarly there should be a thorough review of the literature, a keen grasp of the subject matter, concise writing, adequate research skills, demonstrated importance of the work to psychology, and an understanding of the journal readership (the journal subscribers). Often reviewers are individuals with prior success in publishing their own manuscripts. Once the editor has received the reviews, a decision must be made whether to accept the paper, suggest that the author make some revisions and resubmit, or reject the paper. Journals go through this long, tedious, and expensive process to select the articles to be published (by the way, reviewers do not get paid for this service, and reviews are often done anonymously). This procedure is as fair and objective as possible. Also, in an effort to keep the process fair, the author of the manuscript typically does not know the identity of the reviewers and sometimes the reviewers may not know the name(s) of the author(s) (i.e., a blind review).

This process also differs from a magazine in that magazines pay people to write articles; authors of journal articles are not paid and sometimes even help defray the cost of journal publishing. Whereas magazine articles may be checked for accuracy, they do not undergo the same scrutiny, examination, and review as journal articles. The majority of journal articles are well documented with supporting references noted as to when an idea has been adopted from another source. A magazine article is rarely as extensive in documenting the academic and scholarly work of the author. Another difference between the two is that journals are typically not available for purchase at newsstands but must be subscribed to, whereas magazines are typically available at a newsstand. However, magazines can be a great resource if you are trying to *get* some ideas about research topics.

Now that you are familiar with journal articles, where do you find them? The best place to begin your search is the library. Academic journals are expensive (and foreign journals are *extremely* expensive), and your library likely subscribes to selected journals of particular interest to faculty and students. Care and respect should be given to these resources. Never tear or cut any page out of a journal, and take the journal out of the library only if permissible and if necessary. When you photocopy an article, always copy the entire reference section. Sometimes students try to cut corners by not copying the references, and often regret it later; those references are valuable sources of information on your topic. Also realize that some of your faculty members may subscribe to particular journals—ask to see if someone in your department already has access to the information you need.

The key component of the database for searching the psychological literature is a product called *Psychological Abstracts* (Psych Abstracts, or PA). PA is an APA product, where journal articles published in psychology are indexed into a common database that is made available to the public in various forms. Most journals that publish empirical research of a psychological nature are abstracted or indexed in PA. Technically speaking, *Psychological Abstracts* is the paper version of this index. Each month new indexing information becomes available in hard copy, or in paper/booklet form. Because online indexing products have become much more popular and user-friendly, your library may have discontinued its subscription to PA. Regardless of the format used, a key to success in using this resource is securing the appropriate key words or search terms (more on this later in Exercise 9). The key words used to access *PsycINFO* and PA are contained in the *Thesaurus of Psychological Index Terms.* Your reference librarian should be able to locate this volume for you.

The newest version of PA is an APA service called *PsycINFO. PsycINFO* is an Internet/Web interface where users can do multiple, unlimited searches of the PA database. Although this service provides a great deal of convenience for the user, one additional benefit is that the journal database has been expanded to an index of psychological articles published since 1887—that's right, 1887. In *PsycINFO* you can print out the bibliographic citation as well as the abstract, and you can use search operators (e.g., "and," "or," "not"). Also, some APA journals also have full-text versions available over the Internet. For more information about the variety of costs and services available to psychology students, check the APA Web site at www.apa.org. It is important to note that *PsycINFO* provides *only* citations and abstracts. You need to be sure to get the complete article before you write about it in a paper. You *cannot* write a good research paper from a stack of abstracts.

The resources that are available from *PsycINFO* are staggering. Here's how APA (2004b) describes this resource: "PsycINFO is an electronic bibliographic database that provides citations and abstracts to the scholarly literature in the behavioral sciences and mental health from the 1887 to the present. The database includes nearly 2 million records and is updated weekly. Material of relevance to psychologists and professionals in related fields such as psychiatry, management, business, education, social science, neuroscience, law, medicine, and social work is included in the database. PsycINFO covers more than 1,900 journal titles, doctoral dissertations, authored and edited books, and chapters from edited books" (¶ 3). Table 9.3 contains a listing of the journals published by the APA—these are some of the most prestigious journals published in psychology.

APA also publishes a monthly journal called *Contemporary Psychology: APA Reviews of Books,* which contains reviews of books and other information relevant to psychology. Sometimes book information is more difficult to search for; hence *Contemporary Psychology* is an important resource.

THE INTERNET

In the past 5 years, the Internet via the World Wide Web has become an important source of information about psychology and life in general. Caution should be used in interpreting information taken from the Web. In particular, look for the same signs of scholarship that you would expect to find from a scholarly research article or from a legitimate scientific entity: accuracy, authority, objectivity and reliability, and currency (Brandeis University, 1998). Look for information from reliable sources such as professional organizations (e.g., APA, APS, Psi Chi) or from colleges and universities. Although you should evaluate *any* type of information critically, Web materials necessitate additional scrutiny. It is easy for anyone to post a Web page to the Internet and make it universally accessible—it is not nearly so easy to start your own peer-reviewed scholarly research journal and publish it yourself. Kirk (1996) offers this advice for evaluating information from the Internet, as well as evaluative criteria presented in Table 9.4: "The World Wide Web offers information and data from all over the world. Because so much information is available, and because that information can appear to be fairly "anonymous," it is necessary to develop skills to evaluate what you find. When you use a research or academic library, the books, journals and other resources have already been evaluated by scholars, publishers and

TABLE 9.3 American Psychological Association Journals

American Psychologist	Journal of Experimental Psychology: General
American Journal of Orthopsychiatry	Journal of Experimental Psychology: Human Perception and Performance
Behavioral Neuroscience	
Clinician's Research Digest	Journal of Experimental Psychology: Learning, Memory, and Cognition
Consulting Psychology Journal: Practice and Research	Journal of Family Psychology
Contemporary Psychology: APA Review of Books	Journal of Occupational Health Psychology
	Journal of Personality and Social Psychology
Cultural Diversity and Ethnic Minority Psychology	Journal of Psychotherapy Integration
Developmental Psychology	Neuropsychology
Dreaming	Prevention & Treatment
Emotion	Professional Psychology: Research and Practice
European Psychologist	
Experimental & Clinical Psychopharmacology	Psychoanalytic Psychology
Families, Systems, & Health	Psychological Abstracts
Group Dynamics: Theory, Research, and Practice	Psychological Assessment
	Psychological Bulletin
Health Psychology	Psychological Methods
History of Psychology	Psychological Review
International Journal of Stress Management	Psychological Services
Journal of Abnormal Psychology	Psychology and Aging
Journal of Applied Psychology	Psychology of Addictive Behaviors
Journal of Comparative Psychology	Psychology of Men and Masculinity
Journal of Consulting & Clinical Psychology	Psychology, Public Policy, and Law
Journal of Counseling Psychology	Psychotherapy: Theory, Research, Practice, Training
Journal of Educational Psychology	
Journal of Experimental Psychology: Animal Behavior Processes	Rehabilitation Psychology
	Review of General Psychology
Journal of Experimental Psychology: Applied	

Source: American Psychological Association. (2004b). APA journals. Retrieved July 19, 2004, from http://www.apa.org/journals/journals_list.html

librarians. Every resource you find has been evaluated in one way or another before you ever see it. When you are using the World Wide Web, none of this applies. There are no filters. Excellent resources reside along side the most dubious" (¶ 1).

Below is a brief list of reputable places to start on the Web:

- American Psychological Association: www.apa.org
- American Psychological Society: www.psychologicalscience.org
- PsychWeb by Russ Dewey: www.psywww.com
- Links to Psychology Departments by John Krantz and Yvan Russell: psych.hanover.edu/Krantz/other.html

These sites contain links to many other psychology Web sites—the combinations are virtually endless.

TABLE 9.4 Criteria Used to Evaluate Internet Information

- Authorship is perhaps the major criterion used in evaluating information. Who wrote this? When we look for information with some type of critical value, we want to know the basis of the authority with which the author speaks.

- The publishing body also helps evaluate any kind of document you may be reading. In the print universe, this generally means that the author's manuscript has undergone screening in order to verify that it meets the standards or aims of the organization that serves as publisher. This may include peer review.

- Point of view or bias reminds us that information is rarely neutral. Because data is used in selective ways to form information, it generally represents a point of view. Every writer wants to prove his point, and will use the data and information that assists him in doing so. When evaluating information found on the Internet, it is important to examine who is providing the "information" you are viewing, and what might be their point of view or bias. The popularity of the Internet makes it the perfect venue for commercial and sociopolitical publishing. These areas in particular are open to highly "interpretative" uses of data.

- Referral to or knowledge of the literature refers to the context in which the author situates his or her work. This reveals what the author knows about his or her discipline and its practices allow you to evaluate the author's scholarship or knowledge of trends in the area under discussion.

- Accuracy or verifiability of details is an important part of the evaluation process, especially when you are reading the work of an unfamiliar author presented by an unfamiliar organization, or presented in a nontraditional way.

- Currency refers to the timeliness of information. In printed documents, the date of publication is the first indicator of currency. For some types of information, currency is not an issue: authorship or place in the historical record is more important. For many other types of data, however, currency is extremely important, as is the regularity with which the data is updated.

- All information, whether in print or by byte, needs to be evaluated by readers for authority, appropriateness, and other personal criteria for value. If you find information that is "too good to be true," it probably is. Never use information that you cannot verify. Establishing and learning criteria to filter information you find on the Internet is a good beginning for becoming a critical consumer of information in all forms. Look for other sources that can authenticate or corroborate what you find. Learn to be skeptical and then learn to trust your instincts.

Source: Kirk, E. E. (1996). *Evaluating information found on the internet.* Johns Hopkins University. Retrieved July 19, 2004, from http://www.library.jhu.edu/elp/useit/evaluate/index.html

MORE LITERATURE SEARCH STRATEGIES

Before we conclude this chapter with some of the library skills that a psychology major should have, there are a handful of other strategies that you can use in your search for prior research. "Treeing" is a technique that can be used forward and backward. To tree backward through your references, try to find a great, current article that is right on target with your research idea—then look at that article's reference section. You may find some good leads in the articles you already have. Don't forget about textbooks—they have reference sections that you can use to tree backward.

Treeing forward through the references involves the use of another bibliographic resource, the Social Sciences Citation Index (SSCI) (Institute for Scientific Information, 1998). To tree forward, find a classic article that is commonly referenced in your field of study—perhaps a major article that shaped the direction of research since it was published. By using the SSCI, you can look at all the authors of articles who have cited that classic article since it was published. That is, you can find the more current information related to your area of interest by looking for other researchers who cited that classic article, and then obtain their publications. SSCI is a valuable resource; however, it uses incredibly small print and may be difficult to use initially. Ask your instructor or the reference librarian for help if you have difficulty.

If your library does not carry a journal that you need for a particular article (and you have some time), why not write the author directly? Some authors have reprints (copies) made of each one of their publications. As a professional courtesy, most researchers will send you a free reprint on request. If you know the author's name and affiliation, you should be able to determine a phone number, mailing address, or e-mail address that you can use for contact. Search engines on the Internet can help (www.google.com), and both the APA and APS publish membership directories that may be available in your library (or from faculty members in your department if they belong to either organization). If you have the good fortune to attend a professional conference, you might have the chance to meet the researcher in person and make your request at that time. Similarly, at a conference you can often obtain a preprint, which is a manuscript that is either submitted for publication, or has been accepted for publication but is not yet in print.

The University of California–Santa Cruz (1998) library makes these recommendations when evaluating sources: (a) look for articles published in scholarly journals or sources that require certain standards or criteria to be met prior to publication, (b) use the bibliographies or reference lists cited from scholarly journal articles or books, (c) compare several opinions by scholars in your topic area as another method of evaluating your sources, and (d) consult with an instructor or the faculty member who is supervising the research project. Using these methods does not guarantee that you will have a perfect or complete literature search. The more you do literature reviews and the more familiar you become with the ideas and terminology in psychology, the better you will become as a consumer and evaluator of psychological knowledge.

LIBRARY SKILLS PSYCHOLOGY MAJORS SHOULD HAVE

Merriam, LaBaugh, and Butterfield (1992) proposed minimum training guidelines for library instruction of psychology majors. They suggested that students should become familiar with (a) locating known sources, (b) conducting a literature search, (c) making effective use of those resources that are found, and (d) developing an increased awareness of the places that a person can find information in psychology. This chapter has focused on the importance of the formulation of research ideas, and the pursuit of information related to those ideas. Reviewing the strategies presented in this chapter will allow you to be successful in locating prior research. In the next chapter, we will look at how to put this information and more into creating an APA format paper.

Exercise #9: PsycINFO Author Search

Below is a sample screen shot of how your PsycINFO interface might look (this is the interface from Boise State University). See where it says "Keyword"? If you hit the drop down arrow, you will find that you can search on a number of difference parameters, including journal title, author, etc. For this exercise, search in PsycINFO for journal articles written by faculty members at your college or university. If they have an uncommon last name, that will probably do in the "Search for:" first box (and instead of Keyword in the second box, select Author). If they have a common last name, you'll get plenty of hits, so you'll either have to scroll through those or you'll have to add a first name and/or initials to the search. When done, write down some of the details of your search on the lines below.

PsycINFO_1887 Advanced Search

- Enter search terms in one or more boxes and click on **Search**.

Home	Databases	Searching

Basic Search   Advanced Search   **Expert Search**   Go to page

Subjects News Help   Current database: **PsycINFO_1887 to present**

Search   Clear

Search in database: PsycINFO_1887   ⓘ (Updated: 2004-07-13)
Psychology and related fields since 1887

Search for: [   ]   Keyword

and   [   ]   Keyword

and   [   ]   Keyword

Limit to: Year   [   ]   (format: YYYY-YYYY)
Language Phrase   No Limit
Document Type Phrase   No Limit

Limit to: ☐ 目 Full text ❓

Limit availability to: ☐ 🕮 Subscriptions held by my library (OIP, BOISE STATE UNIV) ❓
match any of the following   Library Code   [   ]   Find codes ...

Rank by: No ranking ❓

Search   Clear

_____
_____
_____
_____

CHAPTER 10

An APA Format Primer

As you begin to read more and more journal articles in psychology, you may wonder, "Why APA format?" For years the APA has published the *Publication Manual of the American Psychological Association;* the 2001 version is the fifth edition. Psychologists all over the world follow these steps and guidelines in the preparation of manuscripts. In fact, a number of scientific disciplines have adopted basic APA format as the *de facto* standard of manuscript preparation. The first formal presentation of manuscript instructions appeared in the *Psychological Bulletin* (an APA journal) in 1929. A six-member panel attending a Conference of Editors and Business Managers of Anthropological and Psychological Periodicals issued a report on manuscript guidelines called "Instructions in Regard to Preparation of Manuscript." This document offered general guidance for authors preparing manuscripts for publication. Although many of the details of page layout and preparation have changed and evolved into the current edition, some of the advice given in 1929 still holds true today. Consider this comment on the general form of the manuscript: "A safe and useful prescription is to be as brief as possible without sacrificing clarity or pertinent facts. Pressure upon space in the scientific journals and the present heavy demands upon the informed reader both reinforce this prescription. Careless writing is usually diffuse, incoherent, and repetitious. Careful reading by a competent critic will usually suggest means for reduction" ("Instructions," 1929, p. 57).

Why the specific format? One of the basic tenets of science and scientific knowledge is communicability (one other basic tenet of scientific knowledge is replication). APA format facilitates communication of scientific, psychological knowledge by the reporting of results in a consistent, reliable format. Any paper written by a psychologist in APA format has information presented in the following order: title page, abstract, introduction, method, results, discussion, and references. Knowing the parts of the manuscript and where they are located gives an advantage to the reader; you may not understand the jargon used, but you know there is a description of how the study was conducted in the Method section, and the statistical findings of the study are recorded in the Results section.

This common format facilitates the communication of ideas in the scientific community. Some students are initially confused by APA format because they have already been taught a paper-writing format such as Turabian (Turabian, 1982), *Chicago Manual of Style* (1993), or MLA (Gibaldi & Achtert, 1988). Other disciplines have their own format as well, such as the Council of Biology Editors (1994). APA format is not necessarily superior to any other of these formats; in fact, APA format can be confusing and tedious at times. However, it is the standard of communication in psychology for all authors. Whether you are submitting your work to a journal for publication or writing a paper in a psychology course, you should follow the established standards and use APA format.

WRITING PSYCHOLOGY PAPERS

Although the APA *Publication Manual* (APA, 2001) is 439 pages long, the basic rules for writing in APA format are relatively straightforward. Much of the APA manual is dedicated to contingencies and events that do not occur very often. For example, in using APA format in the reference section of your paper, the *Publication Manual* lists 95 different methods of referencing; whereas the two basic references are journal articles and books.

Assume that you are eventually going to write a journal-style paper. Perhaps you are writing about your own experiment, a group project, or an experiment proposal. How do you get your notes organized to write the paper? Many authors use the notecard method. The notecard method is a technique of conducting library-type research in such a way that it facilitates later writing of the introduction and discussion sections of a manuscript by increasing the synthesis of a paper. By integrating multiple sources from your library research into the paper, it reads better, it flows better, and is one sign of scholarly writing. The notecard method is an organized procedure for collecting research notes when preparing a major term paper. Students are challenged in such papers to not only analyze information from various sources, but also to synthesize the views and reports of these sources. The difference between a good paper and an excellent paper is often the level of synthesis. By using the notecard method, students organize their thoughts and ideas beforehand, rather than at the moment of paper creation/typing/completion.

Step1. Select a paper topic. Try to generate a topic that interests you. Be sure, however, to keep within the confines of the instructor's assignment. The challenge is to select as specific a topic as possible for which there are library materials readily available (if interlibrary loan is used, plan ahead; it can take at least 2 to 3 weeks to receive materials not found in the library). Try to decide on a paper topic after a trip to the library. This approach allows you to make sure that there are adequate resources available before you are totally committed to a topic. See Chapter 5 for some tips about coming up with research ideas and ways to find information about those ideas.

Step2. Create an outline. Sketch an outline of the major points you want to make in your paper. Again, this step should be done after taking a quick look at the available library materials. You may already know what kinds of points you want to make, but the library quick search may give you more ideas. Try to be as concrete and specific as possible in your outline.

Step3. Make reference notecards. On $3'' \times 5''$ notecards, create your reference list/bibliography. Place only *one* reference on each notecard, and in the upper left corner give each reference a code (A, B, C, etc.). Write each reference in APA style. APA has a very specific format for writing references, and references from books are written differently from those taken from a journal; be sure to note the differences (see the examples in this chapter or at the end of the book). Writing the reference notecard in APA format saves you time later when you type the reference section of your paper; putting one reference per card makes it easy to alphabetize your references.

Step4. Make idea notecards (take notes on sources). On $4'' \times 6''$ notecards, take your notes on each source/reference you have selected. Write down ideas that you may think you might use in your paper. Write only *one* idea on each card. So for Reference A, you may have four separate ideas you might incorporate into your paper, labeled A1, A2, A3, and A4. If you think you might like to use the idea in a direct quote, be sure to note the page number on the idea notecard. It is important to have only one idea on each card so that organizing your paper later is facilitated.

Step5. Plan the paper. Before you actually begin writing the paper, plan the course of the paper. With your revised outline and your idea notecards, organize your paper by selecting ideas (notecards) and grouping them together. Try to integrate the paper as much as possible (i.e., don't talk about all the ideas from your A reference, then your B reference, etc.). The whole point of this system is to help you synthesize similar ideas from different contexts. In this step, you lay out the course of the paper by physically placing your $4'' \times 6''$ idea notecards in the order you are going to use them. How do you know what order? Your outline (Step 2) is your general road map for writing your paper.

Step6. Write the rough draft. Now it is time to actually start writing "the paper." Of course, you've already done much of the writing, which has helped you to become very familiar with your reference materials and the points you want to make. Following your paper plan, write the text by following the notecards you've already organized. You need to make the text readable, providing the necessary transition between ideas. Be sure to include a title with your rough draft. Remember that this is a rough draft, not the finished product. See if your instructor will review your rough draft without assigning a grade. This option may not be available in larger classes; if it is not, try to get one of your classmates to read your paper. If you are not sure about something, try it; the worst that can happen in the draft stage is that you receive some free advice. With the rough draft, your reference list is typically not required (it normally appears at the end of the paper), although you should cite your sources in the text of the paper in APA format. If you see a lot of red ink on your returned draft, just think of it as free advice; remember, the rough draft is not the final version; the comments should improve your paper. At some point we all need outside consultants to help us improve and sharpen our skills.

Step 7. Write the final draft. Consider the comments from the instructor and your classmates. Improve the paper where indicated; these changes may include correcting typographical errors, rewriting paragraphs, or reorganizing the flow of ideas. It is to your benefit to be a careful editor and proofreader of your work. It is strongly recommended that you have a fellow classmate read your paper before handing it in—someone else may catch a mistake that you have overlooked. Simple, repetitive mistakes can be extremely irritating to an instructor. Be sure to follow the APA format rules when preparing the final draft of the paper. There are many rules, so be careful.

THE PARTS: INTRODUCTION, METHOD, RESULTS, AND DISCUSSION

The parts listed above are actually not the only parts to an APA-formatted paper, but they are the major portions of the text. There are various details that must be attended to in preparing a manuscript in APA format, and a discussion of each of these sections follows. Note that, in general, APA has moved toward writing in the active voice (as opposed to the passive voice). Your instructor can help you to make this writing transition. First, Table 10.1 provides a quick overview of these sections.

TABLE 10.1 Major Sections of an APA Manuscript

Title page (Take credit)

    Author's name, affiliation

    Other information as your professor requests

    Page numbering (header) and running head information

Abstract (Quick summary)

    No more than 120 words

    Some assignments will not require an abstract

Introduction (What you are studying)

    Introduce the problem

    Develop the background

    State the purpose and rationale for the present study

Method (What you did)

    Participants, Materials, Procedure

    Should be in enough detail to replicate if desired

Results (What happened)

    Presentation of statistical outcomes; tables and/or figures if necessary

    Presentation, not interpretation

Discussion (What it means)

    Was there support for the research idea? Did the study help resolve the original problem?

    What conclusions can be drawn? Suggest improvements, avenues for further/new research

Reference section (Give credit where credit is due)

    Starts on its own page

    Authors listed alphabetically by last name, no first names used, only initials

    Be sure all citations in the text are referenced

    Shows your scholarly ability and how you did your homework

The Introduction and Literature Review

This section is especially frustrating to persons who are unfamiliar with writing in APA format. The *Publication Manual* (APA, 2001) suggests that authors should try to accomplish three goals in this opening portion of the paper. *First*, introduce the problem. The body of the paper opens with an introduction that presents the specific problem under study and describes the research strategy. Before writing the introduction, consider the following: What is the point of the study? How do the hypotheses and the experimental design relate to the problem? What are the theoretical implications of the study? How does the study relate to previous work in the area? A good introduction answers these questions in a paragraph or two and, by summarizing the relevant arguments and the data, gives the reader a firm sense of what was done and why.

Second, develop the background. Discuss the literature, but do not include an exhaustive historical review. Assume that the reader has knowledge in the field for which you are writing and does not require a complete listing. Although you should acknowledge the contributions of others to the study of the problem, cite only research that is pertinent to the specific issue and avoid references with only general significance. Refer the reader to general surveys or reviews of the topic if they are available. A real challenge for writers is to demonstrate the logical continuity between previous research and the present work (your project). Develop the problem with enough breadth and clarity to make it generally understood by as wide a professional audience as possible. Do not let the goal of brevity mislead you into writing a statement understandable only to the specialist. As you can see in the sample paper (at the end of this chapter), the author takes about five double-spaced pages to develop the idea. You may want to use subheadings (as in the sample paper) to better organize your thoughts.

Third, state the purpose and rationale. After you have introduced the problem and developed the background material, you are in a position to tell what you did. Make this statement in the closing paragraphs of the introduction. At this point, a definition of the variables and a formal statement of your hypotheses give clarity to the paper. Often you will see the sentence containing the hypothesis clearly beginning "It is hypothesized that. . ." Clearly develop the rationale for each hypothesis. End the introduction with a brief overview of your own study. This overview provides a smooth transition into the Method section, which immediately follows. They provide the transition for the reader. Bordens and Abbott (1988) provide a checklist for the introduction and literature review found in Table 10.2.

The Method Section

The goal of this section is to describe your participants, apparatus, and procedures so clearly that another person in your field could replicate or repeat your research. You are inviting others to repeat what you did. This section is conventionally divided under three headings: participants, apparatus or materials, and procedure (a research design heading is sometimes included).

Participants

Describe the major demographic characteristics of the participants, such as age, sex, type of institution they were drawn from, and geographic location. Describe the procedures by which

---

TABLE 10.2 Introduction/Literature Review Checklist

Introduction to the topic under study

Brief review of the research findings and theories related to the topic

Statement of the problem to be addressed by the research (identifying an area in which knowledge is incomplete)

Statement of purpose of the present research

Brief description of the method intended to establish the relationship between the question being addressed and the method being used to address it

Description of any predictions about the outcome and of the hypotheses used to generate those predictions

---

the participants were available for participation, such as student volunteers or students fulfilling course requirements. Include any criteria you used in determining who could be a participant. Describe the procedures by which you assigned participants to groups. If certain participants were dropped from the study, explain why in this section.

Materials

If specialized equipment is an integral part of your research, describe this equipment and how you used it. If the equipment is standard, cite the manufacturer and any relevant identifying labels or numbers (this section might be labeled apparatus in that case). If standardized test materials were used, briefly describe them under a heading of materials. If the materials were specially designed for your study, describe them in enough detail so that someone experienced in your field could reproduce them for replication or further research purposes.

Procedure

Describe the research chronologically, step by step. In descriptive research, describe the conditions under which you observed or tested the participants as well as specific instructions or tasks presented to them. In experimental research, indicate how the participants in each group were exposed to the independent variable, and describe any control procedures used in the design. Instructions to the participants should be included verbatim if they were a key part of the study. Provide clear details on the measurement of participants' behavior.

The Results Section

Verify that all conditions stipulated in the Method section were accomplished. If any variations occurred, describe them here; then briefly describe the procedures used for data collection and analysis. How were your observations converted into analyzable data? What type of statistical analysis was selected, and how was it conducted? It is now time to present the findings. Briefly describe your results in writing. After doing so, repeat the results in numerical form. When reporting the results of statistical tests, include the following: the name of the test (such as t or F), the degrees of freedom, the results of the specific computation, and the alpha level (usually $p < 0.05$). Now, you may elaborate or qualify the overall conclusion if necessary in writing. Be sure to end each section of the results with a summary of where things stand. APA format requires that when you report the mean, you also report the standard deviation. For particular analyses, you will need to report the effect size along with the inferential statistic.

Figures and Tables

Unless a set of findings can be stated in one or two numbers, a table or figure should accompany results that are sufficiently important to be stressed. However, you do not want the information presented in a table or figure to be redundant with information already presented in the text. The basic rule of presentation is that a reader should be able to grasp your major findings either by reading the text or by looking at the tables and figures. Be careful in preparing figures and tables: There are very specific APA rules governing their construction, they are time-consuming, and they are often difficult and expensive for journals to publish.

The Discussion Section

Begin the discussion by telling the reader what you have learned from the study. Open with a clear statement on the support or nonsupport of the hypotheses or the answers to the questions you first raised in the introduction. Do not simply reformulate and repeat points already summarized in the Results section. Each new statement should contribute something new to the reader's understanding of the problem. What inferences can be drawn from the data? What are the theoretical, practical, or even political implications of the results? Next, compare your results with the results reported by other investigators and discuss possible shortcomings of your study—that is, conditions that might limit the extent of legitimate generalizations. Do not dwell compulsively on flaws in your study. Typically there is a section included that considers questions that remain unanswered or have been raised by the study itself, along with suggestions for the kinds of research that would help to answer them.

References

List the scholarly works that you used (cited) in your paper in the reference section. List only works that you actually used; the reference section is *not* a bibliography (in a bibliography, you would list all the research that you gathered, regardless of whether or not that information was used in the paper). Also, note that references have their own rules of capitalization, and these rules are counterintuitive to students at first. For example, most students think that every word of a book title or journal article is always capitalized—in APA format in the reference section, which is not true. There are many, many different types of reference materials that you can use in an APA format paper. Unfortunately, each type has a slightly different APA format. For the listing of examples on how to format references, see the *Publication Manual* (APA, 2001, pp. 239–281). Table 10.3 presents the most common reference formats (note that they are not double-spaced as they would be in true APA format).

APA format concerning citing information from the Internet is much clearer than it used to be. APA has recommendations available (www.apastyle.org). As with all reference materials, the ultimate goal is to provide enough information in the reference so that other researchers are able to follow your path to the same information.

Title and Abstract

The title and abstract of your article permit potential readers to get a quick overview of your study and decide if they wish to read the article itself. Titles and abstracts are also indexed

TABLE 10.3 Examples of APA Format References

Periodicals/Journal Articles

Davis, S. F., & Ludvigson, H. W. (1995). Additional data on academic dishonesty and a proposal for remediation. *Teaching of Psychology, 22,* 119–122.

Landrum, R. E., & Chastain, G. (1998). Demonstrating tutoring effectiveness within a one-semester course. *Journal of College Student Development, 39,* 502–506.

Books

Davis, S. F., & Palladino, J. J. (1997). *Psychology* (2nd ed.). Upper Saddle River, NJ: Prentice Hall.

Horvat, J. J., & Davis, S. F. (1998). *Doing psychological research.* Upper Saddle River, NJ: Prentice Hall.

Smith, R. A., & Davis, S. F. (1997). *The psychologist as detective: An introduction to conducting research in psychology.* Upper Saddle River, NJ: Prentice Hall.

Edited Book

Chastain, G., & Landrum, R. E. (Eds.). (1999). *Protecting human subjects: Departmental subject pools and institutional review boards.* Washington, DC: APA Books.

Book Chapters

Davis, S. F. (1994). You take the high road, I'll take the low road: A satisfying career at a small state university. In P. A. Keller (Ed.), *Academic paths: Career decisions and experiences of psychologists.* Hillsdale, NJ: Erlbaum.

Landrum, R. E., & Chastain, G. (1999). Subject pool policies in undergraduate-only departments: Results from a nationwide survey. In G. Chastain & R. E. Landrum (Eds.), *Protecting human subjects: Departmental subject pools and institutional review boards* (pp. 24–36). Washington, DC: APA Books.

Internet Materials

American Psychological Association. (1997). *A guide to getting into graduate school.* Retrieved November 28, 1998, from http://www.apa.org/ed/getin.html

Lloyd, M. A. (1997, August 28). *Exploring career-related abilities, interests, skills, and values.* Retrieved March 30, 1998, from http://www.psych-web.com/careers/explore.htm

and compiled in reference works *(Psychological Abstracts)* and computerized databases *(PsycINFO)*. For this reason they should accurately reflect the content of the article; write the abstract after you have completed the article and have a firm view of its structure and content. The recommended length for a title is 10 to 12 words. The title should be fully explanatory when standing alone and identify the theoretical issue(s) or the variable(s) under investigation. A good title is hard to write; plan to spend some time on it. The abstract is a short paragraph that summarizes the entire work—it should not exceed 120 words. It should state the problem under investigation, in one sentence if possible, the participants (specifying pertinent characteristics), the experimental method (including apparatus, data-gathering materials, test names), the findings (including statistical significance levels), and the conclusion with the implications or applications. Be warned: a good abstract is often the most difficult portion of the paper to write.

The Appendix

The appendix contains materials important to the research that are too lengthy or detailed for inclusion in the Method section. These items may include technical materials, listing of a computer program, word lists used as stimuli, or an original survey/questionnaire. Try to minimize the use of appendices.

APA Format Typing Instructions

There are a number of specific details that are followed when preparing a manuscript in APA format. Some of the more basic guidelines are presented here. As always, heed your instructor's modifications to this list.

- Do not use underlining in 5th edition APA format—only italics.
- Double-space everything!
- Use a one-inch margin on *all* sides.
- Do not justify lines if using a word processing program (i.e., you should have a ragged right margin).
- Use a 12-point font, preferably Times New Roman or equivalent—always make sure the font is absolutely readable.
- Number every page, including the title page (except figures)—upper right-hand corner, inside the one-inch margin.
- Indent the first line of every paragraph using the tab key (usually set at one-half inch indention), or use five to seven spaces to indent.
- Center the title page information on a page; it should contain the paper's title, the author's name, and the author's affiliation. The running head also appears on the title page—this short description is what would appear at the top of the page if the article were published in a journal. The title is also repeated again on the first page of manuscript text.
- Place the abstract on a page by itself (page 2 of the paper). The word "Abstract" should be centered at the top of the page. The abstract should be about 120 words in length (maximum) and must be typed as one blocked (not indented) paragraph.

Spacing and Punctuation

APA format requires only *one* space after punctuation in the body of the paper and Reference section. Check with your instructor on his or her preference. Some instructors may want you to follow APA format exactly; others will want two spaces because they believe it improves readability; and others won't care. Also leave a space after the period used in the initials of people's names listed in your reference section. The Reference section starts on its own page.

GRAMMAR AND VOCABULARY

You can imagine that with all of these sections, the flow of a research paper might be choppy and the text difficult to read. The skilled writer uses transitions between sections and paragraphs to improve the flow and readability. Here are some of APA's suggestions (2001) for transitions:

Time links: then, next, after, while, since

Cause–effect links: therefore, consequently, as a result

Addition links: in addition, moreover, furthermore, similarly

Contrast links: but, conversely, nevertheless, however, although, whereas

One of the most confusing aspects to the writer new to the use of APA format regards the use of verbs. The verb tense that is used depends upon the section of the paper (see Table 10.4). As a general note, the *APA Manual* does a good job of providing the basics of formatting, and does have helpful examples. You should remember to always consult your instructor to determine his or her particular preferences in the application of APA format rules. At times, instructors may want you to vary from the rules to improve readability or to fulfill a departmental or institutional requirement.

Here are some different types of verb tense and an example of each. When appropriate, use the active voice. Try to increase the frequency of active voice construction—"Davis designed the study." The passive voice is acceptable when you focus on the outcome of the action, rather than who made the action happen. Try to minimize the use of passive voice— "The survey was administered by the students." Use past tense to discuss something that happened at a specific, definite time in the past (e.g., writing about another researcher's work or when reporting your results)—"Landrum (1998) found that 63% of students reporting average work expected a grade of B or a grade of A." Use the present perfect tense to discuss a past action that did *not* occur at a specific, definite time in the past—"Since the completion of the study, we have found further evidence to support our conclusions."

Using Direct Quotes vs. Paraphrasing

Use a direct quote only if the author has stated the idea so perfectly that any paraphrasing of the original would not do justice to it. In general, you should paraphrase information you take from other sources. To paraphrase means that you read and comprehend the material, but then you write it in your own words, not the author's words (as a direct quote would do). *You still need to give the writer credit for his or her work*, even though you have put it in your own words; if you do not, you have plagiarized.

In general (and this is *our* suggestion, not APA format), use direct quotations sparingly. No more than one or two per paper, and do not use block quotes (quotes longer than 40 words). When instructors see a string of quotations or a bunch of block quotes, they are drawn to the conclusion that the student thought that stringing quotes together would look good and

---

TABLE 10.4 Verb Use in Sections of an APA Format Paper

Introduction (Literature review)

　Past tense ("Davis concluded")

　Present perfect tense ("Researchers have concluded")

Method

　Past tense ("Participants completed the task in 5 min")

　Present perfect tense ("The task was completed by the participants in 5 min)

Results

　Past tense ("Scores declined after the intervention")

Discussion (discuss results and present conclusions)

　Present tense ("Participants take the computer task seriously")

---

satisfy the requirement. A scholarly paper is *not* a string of direct quotations. Examples of paraphrasing include some sentences that have phrases like these: (a) Landrum (1998) found that. . . ; (b) . . . as reported in a previous study (Landrum, 1998); and (c) In 1998, Landrum concluded that. . .

A BRIEF NOTE ON PLAGIARISM

In the chapter on student ethics, we will review more about plagiarism, but it is important to mention it now while presenting information on writing papers. You need to avoid plagiarism at all costs. What is plagiarism? According to Landau (2003), "Plagiarism occurs when people take credit for thoughts, words, images, musical passages, or ideas originally created by someone else" (¶ 3). Landau suggested that there are two main types of plagiarism—intentional and unintentional plagiarism. Regarding unintentional plagiarism, Landau suggested two types: (a) students inadvertently present someone else's work as their own (source memory error), or (b) misapprehension, or that students do not know what they were doing was wrong.

There are serious consequences for students who are caught plagiarizing; these vary from instructor to instructor as well as institution to institution. You should be able to find detailed information about this in your student handbook. The consequences could be receiving an F on the assignment, an F in the course, and worse punishments in some cases. In the real world, plagiarism has its consequences too. Read this excerpt by Margulies (2002) about what happened in one case of plagiarism: "Less than two weeks after he was called to task for borrowing liberally from others in his welcome address to the freshman class, the president of Hamilton College resigned on Tuesday. Although some faculty members had criticized Eugene M. Tobin, many people on the campus expressed surprise and disappointment at his resignation. Mr. Tobin stepped down after nine years at the helm of the Clinton, NY, college. He spoke to his colleagues at an afternoon faculty meeting after having consulted with a circle of advisors and constituents almost continuously from the time his act of plagiarism was exposed last month. In a convocation address that focused on the books he had read over the summer, Mr. Tobin used phrases and passages, without citation, from a number of book reviews and descriptions posted on Amazon.com" (¶'s 1–2, 4).

SAMPLE PAPER

We conclude this chapter with a mock-up of a sample paper. In actual APA format, each page is contained on one piece of paper, and pages are printed on one side of the page. Writing an APA format paper early in your academic career can be a daunting and frustrating task—try not to be discouraged. It is a skill and it takes time to acquire skills. As with most other things, practice helps; the more papers you write, the better you will become at writing in this style. The conventions used in APA format will become familiar over time, and you will eventually appreciate the organizational structure and logical sequence of thought that a well-prepared APA paper provides.

Running head: PERSONALITY AND TEACHING EFFECTIVENESS

The Influence of Instructor Personality on Student Ratings of Teaching Effectiveness

Lisa R. Nelsen

Boise State University

Abstract

This study examined the influence of University instructor personality traits on student ratings of teaching effectiveness. Forty-one students, enrolled in 2 upper-division psychology courses, completed 1 of 2 variations of a survey in order to examine the effects of prompting participants to think about instructor personality before completing the evaluation. The first version of the instrument consisted of a 28-item personality trait checklist, followed by an instructor evaluation form. The second version was administered in the opposite order. Analysis of the data revealed significant differences between the groups for 2 of the questions, most notably the overall rating of the instructor. Implications of the study include development of improved evaluation instruments specifically designed to measure influences on student learning.

The Influence of Instructor Personality on Student Ratings of Teaching Effectiveness

Colleges and universities widely use student evaluations that are generally accepted as a useful tool in determining the overall effectiveness of individual educators. The ratings provided by students can affect administrative decisions regarding a faculty member's salary, promotion and even retention. More importantly, though, such ratings can be used by educators who wish to improve their skills in the classroom. With this information in mind, it is important to know exactly what characteristics are associated with highly rated teachers. Knowing more specifically what leads students to differentiate between a "good" teacher and a "bad" teacher would obviously be of significant value. Researchers have been attempting to pinpoint such characteristics for more than 40 years. Much of the research conducted in the past 20 years focuses on how instructor personality traits influence student evaluations (Bendig, 1955; Erdle, Murray, & Rushton, 1985; Sherman & Blackburn, 1975).

One study of this type looked at how student evaluations differ between instructors possessing functional classroom skills (for example, fairness in grading, and relevance of presented material) and those instructors viewed as amicable, dynamic and pragmatic (Sherman & Blackburn, 1975). They found that personal attributes, as opposed to functional classroom skills, are more significant predictors of student ratings of instructor effectiveness. The authors explain that these findings have significant implications for instructors who wish to improve student ratings, and that these instructors would be better off focusing on personality traits than focusing on functional classroom behaviors.

Conclusions such as this one led to the belief that a college teacher's effectiveness is influenced, or even determined, by the personality characteristics that the teacher possesses (Feldman, 1986). Consequently, some colleges implemented training programs that focused on

improving the presentation of subject matter (such as speech and drama training), and follow-up research examined the usefulness of such training as a means of improving student ratings. Murray and Lawrence (1980) found that teachers who participated in the training did showed improvements in their overall effectiveness ratings. A concern raised by these findings was that emphasizing presentation, over a thorough and clear delivery of subject matter, simply "reduces teaching to entertainment or show business" (Murray & Lawrence, 1980, p. 88). On the surface, this concern appears to be legitimate.

One such explanation is that an instructor who presents material in a dynamic fashion will more likely get and keep the attention of students. This explanation is significant because no matter how thorough and concise an instructor is, learning cannot occur unless the instructor keeps the students engaged and actively listening to the material being presented (Frey, 1978; Murray, 1983). The emphasis, therefore, is on the importance of delivering a dynamic presentation of subject matter in order to facilitate learning, not for entertainment purposes.

Another explanation arises from the finding that personality and student ratings correlate with specific behaviors such as speaking expressively, using humor and varying facial expressions, providing multiple examples, and encouraging students to participate (Murray, 1983). As explained by Erdle et al. (1985), this explanation indicates student evaluations are not just a measure of teacher personality, but that instructors who possess certain personality traits exhibit similar patterns of behavior, and that these behaviors are an essential part of effective teaching. These findings suggest that the instructor's personality is reflected in specific behaviors and that these behaviors, rather than personality, influence student evaluations.

Although the research clearly establishes the relation between personality, classroom behavior, and student ratings, this research does not necessarily establish a relation between actual student success and teaching effectiveness (as rated by students). However, establishing such a relation is a difficult task. One measure of student success would appear to be the final grade a student receives in a given course. However, because there are many factors that influence grades other than teaching effectiveness (such as distinct differences in student ability, difficulty of course content, and the different grading practices of individual teachers) grades are not a reliable measure of student success (Feldman, 1986).

Because it is extremely difficult to assess actual student achievement, researchers have concluded that that the best measure of teaching effectiveness, available at this time, are student ratings (Ambady & Rosenthal, 1993). They further agree that student evaluations are reliable because they are consistent over time and across raters, and correlate positively with the ratings of personality done by colleagues, alumni and trained classroom observers (Ambady & Rosenthal, 1993; Erdle et al., 1985; Murray, Rushton, & Paunonen, 1990).

In light of these conclusions, it is important that the writers of student evaluations ensure the validity of ratings, to as great an extent as possible. In other words, make sure that the questions measure how much the student feels he/she learned, rather than questions that simply measure how the student "feels" about the instructor in general. For example, if students "like" the instructor they might be more likely to evaluate the instructor's teaching effectiveness positively. Therefore, it is important to formulate questions that emphasize how much the student feels he/she has actually learned from the instructor.

The purpose of the present study was to examine how prompting students to think about the personality of a given instructor can influence the outcome of responses to various evaluation items, as well as the overall rating of the instructor. I administered two variations of a survey to college students. One type prompted students to think about personality traits of the instructor,

and asked them to rate the instructor. In the second variation students completed the evaluation first, and then completed the personality checklist. The research hypothesis was that if the students in the first group rated the instructor differently than the students in the second group, we can conclude that prompting students to think about the personality characteristics has an effect on how they evaluate the instructor.

Method

Participants

The participant group consisted of 41 students (9 men, 32 women) enrolled in two different upper-division psychology courses at Boise State University. The breakdown based on age, which was defined as traditional students (18-24 years old), or nontraditional students (25 years old and up), resulted in 22 nontraditional and 19 traditional students.

Both of the instructors being rated were full professors who had each taught for more than 5 years at the university. Each professor agreed to participate.

Materials

The materials used in the study consisted of two variations of a two-part survey instrument. One page of the instrument, designed to measure personality, consisted of 28 trait adjectives. Twenty of the items were adapted from The Adjective Checklist Manual (ACL; Gough & Heilbrun, 1983). The remaining 4 items were adapted from a study by Erdle et al. (1985). The researcher selected the trait adjectives based on the idea that are indicative of charismatic individuals. Two demographic items (traditional/nontraditional student and male/female) were added to this part of the instrument. The other page of the instrument was a Course and Instructor Evaluation Questionnaire obtained from the Psychology Department at

Boise State University. This form is regularly used for semester-end student evaluations by the university's College of Social Sciences and Public Affairs.

The two forms were stapled, prior to administration, so that one-half of the forms had the personality checklist on top and the Instructor Evaluation Questionnaire on the bottom. The remaining forms were stapled together in the opposite order.

Procedure

As previously mentioned, prior approval was obtained from the two upper-division psychology instructors and the date/time the study would take place was agreed on prior to the administering the questionnaire. The first administration took place on a Thursday, April 15, 1999 at 7:40 A.M., and the second took place on the same day at 1:45 P.M. The participants were advised that they were part of a study being conducted by a fellow student, but were not informed of the exact purpose of the study.   The students were not asked to supply personal information on the questionnaire, other than traditional/nontraditional and male/female, in order to preserve student anonymity. The instructor was not in the room while the study was being conducted. The survey instruments were then collected in such a way that would preserve student anonymity.

Results

Descriptive Statistics

Students answered 14 items on the Instructor Evaluation Questionnaire. Items 11 and 13 of the questionnaire were eliminated from the analysis because they were found inappropriate for the purposes of this study. The means and standard deviations for the remaining items are presented in Table 1. For Questions 1 through 10 the average response fell between 2.88 and 3.55 indicating that the participants typically agreed or strongly agreed with the statements.

The participants also completed a checklist of 28 trait adjectives. On several of the items, more than half of the students indicated that their instructor possessed the specified trait. As shown in Table 2, the traits most frequently attributed to the instructors were alert, humorous, self-confident and sociable.

Significant Results

For the age variable (traditional versus nontraditional students), 2 of the 14 questions showed significant differences between the groups. Nontraditional students agreed more strongly with the statement "I felt free to participate in class" ($M = 3.77$, $SD = .43$) than traditional students ($M = 3.32$, $SD = .48$). Similarly, older students felt more strongly that "the instructor seemed well prepared for class" ($M = 3.55$, $SD = .60$) than younger students ($M = 3.11$, $SD = .58$). These differences were statistically significant as follows: (a) I felt free to participate in class, $t (39) = -3.23$, $p < .05$, and (b) The instructor seemed well prepared for class, $t (39) = -2.41$, $p < .05$.

Analysis of differences based on the order that the instruments were completed also revealed significant differences between the groups. On Item 8 (the objectives of the course were met), responses for students who completed the evaluation first, followed by the personality checklist averaged 3.55 ($SD = .51$), whereas responses for students who completed the personality checklist first, followed by the evaluation averaged 3.14 ($SD = .57$). The same was true for Item 14 (the overall rating of the instructor). The average response for students who completed the evaluation first was 2.55 ($SD = .51$), and for the opposite order the response averaged 2.14 ($SD = .65$). Each of these differences were statistically significant as follows: (a) The objectives of the course were met, $t (39) = -2.40$, $p < .05$, and (b) Overall, I would rate this instructor as, $t (39) = -2.21$, $p < .05$.

Because most of the items on the personality checklist are considered positive traits (traits typically associated with effective teaching), an examination was made the correlation between the number of items marked and the overall rating of the instructor. The average number of traits marked was 9.32 ($SD = 5.07$) and the average overall rating of the instructor was 2.34 ($SD = .62$). This correlation was statistically significant, r (39) = 0.47, $p < .01$.

Discussion

The most significant finding in this study is that prompting the students to think about the instructor's personality influenced their overall rating of teaching effectiveness. The responses to this particular question are influenced by the manipulation, whereas many of the other questions were not. This result could indicate that carefully formulated questions that pertain to the student's learning, rather than general questions pertaining to their overall feeling about the instructor, are better indicators of teaching effectiveness. This helps to eliminate the concern of researchers that focusing on improvements to delivery of subject matter minimizes the importance of content (Murray & Lawrence, 1980). Students seem to be rating personality rather than actual teaching effectiveness, but only when we ask questions that are too general in nature. This finding emphasizes the importance of formulating good questions for use on instructor evaluations.

The results of the present study, which indicate that personality influences student ratings, support the findings of similar studies done by Sherman and Blackburn (1975), and Feldman (1986). Also, specific traits that were found to be associated with effective teaching in prior studies (Sherman & Blackburn, 1975) were similar to those found in the present study (e.g., alert, humorous, self-confident and sociable).

Another interesting finding of this study is that students who completed the personality checklist first rated the instructor as less effective (as indicated by the negative t values). This finding may have occurred because the list of trait adjectives consisted only of positive personality traits. Therefore, if the students did not mark very many traits, they may not have been thinking positively about the instructor when they went on to complete the evaluation. This explanation is consistent with the finding that students who marked more traits rated the instructor as more effective.

However, because student ratings were not influenced by personality on many of the questions, students are evidently considering factors other than personality. Although it is important for an instructor to deliver an entertaining lecture, apparently it is just as important to students that the material being presented is useful to their learning. This result does not minimize the importance of an entertaining presentation, but indicates that the content of the material being presented is just as important. Much of the research conducted previously focuses on the delivery aspect of instruction rather than the content (Murray, 1983). According to the findings of the present study, we may be placing too much emphasis on personality, and forgetting the content aspect of teaching. Therefore, an instructor who wishes to improve upon teaching effectiveness, as rated by students, should examine his or her strengths and weaknesses in both areas.

The obvious limitations to the present study are the low number of participants, and that all participants were taken from upper-division psychology classes. Therefore, the results may not generalize to the larger population. Another obvious limitation is that, throughout this report, I have assumed that personality influences student ratings, rather than vice versa. There is the possibility that when an instructor is highly rated by students, his overall attitude and behavior in

The Influence of   11

class may change. This scenario, although possible, seems unlikely when we look at the findings of previous studies where student evaluations of new instructors, who had never been rated, were accurately predicted from peer ratings of personality traits (Murray et al., 1990).

Nonetheless, the results of the present study could be of significant value to instructors who wish to improve upon their teaching skills. Simply focusing on presentation style may not be enough, and instructors lacking in this area can take comfort in knowing that students consider content just as important.

The results of this study also have important implications for the development of instructor evaluation instruments. The questions need to be designed to measure actual learning, as perceived by the student, rather than the student's overall feelings about the instructor.

The Influence of   12

References

Ambady, N., & Rosenthal, R. (1993). Half a minute: Predicting teacher evaluations from thin slices of non-verbal behavior and physical attractiveness. *Journal of Personality and Social Psychology, 64*, 431-441.

Bendig, A. W. (1955). Ability and personality characteristics of introductory psychology instructors rated competent and empathetic by their students. *Journal of Educational Research, 48*, 705-709.

Erdle, S., Murray, H. G., & Rushton, J. P. (1985). Personality, classroom behavior, and student ratings of college teaching effectiveness: A path analysis. *Journal of Educational Psychology, 77*, 394-407.

Feldman, K. A. (1986). The perceived instructional effectiveness of college teachers as related to their personality and attitudinal characteristics: A review and synthesis. *Research in Higher Education, 24*, 139-213.

Frey, P. W. (1978). A two-dimensional analysis of student ratings of instruction. *Research in Higher Education, 9*, 69-91.

Murray, H. G. (1983). Low-inference classroom teaching behaviors and student ratings of college teaching effectiveness. *Journal of Educational Psychology, 75*, 138-149.

Murray, H. G., & Lawrence, C. (1980). Speech and drama training for lecturers as a means of improving university teaching. *Research in Higher Education, 13*, 73-90.

Murray, H. G., Rushton, J. P., & Paunonen, S. V. (1990). Teacher personality traits and student instructional ratings in six types of university courses. *Journal of Educational Psychology, 82*, 250-261.

Sherman, B. R., & Blackburn, R. T. (1975). Personal characteristics and teaching effectiveness of college faculty. *Journal of Educational Psychology, 67*, 124-131.

Table 1

Course and Instructor Evaluation Questionnaire Means and Standard Deviations

Question	Mean	Standard Deviation
1. The instructor's presentations increased my knowledge of the subject.	3.37	0.63
2. The instructor's methods of evaluation were fair.	3.30	0.56
3. The instructor was available during office hours.	2.89	0.76
4. I would recommend this instructor to another student.	3.38	0.67
5. I felt free to participate (e.g., ask questions) in this class.	3.56	0.50
6. The instructor seemed well prepared for class.	3.34	0.62
7. The instructor expressed ideas clearly.	3.22	0.76
8. The objectives of this course were met.	3.34	0.57
9. Assignments and exam results were returned in a timely fashion.	3.55	0.50
10. The assignments were of value to my learning.	3.51	0.64
11. I expect to receive the grade of	3.80	1.05
12. Overall, I would rate this course as	2.37	0.58
13. Compared to that of my classmates, the work I performed in this class was	2.48	0.63
14. Overall, I would rate this instructor as	2.34	0.62

Note. Responses to questions 1 through 10 were made on a 5-point Likert scale: 0 = *Strongly Disagree*, 1 = *Disagree*, 2 = *Uncertain*, 3 = *Agree*, 4 = *Strongly Agree*. Responses to questions 12 and 14 were made on a 4-point scale: 0 = *Poor*, 1 = *Fair*, 2 = *Good*, 3 = *Excellent*.

Table 2

Student Ratings of Instructor Personality Traits

Personality Trait	% Yes	% No
Active	51.2	48.8
Alert	68.3	31.7
Attention-seeking	17.1	82.9
Charming	34.1	65.9
Cheerful	39.0	61.0
Clever	51.2	48.8
Energetic	31.7	68.3
Enthusiastic	48.8	51.2
Extraverted	22.0	78.0
Fun-loving	31.7	68.3
Humorous	65.9	34.1
Imaginative	26.8	73.2
Impulsive	0.00	100.0
Jolly	17.1	82.9
Loud	0.00	100.0
Outgoing	39.0	61.0
Outspoken	9.8	90.2
Quick	22.0	78.0
Robust	19.5	80.5
Self-confident	90.2	9.8

Sharp-witted	56.1	43.9
Show-off	2.4	97.6
Sociable	73.2	26.8
Spontaneous	9.8	90.2
Spunky	9.8	90.2
Talkative	26.8	73.2
Uninhibited	29.3	70.7
Witty	39.0	61.0

Exercise #10: Proofreading APA Format

Below are two sample pages from an assignment. This paper was supposed to be prepared in APA format. Mark the mistakes that this person made in preparing his or her paper in APA format. Just for fun, use a red pen!

A. Student

E. Landrum

Psychology 101

11-17-96

Turning Mind

The streets of many cities are homes for thousands of people with no homes, no money and seemingly no lives. When seen talking to themselves or yelling at a wall, ordinary people cross the street or simply look the other way. It never occurred to them that these "crazies" ate often very sick people with the incurable disease schizophrenia. What they don't know also realize is that this disease could just as likely be a friend, cousin, sister, or even them.

Schizophrenia was first recognized by a Belgian, Benoit A. Morel. He called it demence precoce and describes it as a condition in young people, similar to the deterioration of the old, of arrested development. Morel noted "the fact that it led to severe emotional and intellectual deterioration" (Collier's 389).

Because of the age of occurrence, the name was changed to precocious dementia, and changed again in 1911 to two Greek words: schizein(split) and phren (mind) by Swiss psychiatrist Eugen Bleuler (Collier's 389).

In 1896 and well into the 1900's, psychologists predominantly believed in the theories of three men: German Dr. Emil Kraeplin, Dr. Sigmund Freud of Austria, and U.S. Dr. John B. Watson (Long 49). Kraeplin systematically studied the different conditions patients showed of the disease and classified them into four groups: paranoid, hebephrenic, catatonic, and simple (Collier's 389).

Freud brought about the theory that the illness developed because of certain experiences in ones emotional life, "particularly sexual adjustment" (Colleir's 389), which made it impossible or at least difficult to emotionally mature normally with the outside world.

A contribution in another direction is that form "the late R.C. Laing, a British psychiatrist [who] suggested that it is really a 'healthy' response to an insane world. People burdened with terrible stress act 'crazy' in an effort to adapt" (Long 7).

Now, with modern technology and better research, psychologist and doctors have gotten a better understanding on what schizophrenia really is. Though still uncertain on exactly why it happens, we know it isn't caused by a domineering mother, but most likely neurotransmitters in the brain. Brain activity in a normal brain acts differently than the brain of a schizophrenic. Much more neurotransmitters are released between neurons causing an excess of dopamine. This "dopamine hypothesis" is the most widely accepted theory as the cause of symptoms (Health Center 1).

Treatment is shady because the cause is just as grey, but new medication and supportive counseling has been proven to help. Neuroleptic drugs have been developed that interfere with receptors for the chemical onto nerve cells and "evidence is accumulating that some people with schizophrenia may either have too many dopamine receptors that are overly sensitive to dopamine. Because of this, the brain of a person who has schizophrenia may receive too many messages through other chemical pathways, and may result in the production of psychotic symptoms"(Long 16).

Symptoms of schizophrenia are divided into two categories, "positive" and "negative." This is explained by Dr. E. Fuller Torrey that "positive" " ' ...denotes those

What are the mistakes made in this APA format paper assignment? List the big problems here. How would you fix them?

CHAPTER 11

Doing Well in Psychology Classes: Study Tips

If you skimmed chapter, you likely notice that most of our tips to help you do well in *psychology* courses are tips that will help you do well *in college*, whatever be your major. Another feature that you might notice in this chapter is redundancy. When giving study tips, it is difficult to separate out time management from test preparation from study distractions—they all seem to relate to one another. Hopper (1998a) offers these ten tips for surviving college. They serve as a good overview for the materials that follow.

Try not to schedule back-to-back classes. You'll wear yourself out, and you'll miss some of the best times to study—right before and right after class.

Be a student on the first day of class. Don't take the first two weeks of the semester off—even if your classes are off to a slow start. If possible, try to get ahead on reading so you will be able to keep up later in the semester.

Establish a routine time to study for each class. Studying means more than just doing your homework. Studying involves general organizational and planning strategies (finishing assignments early, organizing notes), task preparation strategies (literature reviews in library, rereading textbooks), environmental restructuring (finding the right place to study, minimizing distractions), processing/recall ability (remembering), and typical study strategies (taking notes, studying notes) (Garavalia & Gredler, 1998). Prepare for each class as if there will be a pop quiz.

Establish a place to study. Make your study place a place with *minimal* distractions. The exercise at the end of the chapter will help you to determine the best place to study.

Do as much of your studying in the daytime as you can. Nighttime brings more distractions for adults.

Schedule breaks. Take a brief break after every block of study time. Try to avoid long blocks of studying unless you are sure that is your optimum method of studying. Don't be *unrealistic* in how long you can study—that is, don't schedule an 8-hour study session for Saturday afternoon and evening if that is something that you just won't do when the time comes.

Make use of study resources on campus. Find out about the opportunities for tutoring, study sessions, test review in class, etc. Does your class have teaching assistants that hold office hours? Ask questions in class of your professors.

Find at least one or two students in each class whom you can study with. A fellow student might be able to explain a concept in terms that you can understand better than your professor might. Also, you might feel more comfortable asking questions of another student, and you'll have an opportunity to observe another person's study habits. Try to study with students who are academically equal to, or better than, you; they will stimulate and challenge your abilities.

Study the hardest subject first. Work on the hardest subjects when you are fresh. Putting those subjects off until you are tired compounds their difficulty.

Be good to yourself. Take care of your other needs—physical, emotional, social, financial, etc. If you can minimize other problems in your life, you can use your efforts to study and understand the subject matter.

It also is important to note that some of the study strategies that were successful for you in high school may no longer work in college. Table 11.1 highlights some of the major differences between then and now. When all is said and done, college is probably going to require more persistence and commitment from you to succeed than did high school.

TABLE 11.1 Examples of How College Is Not High School

Then	Now
High school is required of all students.	College is not required of students.
High school has homerooms.	College does not have homerooms.
In high school, you probably had the same daily class schedule.	In college, your schedule might vary every day.
In high school, your textbooks were given to you.	In college, you must buy your own textbooks (and they are expensive).
In high school, teachers take attendance more.	In college, your instructors often do not take attendance.
A high school requires a doctor's note to say that you were too ill to attend school if you miss class.	In college, if you miss class, that is your business; many professors are unlikely to require a doctor's note. Documentation may be required for missing major exams, however.
High schools emphasize teachers teaching.	College emphasizes learners learning.
High school may not require you to devote much time to homework.	To be successful in college, you will have to devote a lot of time to studying
High school is a system with many rules that sometimes restricts freedom.	College is a system with fewer rules that allows a good deal of freedom.

Source: Wahlstrom, C., & Williams, B. K. (2004). *College to career: Your road to personal success.* Mason, OH: South-Western.

GENERAL STUDY TIPS

Many students enter college unprepared or underprepared for the academic challenges ahead. The strategies that worked for you previously may not be effective now, as pointed out earlier. In fact, you may find that different college classes, even different psychology classes, may require different study strategies. The following information is designed to give you some tips on how to improve your study habits, improve your reading, get more out of lectures, and improve your test-taking skills.

Students Are Different

Techniques and strategies that work for one student may not work for another. You need to concentrate on what you know, and you need to discover what works and does not work for you. The studying process involves a complicated sequence of behaviors. One instrument used to assess this complex behavioral pattern is the Learning and Study Strategies Inventory (LASSI) (Weinstein, Palmer, & Schulte, 1987). The following list summarizes the areas of learning and studying that the LASSI measures: (a) attitude and interest; (b) motivation, diligence, self-discipline, and willingness to work hard; (c) use of time management principles for academic tasks; (d) anxiety and worry about school performance; (e) concentration and attention to academic tasks; (f) information processing, acquiring knowledge, and reasoning; (g) selecting main ideas and recognizing important information; (h) use of support techniques and materials; (i) self-testing, reviewing, and preparing for classes; and (j) test strategies and preparing for tests.

If you have an interest in taking the LASSI, ask a psychology instructor about it, or better yet visit your campus Counseling and Testing Center to see if they can administer this inventory to you. If that opportunity is not available to you, Table 11.2 presents a Study Skills Checklist by McConnell (1998) that can give you some insight into several of the same areas covered by the LASSI.

TABLE 11.2 Study Skills Checklist

Yes	No	Items
____	____	1. I spend too much time studying for what I am learning.
____	____	2. I usually spend hours cramming the night before the exam.
____	____	3. If I spend as much time on my social activities as I want to, I don't have enough time left to study, or when I study enough, I don't have time for a social life.
____	____	4. I usually try to study with the radio or TV turned on.
____	____	5. I can't sit and study for long periods of time without becoming tired or distracted.
____	____	6. I go to class, but I usually doodle, daydream, or fall asleep.
____	____	7. My class notes are sometimes difficult to understand later.
____	____	8. I usually seem to get the wrong material into my class notes.
____	____	9. I don't review my class notes periodically throughout the semester in preparation for tests.
____	____	10. When I get to the end of a chapter, I can't remember what I've just read.
____	____	11. I don't know how to pick out what is important in the text.
____	____	12. I can't keep up with my reading assignments, and then I have to cram the night before a test.
____	____	13. I lose a lot of points on essay tests even when I know the material well.
____	____	14. I study enough for my test, but when I get there my mind goes blank.
____	____	15. I often study in a haphazard, disorganized way under the threat of the next test.
____	____	16. I often find myself getting lost in the details of reading and have trouble identifying the main ideas.
____	____	17. I rarely change my reading speed in response to the difficulty level of the selection or my familiarity with the content.
____	____	18. I often wish I could read faster.
____	____	19. When my teachers assign papers, I feel so overwhelmed that I can't get started.
____	____	20. I usually write my papers the night before they are due.
____	____	21. I can't seem to organize my thoughts into a paper that makes sense.

How to score the results—look at the categories below that correspond to the questions in Table 11.2. If you answered yes to two or more questions in any category, you might want to concentrate on those areas.

Items 1, 2, 3—time scheduling   Items 13, 14, 15—exams
Items 4, 5, 6—concentration   Items 16, 17, 18—reading
Items 7, 8, 9—listening and note-taking Items 19, 20, 21—writing papers
Items 10, 11, 12—reading

Fight Delaying Tactics

These are things that you do when you know the task is boring, long, or difficult (Wahlstrom & Williams, 2004). Three strategies for avoiding delaying tactics include (a) facing boring assignments with short concentrations of effort, (b) conquering long assignments by breaking them down into smaller tasks, and (c) fighting difficult tasks by tackling them first and by making sure you understand them. Delaying tactics differ from procrastination because procrastination is defined as intentionally putting things off. Delaying tactics are typically viewed as unintentional (Wahlstrom & Williams, 2004).

DEVELOPING EFFECTIVE STUDY HABITS

There is no doubt about it—studying isn't one of your most enjoyable tasks. Studying is hard work. However, by being efficient, organized, and consistent you can make it easier. Here are some tips.

Create a Regular Schedule for Studying

You probably have more obligations now than before college; hence, finding time to study may be difficult. Set aside times during the week that are specifically used for studying (*and only studying*). Choose times when you are at your mental peak—wide awake and alert. Some people are "morning" people, some are "night" people; choose your time to study accordingly. When scheduling study time, write it down. Many students use appointment books to keep track of classes, assignments, commitments, etc. Get an appointment book that breaks the day into individual hours, and carry the book with you. You can then schedule certain hours for specific activities. Be realistic; don't plan to study for 6 hours if you know that you can't really do that. Also, think in the long term. Get a 6-month wall calendar and map out the entire semester. This way, assignment due dates are less likely to sneak up on you if you can see your entire semester at a glance.

Writing your schedule down helps to make it concrete and allows for time management. *Time management* is even more important if you have many other responsibilities (like working, family, sports). Here are some tips for time management:

- Set aside times and places for work.
- Set priorities; then do things in priority order.
- Break large tasks into smaller ones.
- Plan to do a reasonable number of tasks for the day.
- Work on one important task at a time.
- Define all tasks specifically (e.g., not "write paper").
- Check your progress often.

Once you develop your basic schedule, add school events (exams, papers, presentations). Sticking to a schedule can help you to avoid cramming and procrastination. Cramming isn't a good study idea, because it strains your memory processes, drains you of energy, and exacerbates test anxiety. When people are faced with a number of tasks, most of us do the easy things first, saving the harder tasks for later. Unfortunately, by the time you get to the harder ones, you are tired and not at your best. To avoid this situation, break difficult tasks into smaller tasks. To emphasize this aspect even further, Hopper (1998b) offers these ten principles of scheduling in Table 11.3.

Find a Regular Place to Study Where You Can Concentrate With Minimal Distractions

Avoid TV or listening to conversations (as in the library). Find your special nook somewhere that is *your* study place.

TABLE 11.3 Ideas for Better Scheduling and Time Management

Make use of daylight hours.

Study before a class that requires discussion or frequently has pop quizzes.

Study immediately after lecture classes (this is why it is best not to schedule back-to-back classes).

Study at the same time everyday to establish a study habit.

Plan enough time to study.

Space your study periods.

List your study activities according to priorities, and tackle the most difficult task first.

Study during your own prime time, paying attention to your own daily cycles and levels of alertness.

Leave time for flexibility—if you don't do this, you probably won't get much use out of your schedule.

Analyze your use of time—keep a log every once in a while to see how you are using your time and where you might make improvements.

Reward Your Studying

Try to reward your *successful* study sessions with something you like (watching TV, a healthy snack, or calling a friend). Many of the traditional rewards of studying (good grades, a college degree) take time, so give yourself some immediate rewards. Take breaks and be realistic about what you can accomplish in one study session.

IMPROVING YOUR READING

Much of your study time is spent reading. To be successful, you need to actively think about what you are reading. Highlighting the boldfaced terms isn't enough. A very popular reading system developed by Robinson (1970) is SQ3R, which divides the reading task into these steps: *Survey, Question, Read, Recite,* and *Review.*

1. **Survey.** Before reading the chapter word for word, glance over the topic headings and try to get an overview for the chapter. You will know where the chapter is going.
2. **Question.** Look at the chapter headings. Turn the headings into questions, questions you want to be able to answer when finished reading. If the heading is "Auditory System," ask yourself, "How does the auditory system work?" If the heading is "Multiple-Personality Disorder," ask, "What are the characteristics of multiple-personality disorder?"
3. **Read.** Now you are ready to read the chapter. Your purpose is to answer the questions you just asked. If you finish reading and haven't answered your questions, go back and reread.
4. **Recite.** Once you know the answers to your key questions, recite them out loud to yourself *in your own words*. Personalizing these concepts will help you later when you are tested. Once you've said them, write them down.
5. **Review.** When you are finished with the entire chapter, test your memory by asking yourself the key questions. Try not to look at the written answers.

Practice the SQ3R system and you will find you have developed a method for successful studying. SQ3R works because the reading assignment is divided into more manageable portions.

GETTING MORE OUT OF LECTURES

Lectures can occasionally be boring and tedious; however, poor class attendance is associated with poor grades. Even if the instructor is disorganized, going to class helps you understand how the instructor thinks, which may help with exam questions or assignment expectations.

Most lectures are coherent and understandable, and accurate note-taking is related to better test performance. Here are some *tips on improving your note-taking skills*:

- You need to listen actively to extract what is important. Focus all attention on the speaker, and try to anticipate meanings and what is coming up.
- If the lecture material is particularly difficult, review the material in the text ahead of time.
- Don't try to be a human tape recorder. Try to write down the lecturer's thoughts *in your own words* (as much as you can). Be organized even if the lecture is not. Practice determining what is important and what is not (sometimes instructors give verbal or nonverbal cues).
- Ask questions during lecture. You can clarify points you missed and catch up in your notes. Most lecturers welcome questions and often wish students weren't so bashful.
- If the lecture is fast-paced (or if you are a slow note-taker), try to review your notes right after class if possible. Consult with a fellow classmate to make sure you didn't miss anything important. You may want to form a study group to regularly review lecture materials and textbook readings.

You should note that instructors are often integrating the use of technology into course instruction. Your professor may make additional materials available through Blackboard or some other software package. Many textbooks now come with online support, Web-based materials, and CD-ROMs or DVDs full of support. Be sure to consult with your instructor to know what support materials are available for your particular course.

IMPROVING TEST-TAKING STRATEGIES

Your strategy should relate to the type of test you are taking. Most students study differently for a multiple-choice test compared with an essay exam. One myth about multiple-choice tests is that you should go with your first answer and not go back and change answers. Research indicates that this idea is *wrong*, and that 58% of the time students changed wrong answers to right; 20% of the time students changed right answers to wrong; and 22% of the time students changed a wrong answer to another wrong answer (Benjamin, Cavell, & Shallenberger, 1984). Some of the items in the lists below are from Wahlstrom and Williams (2004).

Here are some **general tips for test-taking situations**:

- When you first receive your test, ". . . flip the examination sheet over and simply unload. Unloading means taking two or three minutes to jot down on the back of the exam sheet any key words, concepts, and ideas that are in your mind" (Wahstrom & Williams, 2004, p. 176). This helps to relieve anxiety as well as to prevent forgetting.
- Pace yourself. Make sure that when half the time is up, you are halfway through the test.
- Don't waste lots of time by pondering difficult questions. If you have no idea, guess (don't leave a question blank). If you think you can answer a question but need more time, skip it and come back later.
- Don't make the test more difficult than it is. Often simple questions are just that—simple.
- Ask a question if you need clarification.
- If you finish all the questions and still have time, review your test. Check for careless mistakes, such as double-checking earlier questions that you may have skipped.

Here are some tips for **multiple-choice exams**:

- As you read the question, anticipate the answer without looking. You may recall it on your own.
- Even if you anticipated the answer, read all the options. A choice further down may incorporate your answer. Read each question completely.
- Eliminate implausible options. Often questions have a right answer, a close answer, and two fillers. Eliminating filler items makes for an easier choice.

- Often tests give away relevant information for one question in another question. Be on the lookout.
- Return to questions that are difficult.
- There are exceptions, but alternatives that are detailed tend to be correct. Pay extra attention to options that are extra long.
- Options that create sweeping generalizations tend to be incorrect. Watch out for words such as *always*, *never*, *necessarily*, *only*, *must*, *completely*, and *totally*.
- Items with carefully qualified statements are often correct. Well-qualified statements tend to include words such as *often*, *sometimes*, *perhaps*, *may*, and *generally*.
- Look for opposite choices. One of the two opposites is likely the correct answer.

If you can guess without penalty, then use these options with your multiple-choice items: (a) choose between similar sounding options; (b) if options are numbers, pick in the middle; (c) consider that the first option is often not correct; (d) pick a familiar term over an unfamiliar one. Be sure to clarify with the instructor first to make sure there is not a penalty for guessing.

Here are some tips for **essay exams**:

- Time is usually a critical factor in essay exams. When reviewing questions, consider what you know, the time you think it will take to answer, and the point value. Answer questions that you know first, but don't neglect questions with high point values.
- Organize your thoughts so you can write them down coherently. Take one or two minutes and plan your essay (make an outline). Then make your answer easier to read by numbering your points.
- The challenge with essays is to be both complete and concise. Avoid the "kitchen-sink" method (you don't know the exact answer, so you write all you know hoping the answer is in there somewhere).
- You have probably learned a great deal of jargon and terminology in the course, so demonstrate what you've learned in your essay.

If possible, try to get your graded test back from your instructor, or at least specific feedback about your test performance. Use the strategies presented in Table 11.4 to make the most from **returned tests** (University of California–Berkeley, 1998).

Study skills, reading, understanding lectures, and test-taking skills are all important to achieving academic success. You cannot develop these skills overnight; however, they will emerge with practice. The rewards can be worth the effort—knowledge gained, a feeling of accomplishment, improved grades, and progress toward your degree.

TABLE 11.4 Making the Most of Returned Tests

If you receive your test back to keep, rework your errors trying to reason out why the correct answer was correct and yours was not.

If you do not receive your test back, visit your instructor's office to take a look at your answer sheet and the questions you missed.

Look for the origin of each question—textbook, class notes, labs, Web information, etc.

Identify the reason you missed a question. Did you read it incorrectly? Was it something that you were not prepared for? Did you run out of time?

Check the level of detail and skill of the test. Were most of the questions over precise details and facts, or over main ideas and principles (the big picture)? Did questions come straight from the text, from lecture and class discussion, or from both?

Did you have any problems with anxiety or blocking during the test?

Success Stories

Dr. Janet F. Carlson
State University of New York—Oswego

Roberto was a student in my Introductory Psychology class. He also was in the Higher Education Opportunity Program (HEOP) at the university, a program designed to assist academically and economically disadvantaged students. The HEOP advisors were very involved with their advisees, often calling course instructors and so on, to ascertain their advisees' progress during the semester.

Roberto was present for every class, and clearly attentive. He was somewhat quiet, but occasionally asked or answered questions, and participated in class activities fully. To my surprise, he failed the mid-term examination. I wrote on his examination words to the effect, "I hope you are not too discouraged by this grade. I believe from the quality of your work in class that you have a much better understanding of the material than is reflected here."

Roberto's advisor from HEOP called me to ask about his standing in my class, wondering whether he should drop it, but unsure just how to proceed (because of my written comment). I reiterated my sense that Roberto had a good grasp of the material and needed to sort out why he was not able to demonstrate that on the examination. He stayed in the class, and received the third highest grade on the final examination. Together with other class requirements, he ended up with a B in the course.

I don't know what happened to Roberto after that, as I left the university (it was a one-year position).

I guess the important messages here are that it is important for students to receive feedback in its many forms and that faculty should not to equate a student's grade/s with the student's ability too swiftly. Grades are an estimate of subject matter mastery, and not every estimate will be accurate. It is important to try your hardest with each opportunity to do so.

MATH ANXIETY

According to Conners, Mccown, and Roskos-Ewoldsen (1998), "Math anxiety is an emotional state of dread of future math-related activities. It interferes with statistics learning by making students so nervous they cannot concentrate and by lowering motivation, which, in turn, lowers effort and achievement" (p. 40). Throughout this book we have tried to emphasize the skills and abilities that are necessary to be successful in psychology. Math skills (especially statistics) are going to be an important part of your undergraduate career, and also your career in psychology. Math anxiety is not insurmountable, and to be successful in your undergraduate and graduate careers, you have to tackle and confront it.

Dealing with this type of anxiety is not something that you can wave your hand at and make go away, and it's not the type of thing where you wake up one morning and your math anxiety is gone. One method of dealing with this anxiety is to shape your behavior using successive approximations. Success in a math course also helps. If you have a problem in this area, try to schedule your math classes during a semester in which you can give math your best level of attention. Do not wait until the end of your career to take all of your required math classes! You'll do better in statistics and research methods, and be a more useful research assistant (and, as this sequence progresses, get better letters of recommendation, score better on the quantitative GRE section, etc.) if you take the math and statistics courses early. If you are serious about graduate school, try to take an advanced statistics course if one is available.

Do not be afraid to look outside your department—sociology, political science, economics, and math departments might also offer useful upper-division advanced-level statistics courses.

BEHAVIORS TO AVOID

This chapter has focused on providing tips for better performance as a psychology major. We end this chapter with a modified list (Table 11.5) of behaviors that tend to irritate professors—their pet peeves about students. This somewhat humorous, somewhat serious list might give you some ideas about how to avoid getting on the bad side of your professors—these are valuable tips for success in any course.

TABLE 11.5 What Professors Do NOT Want to Hear From Students

Are we doing anything important in class today?

Can I be excused from class this week? My cousin/friend is coming in from Nebraska.

I won't be in class tonight. It's my friend's birthday.

I don't understand why I got such a low grade. I really enjoyed the class and I thought you liked me.

I don't understand why I got such a low grade. I came to class every day.

Can I leave class early? I have to run an errand.

I've been trying to reach you all week. You're never in your office.

I haven't had enough time to do the job I think I can do on this paper.

If I had more time, I could have done a better job.

Do you take off for spelling?

(One week before the project is due): I can't find any articles in the library. Can I change my topic?

Can you give me a topic for the project?

(Concerning handing in group reports): I didn't read the final report. Mary said she would put it together and hand it in on time.

I didn't know there was a test today. I wasn't in class when you announced it. Do I have to take it now?

Does the class presentations count? (Notice the grammar!)

I don't have time to go to the library. Can I borrow your copy of the readings?

I hope this class ends on time.

How many sources do I need in my paper?

Which of the assignment readings will be on the test?

I can't make it to class today. I'm working on a paper for another class and it's due tomorrow.

Will the final exam take the ENTIRE two hours?

That's not what Professor Jones told us about that.

(During the week before finals): What can I do to get an "A" in this class?

Did the syllabus really say that?

Do I have to do footnotes?

How many pages does this paper have to be? What if it isn't that long?

Does the paper have to be typed? Why? Are you sure?

I was absent last class. Did we do anything important?

Will we be responsible for EVERYTHING covered in the book and in the class?

Why did I have to read all this if it wasn't going to be on the test?

(Written on top of the final exam): Dear Professor Jones: If this test brings me down below a "B," I would like to take an incomplete.

(After the exam is handed out): I don't feel well. Can I take a make-up exam?

I couldn't find the room. Can I take the exam now?

I forgot the time of the exam. Can I take it now?

I'm not doing well in this class. Can I do some extra credit work?

I think I have a problem. I'm taking another class that meets the same time as yours, and I have a midterm that's scheduled at the same time for both classes. Can I take your test at a later time?

There's nothing written on the subject. I looked for a book in the library and couldn't find one.

I missed class last week. Can you tell me what went on?

It's not fair. I wasn't in class when you gave the assignment.

Source: Zuckerman, R. A. (1995). *Doc Whiz's 40 ways to P.O. the prof.* Retrieved July 21, 2004, from http://www.educ.kent.edu/community/DOCWHIZ/poprof.html

Again, please remember that the listing in Table 11.5 consists of **statements and questions** that professors do *not* want to hear from their students.

DILBERT reprinted by permission of United Feature Syndicate, Inc.

Exercise #11: Locations for Studying

In using the table below, think of the three most common places that you study, and give each an arbitrary label (Place A, Place B, Place C). Answer the true–false questions for each of the locations. *The location that has the most "false" responses may be the least distracting place to study.* Try to plan your day so that the bulk of your studying is done in the most favorable place.

Study Distractions Analysis

Place A		Place B		Place C		Questions
True	False	True	False	True	False	
						1. Other people often interrupt me when I study here.
						2. Much of what I can see here reminds me of things that don't have anything to do with studying.
						3. I can often hear radio or TV when I study here.
						4. I can often hear the phone ringing when I study here.
						5. I think I take too many breaks when I study here.
						6. I seem to be especially bothered by distractions here.
						7. I usually don't study here at regular times each week.
						8. My breaks tend to be too long when I study here.
						9. I tend to start conversations with people when I study here.
						10. I spend time on the phone here that I should be using for study.
						11. There are many things here that don't have anything to do with study or school work.
						12. Temperature conditions here are not very good for studying.
						13. The chair, table, and lighting arrangements here are not very helpful for studying.
						14. When I study here I am often distracted by certain individuals.
						15. I don't enjoy studying here.
						TOTALS

Source: Hopper, C. (1998a). Ten tips you need to survive college. Retrieved on September 28, 1998, at http://www.mtsu.edu/~studskl/10tips.html.

CHAPTER 12

Ethical Issues for Psychology Majors

In this chapter, we will discuss ethical issues from two different perspectives: ethics as a student enrolled in a college or university (whether you are a psychology major or not), and ethics from the perspective of an undergraduate researcher. As discussed earlier, serving as a research assistant for a professor in the psychology department allows you to gain valuable skills/abilities and a potentially strong letter of recommendation. However, the opportunity to serve as a research assistant carries additional responsibilities, such as the guarantee that you will interact ethically with your research study participants. The latter portion of this chapter reviews the guidelines and principles for ethical behavior as a psychologist.

Before we address those principles specific to psychology, however, a broader topic involves your ethical behavior as a person. How do you treat other people? Do you treat everyone you encounter with dignity and respect? Do you show respect for the laws of the land and the rules that your institution imposes on the student body? It is clearly difficult to legislate ethical behavior among people—in fact, some people split hairs between actions and behavior that are probably unethical but not technically illegal. Of course, we would encourage you to seek the higher moral and ethical plane—some people behave in a certain way because they don't think they'll be caught, whereas others know the difference between right and wrong and do what's right, even if they could get away with what's wrong. Houston Nutt, the head football coach at the University of Arkansas (former head coach at Boise State University) tells his players "Do what's right even if nobody's looking."

As an undergraduate psychology major, you should have exposure to ethical concepts and ideas, hopefully in a number of classes that you take in the major. It is clear from the literature that education in ethics is valuable for undergraduate students (Lamb, 1991; Mathiasen, 1998) and that students can learn ethical behavior and beliefs (LaCour & Lewis, 1998). For instance, student researchers who worked with Institutional Review Boards (more on this topic later in this chapter) became more serious about the research process (Kallgren & Tauber, 1996).

THE ETHICS OF BEING A STUDENT

What are the ethical responsibilities of being a college student? Most colleges and universities address this topic with respect to cheating and academic dishonesty. Much of the work in this area has been done by one of the authors of this book, Stephen Davis (Davis, 1997; Davis, Grover, Becker, & McGregor, 1992; Davis & Ludvigson, 1995; Davis, Pierce, Yandell, Arnow, & Loree, 1995). In a series of studies conducted across the nation, 40%–60% of college students self-report that they have cheated at least once during their college career, and over 50% of that number report cheating on a regular basis. Although many colleges and universities have academic dishonesty policies, students still cheat—again, it is hard to legislate ethical behavior.

It is fair to ask, "So what if a student cheats on an exam?" Thinking back to earlier chapters, if you have a career in psychology, at some point someone is going to expect you to know about your major and the discipline. Cheating is a short-term solution that leads to bigger problems—it will probably become apparent at some point postgraduation that you did not "know your stuff," and that lack of knowledge may create some significant employment issues for someone who has cheated. Additionally, it makes your institution look bad, because "we" are graduating students who do not "know their stuff." This perception lowers the value of a degree of other graduates from your institution, and specifically those graduates in your major. Think of it this way—do you want a surgeon operating on you who cheated his or her way through medical school? Do you want a lawyer protecting your legal interests who cheated his or her way through law school? Do you want someone who is having serious psychological problems to see a psychologist who cheated his or her way through graduate school? The bottom line is that someone someday is going to expect you to know about and understand the principles of psychology—why not just learn the material and complete the projects rather than spending an enormous amount of time and effort in schemes based on cheating?

It may be of interest to you to see how schools address this issue of academic dishonesty. In Table 12.1, we present the academic dishonesty policy of the University of Oregon (2001). It is interesting to see how the policy spells out different types of academic dishonesty. The policy statement starts like this (University of Oregon, 2001, ¶ 1): "Members of the university community are expected to be honest and forthright in their academic endeavors. To falsify the results of one's research, to present the words, ideas, data, or work of another as one's own, or to cheat on an examination corrupts the essential process by which knowledge is advanced."

This University of Oregon (2001) Policy on Academic Dishonesty goes on to suggest ideas about what students can do to protect themselves from being charged with academic dishonesty:

- Prepare thoroughly for examinations and assignments.
- Take the initiative to prevent other students from copying exams or assignments; for example, shield answer sheets during examinations, and do not loan completed assignments to other students.
- Check the course syllabus for a section dealing with academic dishonesty for that course. There may be special requirements. If there is no written section in the syllabus, ask the instructor what his or her expectations are, particularly concerning collaboration and citation.
- Do not look in the direction of other students' papers during examinations.
- Utilize a recognized handbook for instruction on citing source materials in papers. Consult with instructors or academic departments when in doubt.
- Discourage dishonesty among other students.
- Refuse to assist students who cheat.
- If extraordinary circumstances cause anxiety over taking an exam or getting an assignment in on time, talk to the instructor in advance. It is better to request special arrangements rather than resort to dishonesty.
- Inform the instructor if you are aware of other students cheating" (¶ 10).

The consequences of academic dishonesty can be serious, including failure on the assignment, failure in the class, and suspension or expulsion from the university. Be sure you are familiar with the particular policies of your institution. It is clear there are ethical responsibilities to being a student, but what about the special responsibilities of being a student researcher? The remainder of this chapter is devoted to that topic.

THE ETHICS OF RESEARCH

Ethics is a commonly used term that has broad applications in psychology. For example, we might question the ethics of a particular researcher, whether or not a procedure is ethical, or if measuring a participant's behavior can be done in an ethically prudent way. Ethics generally refers to a code of honor in science that researchers follow proper procedures and treat the research participants (whether they be human or animal) properly. As you might expect, psychologists trained in research methods occasionally disagree as to what is proper. Fortunately, the APA has developed a set of rules and regulations of ethical behavior (first adopted in 1953, with major revisions in 1982, 1992, and 2002). For the most current version of the code, see www.apa.org/ethics. Portions of this code are presented near the end of this chapter.

In doing psychological research, the overriding consideration is the analysis of cost versus benefit. The researcher must weigh this decision carefully in any situation involving the participation of humans. Do the potential benefits that might be derived from a research study outweigh the potential harms (or costs) to the participant? Researchers do not take this decision lightly. One method to minimize the costs or harms to a participant (at least a human participant) is to fully inform the person about the nature of the research. Thus, if

TABLE 12.1 Forms of Academic Dishonesty

Plagiarism

Plagiarism is the inclusion of someone else's product, words, ideas, or data as one's own work. When a student submits work for credit that includes the product, words, ideas, or data of others, the source must be acknowledged by the use of complete, accurate, and specific references, such as footnotes. Expectations may vary slightly among disciplines. By placing one's name on work submitted for credit, the student certifies the originality of all work not otherwise identified by appropriate acknowledgements. On written assignments, if verbatim statements are included, the statements must be enclosed by quotation marks or set off from regular text as indented extracts.

A student will avoid being charged with plagiarism if there is an acknowledgement of indebtedness. Indebtedness must be acknowledged whenever:

- one quotes another person's actual words or replicates all or part of another's product;
- one uses another person's ideas, opinions, work, data, or theories, even if they are completely paraphrased in one's own words;
- one borrows facts, statistics, or other illustrative materials—unless the information is common knowledge.

Unauthorized collaboration with others on papers or projects can inadvertently lead to a charge of plagiarism. In addition, it is plagiarism to submit as your own any academic exercise (for example, written work, printing, computer program, art or design work, musical composition, and choreography) prepared totally or in part by another. Plagiarism also includes submitting work in which portions were substantially produced by someone acting as a tutor or editor.

Fabrication

Fabrication is the intentional use of information that the author has invented when he or she states or implies otherwise, or the falsification of research or other findings with the intent to deceive.

Examples include, but are not limited to:

- citing information not taken from the source indicated;
- listing sources in a reference not used in the academic exercise;
- inventing data or source information for research or other academic exercises.

Cheating

Cheating is an act of deception by which a student misrepresents or misleadingly demonstrates that he or she has mastered information on an academic exercise that he or she has not mastered, including the giving or receiving of unauthorized help in an academic exercise.

Examples include, but are not limited to:

- copying from another student's test paper, computer program, project, product, or performance;
- collaborating without authority or allowing another student to copy one's work in a test situation;
- using the course textbook or other material not authorized for use during a test;
- using unauthorized materials during a test; for example, notes, formula lists, cues on a computer, photographs, symbolic representations, and notes written on clothing;
- resubmitting substantially the same work that was produced for another assignment without the knowledge and permission of the instructor;
- taking a test for someone else or permitting someone else to take a test for you.

Academic Misconduct

Academic misconduct is the intentional violation of university policies, such as tampering with grades, or taking part in obtaining or distributing any part of an unadministered test or any information about the test. Examples include, but are not limited to:

- stealing, buying, or obtaining in any other unauthorized manner all or part of an unadministered test;
- selling, trading, or giving away all or part of an unadministered test, including answers to an unadministered test;
- attempting to change or changing, altering, or being an accessory to changing or altering a grade in a grade book, work submitted on a test or a final project, a "supplementary grade report" form, or other official academic records of the university which relate to grades;
- entering a building or office for the purpose of obtaining an unadministered test.

Source: University of Oregon (2001). *Policy on academic dishonesty.* Retrieved July 22, 2004, from http://www.uoregon.edu/~conduct/sai.htm

there are potential harms from placing the participant at risk, then the participant can make an informed judgment about whether to participate or not. This judgment is typically called *informed consent*. Formally speaking, informed consent "is a procedure in which people are given an explicit choice about whether or not they would like to participate in the research *prior* to participation but *after* they have been fully informed of any harmful effects of the research and made aware that they are completely free to withdraw from the research at any time" (Jones, 1985, pp. 35–36).

THE DEVELOPMENT AND USE OF APA ETHICAL PRINCIPLES

Although psychologists were self-motivated to generate a code of ethics on their own, events made public after World War II hastened the need for a written code of honor. In many of the Nazi concentration camps in Europe, prisoners were experimented on under horrible conditions and without regard for the sanctity of human life. Out of those events came the Nuremburg Code (Trials of War Criminals Before the Nuremberg Military Tribunals Under Control Council Law No. 10, 1949), from which much of the APA ethical guidelines are based. The ten-point Nuremburg Code is presented in Table 12.2.

As early as 1935 the APA formed a special committee to discuss ethical matters and make recommendations on how to resolve complaints. By 1948, this committee recommended that the informal procedure they had used for years be formalized into a code of ethics for psychologists. The Committee on Ethical Standards for Psychology was formed and used a unique method of forming and organizing the formal code of ethics. This committee surveyed thousands of members of the APA and asked them to describe any situation in which a psychologist would need to make an ethical decision. Based on the responses, the committee developed a code designed to encompass a large variety of ethics-type situations, which at that time condensed into six general categories: responsibility to the public, the relationship between therapist and client, teaching, research, publishing, and professional relationships (Crawford, 1992). After input was received from the membership, this code was published as the *Ethical Standards of Psychology* by the APA in 1953. This basic code has been revised several times, and the general principles are presented in Table 12.3. For more on the ethical standards related to teaching, training supervision, research, and publishing, see the end of this chapter.

THE ROLE OF INFORMED CONSENT AND THE INSTITUTIONAL REVIEW BOARD

In terms of ethical behavior, one of the fundamental concepts that emerge from examining both the Nuremburg Code and the *Ethical Principles* of the American Psychological Association is that participants must be told, at some time or another, about the nature of the research project. In most cases, it is preferable to accomplish this objective prior to the onset of the research. Why? First, it allows participants to make a judgment about whether they want to participate. Second, it gives the participants more information about the general nature of the required tasks. Third, telling participants about the general nature of the research prior to onset allows the researcher to obtain informed consent. Informed consent means that participants have some idea about the research study and have given their permission not only to participate, but that the researcher may collect data.

Who decides whether an experiment (minimal risk, informed consent, or deception) meets the ethical standards of the APA? Although researchers are required always to consider the ethical practices in their research, most colleges and universities also have a standing committee called the *Institutional Review Board (IRB)* (this committee is sometimes called the Human Subjects Committee). The IRB is typically composed of faculty members from various disciplines and individuals from the community; it is charged with one major function: to protect the rights of persons and animals who participate in research. Any college or university that receives federal funding for research is required to have such a committee. Gone are the days when a researcher might design a new experiment in the morning and actually administer that experiment to participants (i.e., "run subjects") that afternoon. The hypotheses, research methodology, and participant recruitment and treatment all come under scrutiny of the IRB. Only after the approval of this board may researchers go forward with their research. The IRB

Success Stories

Dr. Edie Woods
Madonna University

[Contributed by a colleague.] When I was asked to write something about my own "success story" I was thrilled, because I do feel like I have a success story, but success is measured by my own ruler of what it means to feel like I am doing what I was put on this earth to do. For 44 years I floundered in other professions but nothing felt right for me. I always knew I had to do something different, that I needed to be in a profession that would allow me to understand people, and with that understanding be able to help those who suffered. As a child I always wanted to help and I always was very caring and for some reason I always gravitated toward people who were on the fringe.

When I was 44, after I had been an Insurance Underwriter for 20 years, I went back to school. I wanted more, yet I was not sure what that was. I took psychology, and anthropology and criminal justice classes and I had an interest in all three. I kept taking more and more psychology classes and it began to be evident that I was most curious about why people do what they do. After 4 years in Madonna University with a major in Psychology, I graduated with a BS degree. I knew that I needed more education and that I had to have a master's degree to go further and to actually have a career in psychology as a therapist. I applied for the master's program and began the Fall of the year I graduated from the undergrad program.

Two years later, I graduated with a master's in Clinical Psychology and began my career with my own private practice as a therapist. Success!! Yes in many ways, I feel very successful, but that does not end the story. I am continuing my education at the Michigan Psychoanalytic Institute in their Adult 2-year program. So my education continues. I am a perennial student and that is probably one of the reasons I love this field of psychology. You can never learn enough, the learning goes on and on and as a person I feel enriched by this continuous growth.

Today, less than 2 years out of grad school, I am a therapist with about 40 patients, I am also teaching at my alma mater, Madonna University, as well as a community college, I have a position at a community mental health clinic as a contract therapist and I also am a therapist for an organization called Boys Hope Girls Hope. Do I feel like a success? Absolutely, but there is more to come, much more. My success is not measured in dollars, actually I don't make nearly enough money for most people, but I feel completely rewarded when I sit in a room with a patient and that person feels a connection with me and can share his or her life story. It is a humbling experience and the most rewarding and complete feeling of value that I could ever imagine.

My future plans are to continue my learning at Michigan Psychoanalytic Institute, I have applied to the University of Detroit, Mercy to their doctoral program in clinical psychology and I hope to be admitted for the fall of 2005. I will continue my work as a therapist and teaching. Success is a measure of fulfillment, I don't feel full yet, but I do feel fulfilled and finally on the path toward greater and greater personal success.

screens research projects so that no or minimal harm occurs to persons who participate. If minimal harm may occur, the IRB certifies that the proper informed consent procedures are in place. Experiments involving deception come under the close scrutiny of the IRB, especially in weighing the risk of the deception against the potential benefits of the outcomes. For more

TABLE 12.2 The Nuremburg Code

1. Participation of subjects must be totally voluntary and the subject should have the capacity to give consent to participate. Further, the subject should be fully informed of the purposes, nature, and duration of the experiment.

2. The research should yield results that are useful to society and that cannot be obtained in any other way.

3. The research should have a sound footing in animal research and be based on the natural history of the problem under study.

4. Steps should be taken in the research to avoid unnecessary physical or psychological harm to subjects.

5. Research should not be conducted if there is reason to believe that death or disability will occur to the subjects.

6. The risk involved in the research should be proportional to the benefits to be obtained from the results.

7. Proper plans should be made and facilities provided to protect the subject against harm.

8. Research should be conducted by highly qualified scientists only.

9. The subject should have the freedom to withdraw from the experiment at any time if he (or she) has reached the conclusion that continuing in the experiment is not possible.

10. The researcher must be prepared to discontinue the experiment if it becomes evident to the researcher that continuing the research will be harmful to the subjects.

information about the role and status of IRBs, see Chastain and Landrum (1999) or Rosnow, Rotheram-Borus, Ceci, Blanck, and Koocher (1993).

Although the chief function of the IRB is the protection of the participant population, other advantages occur from its use. The IRB also serves as a screening device for the university in knowing what kinds of activities are taking place. If the IRB feels that a particular research project may involve too much risk (risk to the participant as well as risk to the university), it may reject a project. Another advantage of the IRB is for the protection of the researchers. Often the IRB may have procedural suggestions to make and offer improvements.

The decision to conduct psychologically sound research is not a light one. There are a number of factors that must be carefully considered in making this decision—only a handful of those factors have been discussed here. In Table 12.4 we present a listing of the rights and responsibilities of research participants. This listing echoes the sentiments of the Nuremburg Code and the APA *Ethical Principles*. Although we have focused on your responsibilities as a researcher, the participant also has responsibilities in this process. The dual benefit that accrues from student participation in research is that it allows psychologists to study human behavior and collect data to further the human condition; this opportunity gives students a first-hand learning experience with the research process. To read about research in a textbook or journal article is one way to learn it; you gain a very different experience by being an active participant in actual "live" research.

Actually conducting research is a complicated enterprise, not only from the methodological perspective, but also from an ethical perspective. As undergraduate student researchers, you have a responsibility to protect the health and welfare of your research participants, and at the same time pursue research that enables you to test worthy hypotheses. A psychologist must never take lightly the consideration of using humans or animals for research purposes, and the potential benefits from such research enterprises must always outweigh any potential costs or harm to the participant. And please note: the following section (APA Principles 7 and 8) is provided to you as a convenience and as a reference resource. Don't try to memorize this—it is here to show you the various situations in which ethical behavior is required, and sometimes complicated.

TABLE 12.3 General Principles from *Ethical Principles of Psychologists and Code of Conduct*

General Principles

This section consists of General Principles. General Principles, as opposed to Ethical Standards, are aspirational in nature. Their intent is to guide and inspire psychologists toward the very highest ethical ideals of the profession. General Principles, in contrast to Ethical Standards, do not represent obligations and should not form the basis for imposing sanctions. Relying upon General Principles for either of these reasons distorts both their meaning and purpose.

Principle A: Beneficence and Nonmaleficence

Psychologists strive to benefit those with whom they work and take care to do no harm. In their professional actions, psychologists seek to safeguard the welfare and rights of those with whom they interact professionally and other affected persons, and the welfare of animal subjects of research. When conflicts occur among psychologists' obligations or concerns, they attempt to resolve these conflicts in a responsible fashion that avoids or minimizes harm. Because psychologists' scientific and professional judgments and actions may affect the lives of others, they are alert to and guard against personal, financial, social, organizational, or political factors that might lead to misuse of their influence. Psychologists strive to be aware of the possible effect of their own physical and mental health on their ability to help those with whom they work.

Principle B: Fidelity and Responsibility

Psychologists establish relationships of trust with those with whom they work. They are aware of their professional and scientific responsibilities to society and to the specific communities in which they work. Psychologists uphold professional standards of conduct, clarify their professional roles and obligations, accept appropriate responsibility for their behavior, and seek to manage conflicts of interest that could lead to exploitation or harm. Psychologists consult with, refer to, or cooperate with other professionals and institutions to the extent needed to serve the best interests of those with whom they work. They are concerned about the ethical compliance of their colleagues' scientific and professional conduct. Psychologists strive to contribute a portion of their professional time for little or no compensation or personal advantage.

Principle C: Integrity

Psychologists seek to promote accuracy, honesty, and truthfulness in the science, teaching, and practice of psychology. In these activities psychologists do not steal, cheat, or engage in fraud, subterfuge, or intentional misrepresentation of fact. Psychologists strive to keep their promises and to avoid unwise or unclear commitments. In situations in which deception may be ethically justifiable to maximize benefits and minimize harm, psychologists have a serious obligation to consider the need for, the possible consequences of, and their responsibility to correct any resulting mistrust or other harmful effects that arise from the use of such techniques.

Principle D: Justice

Psychologists recognize that fairness and justice entitle all persons to access to and benefit from the contributions of psychology and to equal quality in the processes, procedures, and services being conducted by psychologists. Psychologists exercise reasonable judgment and take precautions to ensure that their potential biases, the boundaries of their competence, and the limitations of their expertise do not lead to or condone unjust practices.

Principle E: Respect for People's Rights and Dignity

Psychologists respect the dignity and worth of all people, and the rights of individuals to privacy, confidentiality, and self-determination. Psychologists are aware that special safeguards may be necessary to protect the rights and welfare of persons or communities whose vulnerabilities impair autonomous decision-making. Psychologists are aware of and respect cultural, individual, and role differences, including those based on age, gender, gender identity, race, ethnicity, culture, national origin, religion, sexual orientation, disability, language, and socioeconomic status and consider these factors when working with members of such groups. Psychologists try to eliminate the effect on their work of biases based on those factors, and they do not knowingly participate in or condone activities of others based upon such prejudices.

Source: American Psychological Association (2002). *Ethical principles of psychologists and code of conduct, 2002.* Washington, DC: Author.

TABLE 12.4 Rights and Responsibilities of Research Participants

Rights of Research Participants

1. Participants should know the general purpose of the study and what they will be expected to do. Beyond this, they should be told everything a reasonable person would want to know in order to decide whether to participate.

2. Participants have the right to withdraw from a study at any time after beginning participation in the research. A participant who chooses to withdraw has the right to receive whatever benefits were promised.

3. Participants should expect to receive benefits that outweigh the costs or risks involved. To achieve the educational benefit, participants have the right to ask questions and receive clear, honest answers. When participants do not receive what was promised, they have the right to remove their data from the study.

4. Participants have the right to expect that anything done or said during their participation in a study will remain anonymous and confidential, unless they specifically agree to give up this right.

5. Participants have the right to decline to participate in any study and may not be coerced into research. When learning about research is a course requirement, an equivalent alternative to participation should be available.

6. Participants have a right to know when they have been deceived in a study and why the deception was used. If the deception seems unreasonable, participants have the right to withhold their data.

7. When any of these rights is violated or participants object to anything about a study, they have the right and the responsibility to inform appropriate university officials, including the chairperson of the Psychology Department and the Institutional Review Board.

Responsibilities of Research Participants

1. Participants have the responsibility to listen carefully to the experimenter and ask questions in order to understand the research.

2. Be on time for the research appointment.

3. Participants should take the research seriously and cooperate with the experimenter.

4. When the study has been completed, participants share the responsibility for understanding what happened.

5. Participants have the responsibility for honoring the researcher's request that they not discuss the study with anyone else who might be a participant.

Source: Korn, J. H. (1988). Students' roles, responsibilities, and rights as research participants. *Teaching of Psychology, 15,* 74-78.

PRINCIPLES SEVEN AND EIGHT OF APA'S ETHICAL PRINCIPLES OF PSYCHOLOGISTS AND CODE OF CONDUCT

PRINCIPLE 7. Education and Training

7.01 Design of Education and Training Programs

Psychologists responsible for education and training programs take reasonable steps to ensure that the programs are designed to provide the appropriate knowledge and proper experiences, and to meet the requirements for licensure, certification, or other goals for which claims are made by the program. (See also Standard 5.03, Descriptions of Workshops and Non-Degree-Granting Educational Programs.)

7.02 Descriptions of Education and Training Programs

Psychologists responsible for education and training programs take reasonable steps to ensure that there is a current and accurate description of the program content (including participation in required course- or program-related counseling, psychotherapy, experiential groups, consulting projects, or community service), training goals and objectives, stipends and benefits, and requirements that must be met for satisfactory completion of the program. This information must be made readily available to all interested parties.

7.03 Accuracy in Teaching

(a) Psychologists take reasonable steps to ensure that course syllabi are accurate regarding the subject matter to be covered, bases for evaluating progress, and the nature of course experiences. This standard does not preclude an instructor from modifying course content or requirements when the instructor considers it pedagogically necessary or desirable, so long as students are made aware of these modifications in a manner that enables them to fulfill course requirements. (See also Standard 5.01, Avoidance of False or Deceptive Statements.)
(b) When engaged in teaching or training, psychologists present psychological information accurately. (See also Standard 2.03, Maintaining Competence.)

7.04 Student Disclosure of Personal Information

Psychologists do not require students or supervisees to disclose personal information in course- or program-related activities, either orally or in writing, regarding sexual history, history of abuse and neglect, psychological treatment, and relationships with parents, peers, and spouses or significant others except if (1) the program or training facility has clearly identified this requirement in its admissions and program materials or (2) the information is necessary to evaluate or obtain assistance for students whose personal problems could reasonably be judged to be preventing them from performing their training- or professionally related activities in a competent manner or posing a threat to the students or others.

7.05 Mandatory Individual or Group Therapy

(a) When individual or group therapy is a program or course requirement, psychologists responsible for that program allow students in undergraduate and graduate programs the option of selecting such therapy from practitioners unaffiliated with the program. (See also Standard 7.02, Descriptions of Education and Training Programs.)
(b) Faculty who are or are likely to be responsible for evaluating students' academic performance do not themselves provide that therapy. (See also Standard 3.05, Multiple Relationships.)

7.06 Assessing Student and Supervisee Performance

(a) In academic and supervisory relationships, psychologists establish a timely and specific process for providing feedback to students and supervisees. Information regarding the process is provided to the student at the beginning of supervision.
(b) Psychologists evaluate students and supervisees on the basis of their actual performance on relevant and established program requirements.

7.07 Sexual Relationships With Students and Supervisees

Psychologists do not engage in sexual relationships with students or supervisees who are in their department, agency, or training center or over whom psychologists have or are likely to have evaluative authority. (See also Standard 3.05, Multiple Relationships.)

PRINCIPLE 8. Research and Publication

8.01 Institutional Approval

When institutional approval is required, psychologists provide accurate information about their research proposals and obtain approval prior to conducting the research. They conduct the research in accordance with the approved research protocol.

8.02 Informed Consent to Research

(a) When obtaining informed consent as required in Standard 3.10, Informed Consent, psychologists inform participants about (1) the purpose of the research, expected duration, and procedures; (2) their right to decline to participate and to withdraw from the research once participation has begun; (3) the foreseeable consequences of declining or withdrawing; (4) reasonably foreseeable factors that may be expected to influence their willingness to participate such as potential risks, discomfort, or adverse effects; (5) any prospective research benefits; (6) limits of confidentiality; (7) incentives for participation; and (8) whom to contact for questions about the research and research participants' rights. They provide opportunity for the prospective participants to ask questions and receive answers. (See also Standards 8.03, Informed Consent for Recording Voices and Images in Research; 8.05, Dispensing With Informed Consent for Research; and 8.07, Deception in Research.)

(b) Psychologists conducting intervention research involving the use of experimental treatments clarify to participants at the outset of the research (1) the experimental nature of the treatment; (2) the services that will or will not be available to the control group(s) if appropriate; (3) the means by which assignment to treatment and control groups will be made; (4) available treatment alternatives if an individual does not wish to participate in the research or wishes to withdraw once a study has begun; and (5) compensation for or monetary costs of participating including, if appropriate, whether reimbursement from the participant or a third-party payer will be sought. (See also Standard 8.02a, Informed Consent to Research.)

8.03 Informed Consent for Recording Voices and Images in Research

Psychologists obtain informed consent from research participants prior to recording their voices or images for data collection unless (1) the research consists solely of naturalistic observations in public places, and it is not anticipated that the recording will be used in a manner that could cause personal identification or harm, or (2) the research design includes deception, and consent for the use of the recording is obtained during debriefing. (See also Standard 8.07, Deception in Research.)

8.04 Client/Patient, Student, and Subordinate Research Participants

(a) When psychologists conduct research with clients/patients, students, or subordinates as participants, psychologists take steps to protect the prospective participants from adverse consequences of declining or withdrawing from participation.

(b) When research participation is a course requirement or an opportunity for extra credit, the prospective participant is given the choice of equitable alternative activities.

8.05 Dispensing With Informed Consent for Research

Psychologists may dispense with informed consent only (1) where research would not reasonably be assumed to create distress or harm and involves (a) the study of normal educational practices, curricula, or classroom management methods conducted in educational settings; (b) only anonymous questionnaires, naturalistic observations, or archival research for which disclosure of responses would not place participants at risk of criminal or civil liability or damage their financial standing, employability, or reputation, and confidentiality is protected; or (c) the study of factors related to job or organization effectiveness conducted in organizational settings for which there is no risk to participants' employability, and confidentiality is protected or (2) where otherwise permitted by law or federal or institutional regulations.

8.06 Offering Inducements for Research Participation

(a) Psychologists make reasonable efforts to avoid offering excessive or inappropriate financial or other inducements for research participation when such inducements are likely to coerce participation.

(b) When offering professional services as an inducement for research participation, psychologists clarify the nature of the services, as well as the risks, obligations, and limitations. (See also Standard 6.05, Barter With Clients/Patients.)

8.07 Deception in Research

(a) Psychologists do not conduct a study involving deception unless they have determined that the use of deceptive techniques is justified by the study's significant prospective scientific, educational, or applied value and that effective nondeceptive alternative procedures are not feasible.

(b) Psychologists do not deceive prospective participants about research that is reasonably expected to cause physical pain or severe emotional distress.

(c) Psychologists explain any deception that is an integral feature of the design and conduct of an experiment to participants as early as is feasible, preferably at the conclusion of their participation, but no later than at the conclusion of the data collection, and permit participants to withdraw their data. (See also Standard 8.08, Debriefing.)

8.08 Debriefing

(a) Psychologists provide a prompt opportunity for participants to obtain appropriate information about the nature, results, and conclusions of the research, and they take reasonable steps to correct any misconceptions that participants may have of which the psychologists are aware.
(b) If scientific or humane values justify delaying or withholding this information, psychologists take reasonable measures to reduce the risk of harm.
(c) When psychologists become aware that research procedures have harmed a participant, they take reasonable steps to minimize the harm.

8.09 Humane Care and Use of Animals in Research

(a) Psychologists acquire, care for, use, and dispose of animals in compliance with current federal, state, and local laws and regulations, and with professional standards.
(b) Psychologists trained in research methods and experienced in the care of laboratory animals supervise all procedures involving animals and are responsible for ensuring appropriate consideration of their comfort, health, and humane treatment.
(c) Psychologists ensure that all individuals under their supervision who are using animals have received instruction in research methods and in the care, maintenance, and handling of the species being used, to the extent appropriate to their role. (See also Standard 2.05, Delegation of Work to Others.)
(d) Psychologists make reasonable efforts to minimize the discomfort, infection, illness, and pain of animal subjects.
(e) Psychologists use a procedure subjecting animals to pain, stress, or privation only when an alternative procedure is unavailable and the goal is justified by its prospective scientific, educational, or applied value.
(f) Psychologists perform surgical procedures under appropriate anesthesia and follow techniques to avoid infection and minimize pain during and after surgery.
(g) When it is appropriate that an animal's life be terminated, psychologists proceed rapidly, with an effort to minimize pain and in accordance with accepted procedures.

8.10 Reporting Research Results

(a) Psychologists do not fabricate data. (See also Standard 5.01a, Avoidance of False or Deceptive Statements.)
(b) If psychologists discover significant errors in their published data, they take reasonable steps to correct such errors in a correction, retraction, erratum, or other appropriate publication means.

8.11 Plagiarism

Psychologists do not present portions of another's work or data as their own, even if the other work or data source is cited occasionally.

8.12 Publication Credit

(a) Psychologists take responsibility and credit, including authorship credit, only for work they have actually performed or to which they have substantially contributed. (See also Standard 8.12b, Publication Credit.)
(b) Principal authorship and other publication credits accurately reflect the relative scientific or professional contributions of the individuals involved, regardless of their relative status. Mere possession of an institutional position, such as department chair, does not justify authorship credit. Minor contributions to the research or to the writing for publications are acknowledged appropriately, such as in footnotes or in an introductory statement.
(c) Except under exceptional circumstances, a student is listed as principal author on any multiple-authored article that is substantially based on the student's doctoral dissertation. Faculty advisors discuss publication credit with students as early as feasible and throughout the research and publication process as appropriate. (See also Standard 8.12b, Publication Credit.)

8.13 Duplicate Publication of Data

Psychologists do not publish, as original data, data that have been previously published. This does not preclude republishing data when they are accompanied by proper acknowledgment.

8.14 Sharing Research Data for Verification

(a) After research results are published, psychologists do not withhold the data on which their conclusions are based from other competent professionals who seek to verify the substantive claims through reanalysis and who intend to use such data only for that purpose, provided that the confidentiality of the participants can be protected and unless legal rights concerning proprietary data preclude their release. This does not preclude psychologists from requiring that such individuals or groups be responsible for costs associated with the provision of such information.

(b) Psychologists who request data from other psychologists to verify the substantive claims through reanalysis may use shared data only for the declared purpose. Requesting psychologists obtain prior written agreement for all other uses of the data.

8.15 Reviewers

Psychologists who review material submitted for presentation, publication, grant, or research proposal review respect the confidentiality of and the proprietary rights in such information of those who submitted it.

Exercise #12: Ethics Scenarios

For each of the following scenarios, think about the ethical ramifications of such research. What are the ethical violations, if any? How does the design of the study impact the possible results as well as impact the ethics code? Are there right or wrong answers to these scenarios? We encourage you to talk to classmates and your instructor about these situations.

1. An investigator is interested in the effect of manipulating the initial level of self-esteem. The proposed research would involve having two people compete for the attention of a member of the opposite sex. The experimenter would arrange the situation in such a way that one competitor would experience an embarrassing defeat whereas the other competitor would be victorious. In this case there is no way to inform the participants about the factors that may influence their willingness to participate and still make the desired manipulation. Is it possible to do this research without violating ethical standards?

2. The participants were informed correctly regarding the basic procedures that would be used, but they were misinformed about the purpose of the experiment. They were told the experiment was designed to test the speed of the visual system. Actually, the experimenter was interested in testing long-term memory. The participants were not told the real purpose because the investigator was afraid this knowledge would influence their performance. The experimenter reasoned that a participant who would participate for the stated reason would also participate for the real reason? Is this procedure acceptable?

3. A doctoral student was interested in factors influencing cheating. The doctoral student administered an examination, collected the papers, and then photocopied each one. The students were not informed about the photocopies. The papers were returned unscored and the students were given the opportunity to cheat while scoring their papers. The papers were collected again and were compared with the photocopies. Is this an ethical procedure?

4. A professor of psychology worked on the production line in a factory for one semester. He did not reveal his identity to his coworkers or his reasons for being there. His purpose was to study the interactions of his coworkers. The findings proved useful in his subsequent teaching and research. His coworkers, some of whom he became very close to, were not informed of his purpose until their observation session was completed. Is this type of data collection unethical?

5. An investigator, who was using Galvanic Skin Response procedures, had a participant become extremely upset during a testing session. The eight-year-old child discontinued the experiment and went home. The experimenter was unaware of the child's reason for leaving. Later, it was determined that the child thought that blood was being extracted from his body because the electrode wires had a red plastic covering and red ink was used in the recording pens. Was the experimenter's behavior unethical?

6. The respondents to a mailed questionnaire were told that they would not be identified with their responses. A self-addressed return envelope was included for the "convenience" of the responder. The type and location of the stamp were such that the investigator could identify 100 of the respondents to the questionnaire. Is this procedure unethical?

Source: Wood, G. (1981). *Fundamentals of psychological research* (3rd ed.). Boston: Little Brown.

CHAPTER 13

Psychology and Other Options: Nurturing Your Career

If you have read every chapter of this book, you know that we have covered a myriad of topics. We opened with details about majoring in psychology and what psychology majors can do with a bachelor's degree and higher degrees. Opportunities outside the classroom play a considerable role in your success during your undergraduate years of study. We then refocused on some of the skills and abilities that you will need for success in almost any major, but particularly in psychology: locating prior research, tips for writing in APA format, tips for doing well in classes in general, the ethics of being a college student, and doing research in psychology. We now try to bring this journey full circle by addressing issues related to the psychology major, and other disciplines related to psychology that you might not have considered, and by directing you toward some self-reflection and assessment. This chapter is not designed to talk you "into" or "out of" the psychology major—rather, we think it's best for you to consider all of your options.

Readers of this book are either psychology majors or students seriously considering the major. Given that situation, it would be interesting to know how our profession is regarded, especially in the context of other professionals (such as psychiatrists, physicians, counselors, teachers, and scientists). Webb and Speer (1986) asked various samples of students and their parents to rate the six different professions (the five listed above plus psychology). The results were interesting—each profession was rated on a variety of dimensions that yielded mean scores. Webb and Speer found that "compared to the five other professions, psychologists scored above the group means on rich, patient, inquisitive, understanding, psychological, and helpful. Scores were below the group means on unappreciated, scholarly, dedicated, alienated, and arrogant" (p. 7). The authors concluded from these data that the public image of psychologists is favorable, confused with the role of psychiatrists, clinically biased, and based on limited information. It seems that there were no negative attitudes about psychology; this finding is good news for students planning to major in psychology!

THE PSYCHOLOGY MAJOR, REVISITED

We would like to mention three topics of interest. First, why do students major in psychology? Although not much work has been done in this area, the results we do have are interesting. Second, what are the factors that lead to success in the major? Various sections of this book are designed to lead you to success—what else does the available research say? Third, how satisfied are students with the psychology major, and how prepared are they for careers in psychology? But first, a reminder of just how important the selection of a major can be: "But you should keep in mind that choosing a major is an important part of your college experience and one that's worth carefully thinking about. The world is much too vast to tackle all at once. You have to stake your claim on a little piece of it and build a home. Choosing a major is not irrelevant or unimportant. Your field of study will speak to you constantly—through advisors, professors, course requirements, and fellow students. Whatever choices you make after college, your chosen major will continue to matter through the years. It will affect you, enrich your mind, expand your options, and for some, define the course of your life. Make an effort to find the right major, and you might get more out of college than you ever expected" (Natavi Guides, 2002, p. 3).

Why do students choose to major in psychology? Gallucci (1997) surveyed students at a variety of locations, including conferences that were held in different parts of the country (see Table 13.1). Students rated the reasons on a 1–5 scale, with 1 indicating *not a reason*, and 5 indicating a *very important reason* for majoring in psychology.

Gallucci (1997) concluded that "these results indicated that the most important reason for choosing psychology as an undergraduate major was a very strong interest in the subject matter of psychology. Career concerns were also salient, as undergraduates rated preparation for

TABLE 13.1 Reasons for Becoming a Psychology Major

Reasons	Mean	Standard Deviation
I have a very strong interest in the subject matter of psychology.	4.59	0.71
I want to become a professional psychologist.	3.89	1.17
Psychology is a good undergraduate degree to prepare me for a graduate or professional (e.g., MD, JD) degree.	3.73	1.43
A bachelor's degree in psychology will prepare me for a job.	3.21	1.41
I want to become an academic psychologist.	2.74	1.47
Psychology is a good undergraduate degree to prepare me for teaching.	2.45	1.39
I want to figure myself out.	2.31	1.34
I want to become a professional social worker.	1.62	1.26
I want to become an industrial or organizational psychologist.	1.35	0.87
Psychology is an easy major.	1.27	0.68

Source: Gallucci, N. T. (1997). An evaluation of the characteristics of undergraduate psychology majors. *Psychological Reports, 81,* 879–889.

graduate study in professional psychology, other graduate or professional study, and employment as important reasons for selecting the psychology major" (p. 886). The lowest rated item is also of interest: "Psychology is an easy major." Clearly, psychology majors do not select psychology because they think it is easy. This result provides some good truth in advertising about the major and what to expect from it—don't choose it because you think it will be easy. In fact, there are a number of universities now that offer "Introduction to the Psychology Major"-type courses (Dillinger & Landrum, 2002; Landrum, Shoemaker, & Davis, 2003; Mulcock & Landrum, 2002). In an evaluation of the effectiveness of such courses, Thomas and McDaniel (2004) developed a Career Information Survey for psychology majors (see Table 13.2). Students rated each item on a scale from 1 = strongly disagree to 5 = strongly agree. Not only does this scale highlight information necessary for psychology majors, but also it points to some of the major goals you can accomplish by utilizing the advice of this book!

In another study, Meeker, Fox, and Whitley (1994) studied the predictors of academic success for undergraduate psychology majors. Specifically, they looked at high school grades, college admission scores, and college grades to determine the best predictors of psychology GPA in college. They examined the number of semesters of classes taken in high school (e.g.,

TABLE 13.2 Psychology Major Career Information Survey Items

1. I have a clear understanding of the kinds of work done by different types of psychologists (e.g., clinical, social, experimental, organizational).
2. If I decide to become a psychologist, I know what steps I will have to take to accomplish this goal.
3. I know how to go about preparing for, selecting, and getting admitted into graduate school.
4. I can identify several different fields of study that would allow me to do counseling/therapy and I understand what each of them involves.
5. I can identify a number of "people helping" careers outside of psychology and I have some understanding of the preparation required for each of these careers.
6. I can identify several areas within the business world in which a psychology major may be valuable and I know how to pursue a career in business if I should decide to do so.

Source: Thomas, J. H., & McDaniel, C. R. (2004). Effectiveness of a required course in career planning for psychology majors. *Teaching of Psychology, 31,* 22–27.

English), average high school grades in certain areas (e.g., average grades in math classes), high school demographics (GPA, class rank, class size), Scholastic Aptitude Test (SAT) scores, college grades in core/general studies courses (e.g., history, speech), grade in introductory psychology, applied statistics, and research methods. The strongest factor that emerged to predict college psychology GPA was performance in core/general studies classes, such as research methods, mathematics, English, history, and science.

Interestingly, in the Meeker et al. (1994) study, grade in the introductory psychology course was not a strong enough variable to be included in any of the three factors that emerged as predictors of psychology GPA and success in the major. Because many students become attracted to psychology through the introductory course, the results can be interpreted to mean that the grade in the introductory course alone should not drive the decision to major in the discipline. Considering that we have some information about why students choose the major and what leads them to be successful in their psychology courses, what about student satisfaction with the major? If they had it to do all over again, would psychology graduates (i.e., alumni) select the same major? Kressel (1990) conducted a survey of social science (including psychology) alumni and asked a series of questions about degree satisfaction and job satisfaction (see also Braskamp, Wise, & Hengstler, 1979; Finney, Snell, & Sebby, 1989; Keyes & Hogberg, 1990; McGovern & Carr, 1989). Kressel found that 39% of the respondents said they would probably select the same major. The strongest predictor of degree satisfaction was the job-relatedness to the major. The factors that lead to higher satisfaction with the psychology degree include having a higher degree, being female, more course enjoyment, more course difficulty, income satisfaction, and job satisfaction. See Table 13.3 for excellent examples of work-related skills and how you can gain these skills while an undergraduate (Ware, 2001, p. 24).

Based on his research, Kressel (1990) suggests there are several strategies that can be used to enhance degree and job satisfaction of social science graduates: (a) improve instructor and advisor education about career options in psychology, (b) implement career development courses for undergraduate majors, and (c) incorporate business training into psychology curricula. Clearly, the use of this book can help achieve two of these goals. Psychology instructors who read the earlier chapters of this book will be up to date on the latest information related to job opportunities. Second, we wrote this book for career development courses, whether the course is an "Introduction to the Psychology Major" for undergraduate students or "The Professional Psychologist" for the new graduate student. Students attracted to studying psychology are from diverse backgrounds with varied interests. This diversity provides for a valuable learning experience; psychology, by its very nature, is a discipline that strives to understand human behavior—all human behavior.

DIVERSITY IN PSYCHOLOGY

You can think about diversity in many ways. A person can have number of diverse experiences, or receive his or her education at a diverse collection of schools. Typically, however, we think of diversity as in cultural diversity or ethnic diversity. Some dramatic demographic shifts have occurred in psychology in the past 25 years or so. For instance, considering gender diversity, the number of women receiving their bachelor's degree in psychology has increased from 46% of all degrees in 1971 to 73% of all bachelor's degrees in 1993. With respect to graduate school enrollments, in 1977 women comprised 47% of graduate students in psychology, and in 1997 that number had risen to 71%. In 1976, women received 33% of the new doctorates awarded in psychology, and in 1996 that number was 69%. Finally, among Ph.D.'s in the workforce, women accounted for 20% in 1973, and 44% in 1997 (APA, 1998b). When considering people of color, there have also been a number of important changes. For example, the percentage of people of color receiving bachelor's degrees went from 11.6% of all degree recipients in 1976 up to 16.0% in 1993. When considering graduate enrollments, people of color comprised 11.8% of all graduate enrollments in psychology in 1980, and in 1997 that number had risen to 17.0%. When considering the number of new doctorates awarded, people of color received 7.5% of all new doctorates in psychology in 1977, and in 1997 that percentage was 13.9%. Finally, the percentage of people of color in the workforce with Ph.D.'s in psychology rose from 2.0% in 1973 to 8.5% in 1997 (APA, 1998b).

Diversity seems to be an important component of higher education. Why? We think this is a fair question to ask. In a civilized society, the qualities to which we aspire sometimes are hard

TABLE 13.3 Transferable Work-Related Skills, and Examples of Skill Acquisition

	Skills Employers Seek	Student Products, Experiences
Communication Skills	Writing	• Wrote essays for scholarships while applying to colleges and graduate schools
		• Prepared a research article and submitted it for publication
		• Presented a speech to a group of students on a retreat
	Speaking	• Explained the strengths of our university to parents and prospective students
		• Discussed research projects in small groups, explained the project to participants, and talked to professor about research findings
Cognitive Skills	Coping with Deadlines	• Prepared manuscripts in advance of deadlines
		• Completed reports on time when they were vital to patient treatment
		• Evaluated new ways to solve daily problems
	Research	• Wrote numerous manuscripts that required gathering information from a variety of sources
		• Conducted a job search and made contacts with people, asking them about the nature of their work
	Planning	• Scheduled study time in preparation for several major tests
		• Balanced homework, classes, extracurricular time, and time for myself
		• Balanced when to study and when to write papers
Social Skills	Human Relations	• Dealt with older patients, sick children, and families as a hospital volunteer
		• Worked as a physical therapy aide to maximize quality of care and minimize waste of time
		• Mediated between my roommates to ensure that tasks (e.g., paying bills) were completed
		• Resolved differences between players and coaches
	Negotiation/Organization	• Organized a benefit concert
		• Organized workers for a Habitat for Humanity project
		• Coordinated dates, space, exhibitors, advertisers, and nurses for health fair
	Supervision	• Monitored and directed the members of a team in my capacity as captain
		• Ensured that personnel in training attended clinics and completed research projects and manuscripts
		• Monitored a research team and gave directions

Source: Ware, M. E. (2001). Pursuing a career with a bachelor's degree in psychology. In S. Walfish & A. K. Hess (Eds.) *Succeeding in gradu-ate school: The career guide for psychology students* (pp. 11–30). Mahwah, NJ: Erlbaum.

to pinpoint, and for some people, hard to justify. In February 1999, 67 learned societies banded together to publish a statement titled "On the Importance of Diversity in Higher Education" (Chronicle of Higher Education, 1999). Although we cannot provide the entire statement below (it is too long), here are some of the key points:

Many colleges and universities share a common belief, born of experience, that diversity in their student bodies, faculties, and staff is important for them to fulfill their primary mission: providing a high-quality education. The public is entitled to know why these institutions believe so strongly that racial and ethnic diversity should be one factor among the many considered in admissions and hiring. The reasons include:

- Diversity enriches the educational experience. We learn from those whose experiences, beliefs, and perspectives are different from our own, and these lessons can be taught best in a richly diverse intellectual and social environment.
- It promotes personal growth—and a healthy society. Diversity challenges stereotyped preconceptions; it encourages critical thinking; and it helps students learn to communicate effectively with people of varied backgrounds.
- It strengthens communities and the workplace. Education within a diverse setting prepares students to become good citizens in an increasingly complex, pluralistic society; it fosters mutual respect and teamwork; and it helps build communities whose members are judged by the quality of their character and their contributions.
- It enhances America's economic competitiveness. Sustaining the nation's prosperity in the 21st century will require us to make effective use of the talents and abilities of all our citizens, in work settings that bring together individuals from diverse backgrounds and cultures" (p. A42).

If you believe in the values of diversity as outlined above, then you can be confident that psychology as a profession seems to be headed in a good direction. Given the emphasis of understanding human beings and the study of individual differences, it is hard to think of someone who would not value diversity *but* be truly interested in understanding human behavior.

Success Stories

Dr. Kenneth A. Weaver
Emporia State University

Jeremy Kohomban: Using Psychology to Improve Children's Lives

I first met Jeremy Kohomban when I had him in class in the fall 1987 semester, one year after finishing my Ph.D. and beginning my work at Emporia State University (ESU). My first impression was extremely favorable for three reasons—he was at the time the only psychology major who was an international student, he was from Sri Lanka and I had spent 3 months in Sri Lanka in 1976, and his first course with me was a demanding cooperative education placement working with boys who were wards of the court. That impression was reinforced when Jeremy completed a second semester at the same placement, knowing that he could make a difference in the lives of these boys.

Jeremy ended up taking four courses from me before he graduated in May, 1989 with his BS in Psychology with Honors from ESU. His accomplishments at Emporia State were many. He was a member of the Psychology Club and was initiated into Psi Chi. He belonged to the International Club all 4 years, serving in a number of positions and was a member of the ESU Choir for all 4 years. He served a term as an Associated Student Government Senator and participated in the ESU Rugby Club and the Intervarsity Christian Fellowship. During the time that Jeremy was at ESU, we offered the U.S. Army Reserve Officers Training Command (ROTC) curriculum. He was in ROTC all 4 years, eventually becoming leader of the entire squadron.

He was named to the Dean's Honor Roll, President's Honor Roll, and National Dean's List just about every semester and received several scholarships for academic excellence. In addition, Jeremy received the American Legion Award for Scholastic Excellence, the ROTC Commandant's Award, and the ROTC Superior Cadet Award. ESU President Robert Glennen appointed Jeremy to the Council on International Education, which designed and implemented Emporia State's Student Exchange Program. In his Senior year he was named to Who's Who in American Colleges and Universities.

These amazing accomplishments are heightened when one learns that Jeremy was totally responsible financially for all his tuition and living expenses and eventually for those of his younger brother, who joined him at Emporia State for 2 years. At one time, Jeremy was working a full-time job and two part-time jobs simultaneously. Jeremy spent the summer between his junior and senior years in New York City working for St. Christopher's- Jennie Clarkson Family Services, one of 68 private agencies providing foster care services in New York state. The agency recruits and trains foster parents, oversees cases, and coordinates the services needed to either reunite families or free children for adoption. After his ESU graduation, Jeremy moved to New York City to work with St. Christopher's full time.

Jeremy has played a central role in changing the way the foster care system in New York works. Before 1993, agencies housing foster children were reimbursed a daily fee for taking care of each child. The longer the child stayed in the system, the more money the agency generated, which was good for the agency but not good for quickly returning the child back to the family or freeing the child for adoption. Jeremy and other St. Christopher's leaders proposed that the state reimburse agencies a flat, guaranteed fee for each child. This approach gave the agencies the financial incentive to resolve the children's futures more quickly because the agency got to keep the full fee no matter how long the child stayed in foster care.

In a 1995 *New York Times* front page article highlighting St. Christopher's and Jeremy's work, the new approach was credited with returning children to families sooner, thereby keeping the families together. At St. Christopher's, Jeremy started as After-Care Services Coordinator and then gradually moved up through the ranks to become Assistant Program Director for Foster Boarding Homes and Adoption, then Director of Family Services, then Resident Director of the Jennie Clarkson Residential Treatment Center and Group Homes, and then Director of Education and Residential Services where he oversaw the operations of all five residential homes.

In November of 1998, he left St. Christopher's to become Senior Vice-President of Easter Seals of New York, where he continues to dedicate his life to improving children's lives. Jeremy is married with two sons. He earned his Master of Science degree in Clinical Psychology from Long Island University and is currently a Doctor of Philosophy candidate in Organizational Leadership at the Center for Leadership Studies at Regent's University in New York. He is a nationally · recognized speaker who has presented at numerous local and national conferences on system reform and family-focused service delivery. He also consults nationally on system reform.

He is active in his volunteer work. For the last 8 years he has worked with the National Association for Family-Based Services in Washington, DC, serving first as New York State's Representative; then being elected Treasurer of the Association; and then elected Director on the National Board of Directors. Currently, he is the Association's President. He also completed a 2-year term as a school board member for the Greenburgh North Castle Union Free School District in New York. Jeremy will gladly tell anyone how his training in psychology has been instrumental in his work, helping him frame problems and then giving him both the knowledge to create solutions and the methods to identify the best one. He has worked diligently and persevered, using psychology to improve children's lives. Jeremy is one of my heroes.

OTHER RELATED OPTIONS

The bulk of our efforts have been to address psychology and students choosing to major in it. There are a number of related disciplines that we want to discuss briefly to make the picture complete. A common response students give when they are asked, "Why are you majoring in psychology?" is "Because I want to help people." Although this is a noble reason, it is also broad and vague. Many disciplines also strive to help people—in this section we will focus on anthropology, criminal justice, political science, social work, and sociology. We do not present this information to try to talk you out of psychology but to make you aware of the full palette of possibilities available in the social sciences. Even though you may feel *strongly* that psychology is the major for you, we would be remiss if we did not mention that there are other opportunities for careers that help people. Our ultimate goal is for *you* to be satisfied in your choice of major and career. Below we present some brief descriptions of the disciplines mentioned. Note that it is extremely difficult to convey the essence of any discipline in a single paragraph.

Anthropology

Anthropology is the study of humankind. The word *anthropology* itself tells the basic story—from the Greek *anthropos* ("human") and *logia* ("study")—it is the study of humankind, from its beginnings millions of years ago to the present day. Nothing human is alien to anthropology. Indeed, of the many disciplines that study our species, *Homo sapiens*, only anthropology seeks to understand the whole panorama—in geographic space and evolutionary time—of human existence. Its subject matter is both exotic (e.g., star lore of the Australian aborigines) and commonplace (e.g., the anatomy of the foot). Its focus is both sweeping (the evolution of language) and microscopic (the use-wear of obsidian tools). Anthropologists may study ancient Mayan hieroglyphics, the music of African Pygmies, and the corporate culture of a U.S. car manufacturer. A common goal links these vastly different projects: to advance knowledge of who we are, how we came to be that way—and where we may go in the future (American Anthropology Association, 1998).

Criminal Justice

The nature and control of crime are important social phenomena that affect all of our lives. The criminal justice program provides an in-depth analysis of this subject to students. Students who choose this major will study the development, functions, and structure of the criminal justice system. They will examine the roles of law enforcement agencies, the courts, correctional agencies, and private agencies that aid in the prevention and control of crime and delinquency. The in-depth study of pertinent justice issues is designed to foster the capacity for balanced and critical evaluation of criminal justice problems. The criminal justice administration major will appeal to undergraduates who are interested in preparing for a career in criminal justice, law, or a related field; to persons currently employed in the criminal justice community; and to individuals who are generally interested in studying how public policies about crime and its control, as well as deviance and its treatment, are created and implemented (San Diego State University, 1998).

Political Science

Political science is the study of political behavior and the groups and institutions through which power is exercised. Students examine the purposes and problems of politics and evaluate many of the controversial issues of political life. They examine different viewpoints about the world community, analyzing political issues and relating them to ethical decisions (Marietta College, 1998).

Social Work

Social work is a profession for people with a strong desire to help people. Social workers help people deal with their relationships with others; solve their personal, family, and community problems; and grow and develop as they learn to cope with or shape the social and environmental forces affecting daily life. Social workers often encounter clients facing a life-threatening disease or a social problem requiring a quick solution. They also assist families that have serious conflicts, including those involving child or spousal abuse. Social workers practice in a variety of settings, including hospitals, schools, mental health clinics and psychiatric hospitals, and public agencies. Through direct counseling, social workers help clients identify their concerns, consider solutions, and find resources. Social workers typically arrange for services in consultation with clients, following through to assure the services are helpful (Occupational Outlook Handbook, 1998b).

Sociology

Sociology is the study of society, of the social frameworks within which we live our lives. It is a study of social life at every level, from two-person relationships to the rise and fall of nations and civilizations. More than any other discipline it is a meeting place of the social sciences, combining its own ideas and methods with insights from history, anthropology, economics, political science, and psychology in an extended examination of the ways societies work—or fail to work (Harvard University, 1998).

Clearly, there are a variety of methods that you can use to help people—these are just samples of some of the disciplines related to psychology. In addition, the undergraduate degree is good preparation for graduate work in many of the disciplines mentioned above—a career path that students sometimes overlook. Don't limit your horizons and career choices.

SELF-REFLECTION, SELF-ASSESSMENT, AND CAREER DEVELOPMENT

Our focus of this book has been to provide information that we feel is critical for you to be a successful psychology major. That goal rests on the notion that you want to be a psychology major. In the previous section, we reviewed several options that share some similarity with psychology. In this section we explore career interest tools as well as life development ideas. In particular, we focus on the Self-Directed Search (SDS), a career-planning tool developed by John L. Holland (1994). The SDS developed out of Holland's theories of vocational choice (1958, 1959). According to Holland (1973), four working assumptions drive the theory:

1. In this culture, most persons can be categorized as one of six types: realistic, investigative, artistic, social, enterprising, or conventional.

2. There are six kinds of environments: realistic, investigative, artistic, social, enterprising, and conventional.

3. People search for environments that will let them exercise their skills and abilities, express their attitudes and values, and tackle agreeable problems and roles.

4. A person's behavior is determined by an interaction between his or her personality and the characteristics of his or her environment.

The basic notion of this theory is that people are happier and more successful in a job that matches their interests, values, and skills. Scoring of the SDS is linked to occupational codes and titles. Thus, by determining your preferences for styles or types, the SDS gives you some indication of the jobs that you might like and would make the most of your skills and interests. The fundamental idea is that people and work environments can be classified according to Holland's six types; thus, if you know your own type and understand the types that are associated with particular careers, you can find a match. Holland's SDS (1994) is a relatively straightforward inventory. There is an Internet version (http://www.self-directed-search.com/index.html), which, for $9.95 (at the time of this writing), you can take on your computer and receive a personalized report with your results. Individuals answer questions about their aspirations, activities, competencies, occupations, and other self-estimates. These scores yield a three-letter Summary Code that designates the three personality types an individual most closely resembles. With this code, test-takers use the Occupations Finder to discover those occupations that best match their personality types, interests, and skills. This comprehensive booklet lists over 1,300 occupational possibilities—more than any other career interest inventory. Although it is not possible for you to take the SDS here, we describe the six personality types and examples of corresponding careers in Table 13.4. If you are interested in taking the SDS, you might want to contact your campus Counseling and Testing Center or Career Center. There may be a small fee for this service, but the insight and self-reflection gained from the SDS is worth it.

The SDS presents some interesting options for persons thinking about a career. Although you haven't taken the SDS, you can look at the six different types and realize that perhaps one or two of them fit you very well. The idea here is to not be afraid of some self-exploration; it is important for you to figure out what you would like to do for a career. College is a great time for career exploration; if you put some work into it, you will enjoy the rewards you reap.

TABLE 13.4 Types and Occupations of the Self-Directed Search

Realistic		Investigative	
Personality Type	**Occupations**	**Personality Type**	**Occupations**
• Have mechanical ability and athletic ability? • Like to work outdoors? • Like to work with machines and tools? • Genuine, humble, modest, natural, practical, realistic?	• Aircraft controller • Electrician • Carpenter • Auto mechanic • Surveyor • Rancher	• Have math and science abilities? • Like to explore and understand things and events? • Like to work alone and solve problems? • Analytical, curious, intellectual, rational?	• Biologist • Geologist • Anthropologist • Chemist • Medical technologist • Physicist

Artistic		Social	
Personality Type	**Occupations**	**Personality Type**	**Occupations**
• Have artistic skills and a good imagination? • Like reading, music, or art? • Enjoy creating original work? • Expressive, original, idealistic, independent, open?	• Musician • Writer • Decorator • Composer • Stage director • Sculptor	• Like to be around other people? • Like to cooperate with other people? • Like to help other people? • Friendly, understanding, cooperative, sociable, warm?	• Teacher • Counselor • Speech therapist • Clergy member • Social worker • Clinical psychologist

Enterprising		Conventional	
Personality Type	**Occupations**	**Personality Type**	**Occupations**
• Have leadership and public speaking ability? • Like to influence other people? • Like to assume responsibility? • Ambitious, extroverted, adventurous, self-confident?	• Manager • Salesperson • Business executive • Buyer • Promoter • Lawyer	• Have clerical and math abilities? • Like to work indoors? • Like organizing things and meeting clear standards? • Efficient, practical, orderly, conscientious?	• Banker • Financial analyst • Tax expert • Stenographer • Production editor • Cost estimator

Source: Psychological Assessment Resources (2001). *Welcome to the self-directed search*. Retrieved July 25, 2004, from http://www.self-directed-search.com/index.html

Your career can take many different paths, and progress through different stages or models. For instance, Harr (1995; as cited in Wahlstrom & Williams, 2004) differentiated job, occupation, and career this way: Your job is defined by the specific job duties that you fulfill within your occupation. Your occupation is the specific form that your career might take at any given time. Your career is the overall path you will take through your work life. There are different depictions of how a career might progress. Driver (1988; as cited in Wahlstrom & Williams, 2004) describes some of these career progressions: The linear career looks like climbing the stairs, in that you are climbing in the organization's hierarchy. Each job along the way imparts more responsibility and requires more skill. In the steady-state career, you discover that you are comfortable with a particular occupation and you stay put. A promotion might mean more responsibility and more job stress, and you want to avoid that. The spiral career suggests that one job builds on the other, being upwardly mobile. You might have a number of jobs that are different yet they build on one another.

Journalizing is powerful because answering powerful questions yields powerful, clear answers. When you write in a journal regularly, you become the type of person who can define what they want, has definite plans, and can articulate your desires. Combs (2000) suggests the following journalizing questions:

- What are the most important things in your life?
- What are the activities that you love and enjoy most today?
- What would be your ideal work environment today?
- How would your ideal work day go today?
- How would you define success today?
- What might be your purpose or destiny?
- How do you want to be perceived by your friends? Coworkers? Parents? Significant other?
- What magazine would you most like to be featured in for your tremendous accomplishments in 10 years?
- What would you like to be the best in the world at?
- Who are your heroes and what is it about them that you most want to be like?
- What do you really think should be changed in the world?
- What do you most want to be remembered for at the end of your life?
- Whom do you envy and what is it about them that you envy?

As you can see, these are powerful questions, and should provoke thoughtful responses. Not only is college a good time for career exploration, but a good time for life exploration as well. In that vein, we offer the following "Rules for Being Human" which appeared in Combs (2000), but the original author is unknown (see Table 13.5).

TABLE 13.5 The Rules for Being Human

1. You will receive a body. You may like it or hate it, but it will be yours for the entire period this time around.

2. You will learn lessons. You are enrolled in a full-time informal school called life. Each day in this school you will have the opportunity to learn lessons. You may like the lessons or think them irrelevant and stupid.

3. There are no mistakes, only lessons. Growth is a process of trial and error, experimentation. The "failed" experiments are as much as part of the process as the experiment that ultimately "works."

4. A lesson is repeated until it is learned. A lesson will be presented to you in various forms until you have learned it. When you have learned it, you can go on to the next lesson.

5. Learning lessons does not end. There is no part of life that does not contain lessons. If you are alive, there are lessons to be learned.

6. "There" is no better than "here." When your "there" has become a "here," you will simply obtain another "there" that will, again, look better than "here."

7. Others are merely mirrors of you. You cannot love or hate something about another person unless it reflects to you something you love or hate about yourself.

8. What you make of your life is up to you. You have all the tools and resources you need; what you do with them is up to you. The choice is yours.

9. The answers lie inside you. The answers to life's questions lie inside you. All you need to do is look, listen, and trust.

10. You will forget all this.

MORE RESOURCES

We designed this entire book to include a listing of valuable resources for you. Be sure to take advantage of the references section (which lists everything we have referenced). As you can tell from our citations, the Internet is becoming a valuable resource for information about psychology. For more information, especially about careers, check out some of the resources listed in Table 13.6.

We have previously mentioned many of these resources. Keep them in mind as you make your career plans. Knowledge is power, so we hope you will gather all the information you can and then make intelligent decisions.

Psychology is an exciting profession with a positive and growing future. The complications of current lifestyles and choices make understanding behavior even more important and imperative. Behavioral problems and difficulties are all the more commonplace nowadays. Compared to other sciences, psychology is relatively young, with many frontiers still to be blazed and a number of behavioral phenomena yet to be explored or understood. We do have a bias, however—we think that psychology is inherently fascinating, and when you are passionate about a topic such as this, it's natural to want to share that feeling and hope it is infectious. We hope that you come away from this book feeling more positive and more informed about what psychology has to offer, and how you can do well in the psychology major. As we discussed at the beginning, the choice of psychology as a discipline to study and as a career can take many different directions and occur in many different settings. We hope that your use of this book will continue as you journey through the major—at different times you may need to refer to different sections.

TABLE 13.6 Recommended Resources

American Psychological Association. (1997). *Getting in: A step-by-step plan for gaining admission to graduate school in psychology.* Washington, DC: Author.

Appleby, D. (1997). *The handbook of psychology.* Reading, MA: Longman.

Career Communications, Inc. (2004). *Career success catalog.* Harleysville, PA: Author.

Combs, P. (2000). *Major in success: Make college easier, fire up your dreams, and get a very cool job.* Berkeley, CA: Ten Speed Press.

DeGalan, J., & Lambert, S. (1995). *Great jobs for psychology majors.* Lincolnwood, IL: VGM Career Horizons.

Field, S. (1996). *100 best careers for the 21st century.* New York: Macmillan.

Hettich, P. I., & Helkowski, C. (2005). *Connect college to career.* Belmont, CA: Thomson Wadsworth.

Keith-Spiegel, P., & Wiederman, M. W. (2000). *The complete guide to graduate school admission: Psychology, counseling, and related professions* (2nd ed.). Mahwah, NJ: Erlbaum.

Kuther, T. L. (2003). *The psychology major's handbook.* Belmont, CA: Wadsworth.

Morgan, B. L., & Korschgen, A. J. (2001). *Majoring in psych? Career options for psychology undergraduates* (2nd ed.). Boston: Allyn & Bacon.

Reingold, H. (1994). *The psychologist's guide to an academic career.* Washington, DC: American Psychological Association.

Sternberg, R. J. (Ed.). (1997). *Career paths in psychology: Where your degree can take you.* Washington, DC: American Psychological Association.

Super, C. M., & Super, D. E. (1994). *Opportunities in psychology careers.* Lincolnwood, IL: VGM Career Horizons.

Wahlstrom, C., & Williams, B. K. (2004). *College to career: Your road to personal success.* Mason, OH: South-Western.

Walfish, S., & Hess, A. K. (Eds.). (2001). *Succeeding in graduate school: The career guide for psychology students.* Mahwah, NJ: Erlbaum.

What can be more interesting than understanding human behavior? Many psychologists have found that attempting to answer that question can make for a pleasant and rewarding career choice.

Exercise #13: Attitudes and Options

This exercise is adapted from a self-quiz by Carole Kanchier that appeared in the *USA Weekend Magazine* issue dated April 12–14, 2002. The quiz examines your attitudes toward growth in a career. Answer the following Yes/No questions and then use the scoring key below to ascertain your level of positive, growth-oriented attitudes.

Career Quiz

Yes	No	Items
Y	N	1. I welcome criticism as a way to grow.
Y	N	2. I do what I "should" rather than what I want.
Y	N	3. I periodically assess my career and life goals.
Y	N	4. I prefer activities I know to those I've never tried.
Y	N	5. I enjoy challenge and a sense of achievement.
Y	N	6. I'm too old to compete with younger job applicants.
Y	N	7. I expect good things to happen.
Y	N	8. I won't consider relocating for an attractive job.
Y	N	9. I accept responsibility for my successes and failures.
Y	N	10. I'll take a job I don't like for money or prestige.
Y	N	11. My job gives my life meaning and direction.
Y	N	12. I look forward to retirement so I can do what I want.
Y	N	13. I make my own decisions, even swim against the tide.
Y	N	14. Career success means having social standing and money.
Y	N	15. I'll take a lower-level job.
Y	N	16. If I'm laid off, I'll take the first offer in the same field.

Scoring: Give yourself 1 point for each "YES" for the odd-numbered items._____

Give yourself 1 point for each "NO" for the even-numbered items._____

Now add your scores together. Kanchier (2002) suggests that the higher your score, the more you possess positive, growth-oriented attitudes, and that you believe in the "new view" of career. She suggests that if you scored less than 7, you may want to reevaluate your attitudes concerning a career. For more information on working on yourself, see daretochange.com.

Source: Kanchier, C. (2002, April 12–14). Does your attitude limit your options? *USA Weekend Magazine*, p. 9.

References

Actkinson, T. R. (2000, Winter). Masters & myth: Little-known information about a popular degree. *Eye on Psi Chi, 4* (2), 19–21, 23, 25.

American Anthropology Association (1998). What is anthropology? Retrieved January 4, 1999, at http://www.ameranthassn.org/anthbroc.htm.

American Psychological Association (1986). *Careers in psychology*. Washington, DC: Author.

American Psychological Association (1996). *Psychology: Careers for the twenty-first century*. Washington, DC: Author.

American Psychological Association (1997a). A guide to getting in to graduate school. Retrieved November 28, 1998, at http://www.apa.org/ed/getin.html.

American Psychological Association (1997b). Employment activities of 1992 baccalaureate recipients in psychology. Retrieved November 20, 1998, at http://research.apa.org/bac10.html.

American Psychological Association (1997c). *Getting in: A step-by-step guide for gaining admission to graduate school in psychology*. Washington, DC: Author.

American Psychological Association (1998a). Data on education and employment–master's. Retrieved November 28, 1998, at http://research.apa.org/mas2.html.

American Psychological Association (1998b). Data on education and employment–doctorate. Retrieved November 28, 1998, at http://research.apa.org/doc1.html.

American Psychological Association (2000). *Graduate study in psychology* (34th ed.). Washington, DC: Author.

American Psychological Association (2001). *Publication manual of the American Psychological Association* (5th ed.). Washington, DC: Author.

American Psychological Association (2002). *Ethical principles of psychologists and code of conduct, 2002*. Washington, DC: Author.

American Psychological Association (2003). Applications, acceptances, and new enrollments in Graduate Departments of Psychology, by degree and subfield area, 2001–2002 [Table]. Source: *Graduate study in psychology 2003*. Washington, DC: Author.

American Psychological Association (2004a). About APA. Retrieved July 17, 2004, from http://www.apa.org/about/

American Psychological Association (2004b). Library research in psychology. Retrieved July 17, 2004, from http://www.apa.org/science/lib.html.

American Psychological Association (2004c). Student affiliate. Retrieved July 17, 2004, from http://www.apa.org/membership/students.html.

American Psychological Society (2004a). About APS. Retrieved July 17, 2004, from http://www.psychologicalscience.org/about/

American Psychological Society (2004b). Student member benefits. Retrieved July 17, 2004, from http://www.psychologicalscience.org/join/stu_benefits.cfm.

APA Research Office (2003). *Work settings for baccalaureate degree recipients in psychology: 1999*. Washington, DC: American Psychological Association.

Appleby, D. C. (1990). Characteristics of graduate school superstars. Retrieved September 28, 1998, at http://www.psychwww.com/careers/suprstar.htm.

Appleby, D. (1997). *The handbook of psychology*. Reading, MA: Longman.

Appleby, D. (1998a, August). *The teaching-advising connection: Tomes, tools, and tales*. G. Stanley Hall lecture, American Psychological Association meeting, San Francisco.

Appleby, D. (1998b, August). *Professional planning portfolio for psychology majors*. Indianapolis, IN: Marian College.

Appleby, D. (1999, April). *Advice and strategies for job-seeking psychology majors*. Presented at the Midwestern Psychological Association, Chicago, IL.

Appleby, D. (2000, Spring). Job skills valued by employers who interview psychology majors. *Eye on Psi Chi*, 4 (3), 17.

Appleby, D. C. (2001, Spring). The covert curriculum: The lifelong learning skills you can learn in college. *Eye on Psi Chi*, 5 (3), 28–31, 34.

Arnold, K. L., & Horrigan, K. L. (2002). Gaining admission into the graduate program of your choice. *Eye on Psi Chi*, 7 (1), 30–33.

Banerji, A. (1998, June 5). College degree is not necessary for economic success, U. of Michigan study finds. Retrieved June 8, 1998, at http://www.chronicle.com/daily/98/06/9806506n.shtml.

Bates College (2000). Letter of recommendation worksheet. Retrieved February 9, 2000, at http://www.bates.edu/career/glance/reference/recletter.html.

Benjamin, L. T., Jr., Cavell, T. A., & Shallenberger, W. R., III (1984). Staying with initial answers on objective tests: Is it a myth? *Teaching of Psychology*, 11, 133–141.

Blanton, P. G. (2001). A model of supervising undergraduate internships. *Teaching of Psychology*, 28, 217–219.

Bloom, L. J., & Bell, P. A. (1979). Making it in graduate school: Some reflections about the superstars. *Teaching of Psychology*, 6, 231–232.

Bordens, K. S., & Abbott, B. B. (1988). *Research design and methods: A process approach*. Mountain View, CA: Mayfield Publishing Co.

Bottoms, B. L., & Nysse, K. L. (1999). Applying to graduate school: Writing a compelling personal statement. *Eye on Psi Chi*, 4 (1), 20–22.

Brandeis University (1998). Library research guides—psychology. Retrieved October 27, 1998, at http://www.library.brandeis.edu/resguides/subject/psycguide.html.

Braskamp, L. A., Wise, S. L., & Hengstler, D. D. (1979). Student satisfaction as a measure of departmental quality. *Journal of Educational Psychology*, 71, 494–498.

Buckalew, L. W., & Lewis, H. H. (1982). Curriculum needs: Life preparation for undergraduate psychology majors. *Psychological Reports*, 51, 77–78.

Buskist, W. (2002, Spring). Seven tips for preparing a successful application to graduate school in psychology. *Eye on Psi Chi*, 5 (3), 32–34.

Butler, D. L. (1997, May 7). Getting a job with an undergraduate degree in psychology. Retrieved March 30, 1998, at http://www.bsu.edu/psysc/what/ujob.html.

Career Communications, Inc. (2004). *Career success catalog*. Harleysville, PA: Author.

CareerMosaic (1997). Resume writing tips. Retrieved September 28, 1998, at http://www.careermosaic.com/cm/rwc/rwc3.html.

Carmody, D. P. (1998). Student views on the value of undergraduate presentations. *Eye on Psi Chi*, 2, 11–14.

Cashin, J. R., & Landrum, R. E. (1991). Undergraduate students' perceptions of graduate admissions criteria in psychology. *Psychological Reports*, 69, 1107–1110.

Chastain, G., & Landrum, R. E. (Eds.) (1999). *Protecting human subjects: Departmental subject pools and institutional review boards.* Washington, DC: APA Books.

Chen, E. K. Y. (2004). What price liberal arts education. In Siena College (Ed.), *Liberal education and the new economy.* Loudonville, NY: Siena College.

Chicago Editorial Staff (1993). *The Chicago manual of style: The essential guide for authors, editors, and publishers* (14th ed.). Chicago: University of Chicago Press.

Chickering, A. W., & Reisser, L. (1993). *Education and identity* (2nd ed.). San Francisco: Jossey-Bass.

Chronicle of Higher Education (1999, February 12). On the importance of diversity in higher education [Advertisement]. *Chronicle of Higher Education*, p. A42.

Chronicle of Higher Education (2001). Projections of college enrollment, degrees conferred, and high-school graduates, 1999 to 2010. Retrieved July 29, 2001, at http://www. chronicle.com/ weekly/almanac.2000/facts/ 2501stu.htm.

Clark, R. A., Harden, S. L., & Johnson, W. B. (2000). Mentor relationships in clinical psychology doctoral training: Results of a national survey. *Teaching of Psychology, 27,* 262–268.

Clay, R. A. (2000, May). The postdoc trap [Electronic version]. *Monitor on Psychology, 31* (5). Retrieved July 6, 2004 from http://www.apa.org/ monitor/may00/postdoc.html.

Clay, R. A. (1998). Is a psychology diploma worth the price of tuition? Retrieved December 1, 1998, at http://www.apa.org/monitor/sep96/ tuition.html.

CollegeGrad (2001). The simple key to interview success. Retrieved July 11, 2001, at http:// www.collegegrad.com/ezine/20simkey.shtml.

Combs, P. (2000). *Major in success: Make college easier, fire up your dreams, and get a very cool job.* Berkeley, CA: Ten Speed Press.

Conners, F. A., Mccown, S. M., & Roskos-Ewoldsen, B. (1998). Unique challenges in teaching undergraduate statistics. *Teaching of Psychology, 25,* 40–42.

Council of Biology Editors (1994). *Scientific style and format: The CBE manual for authors, editors, and publishers* (6th ed.). Cambridge, MA: Cambridge University Press.

Council of Graduate Schools (1989). *Why graduate school?* Washington, DC: Author.

Cowart, S. C. (1987). *What works in student retention in state colleges and universities.* Washington, DC: American Association of State Colleges and Universities (ERIC Document Reproduction Service No. ED347928).

Coxford, L. M. (1998). How to write a resume. Retrieved September 28, 1998, at http://www. aboutwork.com/rescov/resinfo/ cosford.html.

Crawford, M. P. (1992). Rapid growth and change at the American Psychological Association: 1945 to 1970. In R. B. Evans, V. S. Sexton, & T. C. Cadwallader (Eds.), *The American Psychological Association: A historical perspective* (Chapter 7, pp. 177–232). Washington, DC: American Psychological Association.

Davis, S. F. (1995). The value of collaborative scholarship with undergraduates. *Psi Chi Newsletter, 21* (1), 12–13.

Davis, S. F. (1997). "Cheating in high school is for grades, cheating in college is for a career": Academic dishonesty in the 1990s. *Kansas Biology Teacher, 6,* 79–81.

Davis, S. F., Grover, C. A., Becker, A. H., & McGregor, L. N. (1992). Academic dishonesty: Prevalence, determinants, techniques, and punishments. *Teaching of Psychology, 19,* 16–20.

Davis, S. F., & Ludvigson, H. W. (1995). Additional data on academic dishonesty and a proposal for remediation. *Teaching of Psychology, 22,* 119–122.

Davis, S. F., Pierce, M. C., Yandell, L. R., Arnow, P. S., & Loree, A. (1995). Cheating in college and the Type A personality: A reevaluation. *College Student Journal, 29*, 493–497.

Day, J. C., & Newburger, E. C. (2002). *The big pay-off: Educational attainment and synthetic estimates of work-life earnings* (Publication P23-210). Washington, DC: U.S. Census Bureau.

DeGalan, J., & Lambert, S. (1995). *Great jobs for psychology majors.* Lincolnwood, IL: VGM Career Horizons.

DeLuca, M. J. (1997). *Best answers to the 201 most frequently asked interview questions.* New York: McGraw-Hill.

Descutner, C. J., & Thelen, M. H. (1989). Graduate school and faculty perspective about graduate school. *Teaching of Psychology, 16*, 58–61.

Diehl, J., & Sullivan, M. (1998). Suggestions for application for graduate study in psychology. Retrieved September 28, 1998, at http://psych.hanover.edu/handbook/gradapp2.html.

Dillinger, R. J., & Landrum, R. E. (2002). An information course for the beginning psychology major. *Teaching of Psychology, 29*, 230–232.

Dodson, J. P., Chastain, G., & Landrum, R. E. (1996). Psychology seminar: Careers and graduate study in psychology. *Teaching of Psychology, 23*, 238–240.

Educational Testing Service (1998). *Graduate Record Examinations®: Guide to the use of scores.* Princeton, NJ: Author.

Educational Testing Service (2001). *Coming in October 2002: A new GRE General Test.* [Pamphlet]. Princeton, NJ: Author.

Edwards, J., & Smith, K. (1988). What skills and knowledge do potential employers value in baccalaureate psychologists? In P. J. Woods (Ed.), *Is psychology for them? A guide to undergraduate advising.* Washington, DC: American Psychological Association.

Ellis, D. (1997). *Becoming a master student* (8th ed.). Boston: Houghton Mifflin.

Field, S. (1996). *100 best careers for the 21st century.* New York: Macmillan.

Finney, P., Snell, W., Jr., & Sebby, R. (1989). Assessment of academic, personal, and career development of alumni from Southeast Missouri State University. *Teaching of Psychology, 16*, 173–177.

Gallucci, N. T. (1997). An evaluation of the characteristics of undergraduate psychology majors. *Psychological Reports, 81*, 879–889.

Garavalia, L. S., & Gredler, M. E. (1998, August). *Planning ahead: Improved academic achievement?* Presented at the American Psychological Association, San Francisco.

Gibaldi, J., & Achtert, W. S. (1988). *MLA handbook for writers of research papers* (3rd ed.). New York: Modern Language Association of America.

Giordano, P. (2004, April). *Deciding if graduate school is right for you.* Paper presented at the Midwestern Psychological Association meeting, Chicago, IL.

Grayson, J. (n.d.). *Principles for successful psychology field placement.* Handout, James Madison University.

Hammer, E. Y. (2003). The importance of being mentored. *Eye on Psi Chi, 7* (3), 4–5.

Harvard University (1998). Sociology. Retrieved January 4, 1999, at http://www.registrar.fas.harvard.edu/handbooks/student/chapter3/sociology.html.

Hayes, L. J., & Hayes, S. C. (1989, September). How to apply to graduate school. Retrieved September 28, 1998, at http://psych.hanover.edu/handbook/applic2.html.

Hayes, N. (1996, June). The distinctive skills of a psychology graduate. Retrieved March 30, 1998, at http://www.apa.org/monitor/jul97/skills.html.

Hettich, P. (1998). *Learning skills for college and career* (2nd ed.). Pacific Grove, CA: Brooks/Cole.

Hettich, P. I. (2004, April). *From college to corporate culture: You're a freshman again.* Paper presented at the Midwestern Psychological Association meeting, Chicago.

Hettich, P. I., & Helkowski, C. (2005). *Connect college to career.* Belmont, CA: Thomson Wadsworth.

Holder, W. B., Leavitt, G. S., & McKenna, F. S. (1958). Undergraduate training for psychologists. *American Psychologist, 13,* 585–588.

Holland, J. L. (1958). A personality inventory employing occupational titles. *Journal of Applied Psychology, 42,* 336–342.

Holland, J. L. (1959). A theory of vocational choice. *Journal of Counseling Psychology, 6,* 35–45.

Holland, J. L. (1973). *Making vocational choices: A theory of careers.* Englewood Cliffs, NJ: Prentice Hall.

Holland, J. L. (1994). Self-Directed Search® (SDS®) Form R (4th ed.). [Instrument]. Odessa, FL: Psychological Assessment Resources.

Hopper, C. (1998a). Ten tips you need to survive college. Retrieved on September 28, 1998, at http://www.mtsu.edu/~studskl/10tips.html.

Hopper, C. (1998b). Time management. Retrieved on September 28, 1998, at http://www.mtsu.edu/~studsk1/tmt.html.

Idaho Department of Labor (1998, October). *Job application tips.* Meridian, ID: Author.

Institute for Scientific Information (1998). *Social sciences citation index.* Philadelphia: Author.

Instructions in regard to preparation of manuscript (1929). *Psychological Bulletin, 26,* 57–63.

Jessen, B. C. (1988). Field experience for undergraduate psychology students. In P. J. Wood (Ed.), *Is Psychology for Them? A Guide to Undergraduate Advising.* Washington, DC: American Psychological Association.

Jobweb (2001). How to prepare an effective resume. Retrieved July 11, 2001 at http://www.jobweb.com/catapult/guenov/how_to.html.

Jones, R. A. (1985). *Research methods in the social and behavioral sciences.* Sunderland, MA: Sinauer Associates.

Kallgren, C. A., & Tauber, R. T. (1996). Undergraduate research and the institutional review board: A mismatch or happy marriage? *Teaching of Psychology, 23,* 20–25.

Kampfe, C. M., Mitchell, M. M., Boyless, J. A., & Sauers, G. O. (1999). Undergraduate students' perceptions of the internship: An exploratory study. *Rehabilitation Education, 13,* 359–367.

Kanchier, C. (2002, April 12–14). Does your attitude limit your options? *USA Weekend Magazine,* p. 9.

Karlin, N. J. (2000). Creating an effective conference presentation. *Eye on Psi Chi, 4* (2), 26–27.

Keith-Spiegel, P. (1991). *The complete guide to graduate school admission: Psychology and related fields.* Hillsdale, NJ: Erlbaum.

Keith-Spiegel, P., & Wiederman, M. W. (2000). *The complete guide to graduate school admission: Psychology, counseling, and related professions* (2nd ed.). Mahwah, NJ: Erlbaum.

Kennedy, J. H., & Lloyd, M. A. (1998, August). *Effectiveness of a careers in psychology course for majors.* Poster presented at the meeting of the American Psychological Association, San Francisco.

Kerckhoff, A. C., & Bell, L. (1998). Hidden capital: Vocational credentials and attainment in the United States. *Sociology of Education, 71,* 152–174.

Keyes, B. J., & Hogberg, D. K. (1990). Undergraduate psychology alumni: Gender and cohort differences in course usefulness, postbaccalaureate education, and career paths. *Teaching of Psychology, 17,* 101–105.

Kirk, E. E. (1996). *Evaluating information found on the internet*. Johns Hopkins University. Retrieved July 19, 2004, from http://www.library.jhu.edu/elp/useit/evaluate/index.html.

Knouse, S. B., Tanner, J. R., & Harris, E. W. (1999). The relation of college internships, college performance, and subsequent job opportunity. *Journal of Employment Counseling, 36*, 35–43.

Kohout, J., & Wicherski, M. (2003). *1999 Doctorate employment survey*. Washington, DC: American Psychological Association.

Korn, J. H. (1988). Students' roles, responsibilities, and rights as research participants. *Teaching of Psychology, 15*, 74–78.

Kressel, N. J. (1990). Job and degree satisfaction among social science graduates. *Teaching of Psychology, 17*, 222–227.

Kuther, T. L. (2003). *The psychology major's handbook*. Belmont, CA: Wadsworth.

La Sierra University (2000). Resumes, letters and interviews. Retrieved October 28, 2002 from www.lasierra.edu/departments/psychology/careers/resumes.html.

LaCour, J., & Lewis, D. M. (1998). Effects of a course in ethics on self-rated and actual knowledge of undergraduate psychology majors. *Psychological Reports, 82*, 499–504.

Lamb, C. S. (1991). Teaching professional ethics to undergraduate counseling students. *Psychological Reports, 69*, 1215–1223.

Landau, J. D. (2003). Understanding and preventing plagiarism. Retrieved April 28, 2003 from http://www.psychologicalscience.org/teaching/tips/tips_0403.html.

Landers, A. (1997, June 18). Job hunters should be aware of rules. *The Idaho Statesman*, Section D, p. 3.

Landrum, R. E. (1998, April). *Career opportunities in research, industry, & consulting*. In "Good Jobs for B.A.'s in Psychology" symposium, Midwestern Psychological Association, Chicago.

Landrum, R. E. (2004a). New odds for graduate admissions in psychology. *Eye on Psi Chi, 8* (3), 20–21, 32.

Landrum, R. E. (2004b, April). *Building blocks of a personal statement*. Presented at the Rocky Mountain Psychological Association meeting, Reno, NV.

Landrum, R. E., Jeglum, E. B., & Cashin, J. R. (1994). The decision-making processes of graduate admissions committees in psychology. *Journal of Social Behavior and Personality, 9*, 239–248.

Landrum, R. E., & Chastain, G. (1995). Experiment spot-checks: A method for assessing the educational value of undergraduate participation in research. *IRB: A Review of Human Subjects Research, 17*(4), 4–6.

Landrum, R. E., & Clark, J. (2004). Graduate admissions criteria in psychology: An update. Unpublished manuscript, Boise State University.

Landrum, R. E., & Harrold, R. (2003). What employers want from psychology graduates. *Teaching of Psychology, 30,* 131–133.

Landrum, R. E., & Nelsen, L. R. (2002). The undergraduate research assistantship: An analysis of the benefits. *Teaching of Psychology, 29*, 15–19.

Landrum, R. E., Shoemaker, C. S., & Davis, S. F. (2003). Important topics in an "Introduction to the Psychology Major" course. *Teaching of Psychology, 30*, 48–51.

Lefton, L. A. (1997). *Psychology* (6th ed.). Boston: Allyn & Bacon.

Library of Congress (1990). *LC classification outline*. Washington, DC: Author.

Lindgren, A. (2003, August 11). Research the key to successful interviews, CEO says. *The Idaho Statesman*, p. CB2.

Lloyd, M. A. (1997a, August 28). Exploring career-related abilities, interests, skills, and values. Available at http://www.psych-web.com/careers/explore.htm.

Lloyd, M. A. (1997b, September 23). Entry-level positions obtained by psychology majors. Retrieved on March 30, 1998, at http://www.psych-web.com/careers/entry.htm.

Lloyd, M. A., Kennedy, J. H., & Dewey, R. A. (1997, August 28). Suggested courses to develop skills that prospective employers want. Available at http://www.psych-web.com/careers/suggest.htm.

Lord, C. G. (2004). A guide to PhD graduate school: How they keep score in the big leagues. In J. M. Darley, M. P. Zanna, & H. L. Roediger III (Eds.), *The complete academic: A career guide* (2nd ed.) (pp. 3–15). Washington, DC: American Psychological Association.

Lore, N. (1997). How to write a masterpiece of a resume. Retrieved September 28, 1998, at http://www.his.com/~rockport/resumes.htm.

Lunneborg, P. W., & Baker, E. C. (1986). Advising undergraduates in psychology: Exploring the neglected dimension. *Teaching of Psychology*, *13*, 181–185.

Margulies, J. (2002). President of N.Y.'s Hamilton College steps down amid controversy over speech. *The Chronicle of Higher Education*, retrieved October 2, 2002, from http://chronicle.com/daily/2002/10/20021002n.htm.

Marietta College (1998). Political science. Retrieved January 4, 1999, at http://www.marietta.edu/~poli/index.html.

Martin, D. W. (1991). *Doing psychology experiments* (3rd ed.). Pacific Grove, CA: Brooks/Cole.

Mathiasen, R. E. (1998). Moral education of college students: Faculty and staff perspectives. *College Student Journal*, *32*, 374–377.

McConnell, K. (1998). Study skill checklist. Retrieved September 28, 1998, at http://wwwmc.nhmccd.edu/elc/reading_writing_area/studycl.html.

McGovern, T. V., & Carr, K. F. (1989). Carving out the niche: A review of alumni surveys on undergraduate psychology majors. *Teaching of Psychology*, *16*, 52–57.

McGovern, T. V., Furumoto, L., Halpern, D. F., Kimble, G. A., & McKeachie, W. J. (1991). Liberal education, study in depth, and the arts and sciences major—psychology. *American Psychologist*, *46*, 598–605.

Meeker, F., Fox, D., & Whitley, Jr., B. E. (1994). Predictors of academic success in the undergraduate psychology major. *Teaching of Psychology*, *21*, 238–241.

Menges, R. J., & Trumpeter, P. W. (1972). Toward an empirical definition of relevance in undergraduate instruction. *American Psychologist*, *27*, 213–217.

Merriam, J., LaBaugh, R. T., & Butterfield, N. E. (1992). Library instruction for psychology majors: Minimum training guidelines. *Teaching of Psychology*, *19*, 34–36.

Messer, W. S., Griggs, R. A., & Jackson, S. L. (1999). A national survey of undergraduate psychology degree options and major requirements. *Teaching of Psychology*, *26*, 164–171.

Morgan, B. L., & Korschgen, A. J. (2001). *Majoring in psych? Career options for psychology undergraduates* (2nd ed.). Boston: Allyn & Bacon.

Mount Saint Vincent University (1998). Benefits to the co-op student. Retrieved on December 1, 1998, at http://serf.msvu.ca/coop/st_ben.htm.

Mulcock, S. D., & Landrum, R. E. (2002, May). *The academic path of students that complete an 'Introduction to the Psychology Major'-type course*. Midwestern Psychological Association, Chicago.

Murray, B. (2002, June). Debating the doctorate's future: Education or vocational training? *Monitor on Psychology*, *33* (6), 36–38.

Murray, B. (2002, June). Good news for bachelor's grads. *Monitor on Psychology*, *33* (6), 30–32.

Natavi Guides (2002). *Fishing for a major*. New York: Author.

National Center for Education Statistics (2003). *Digest of education statistics 2002* (Publication NCES 2003-060). Washington, DC: U.S. Department of Education.

National Centre for Vocational Education Research (2004). Generic skills for the new economy. In Siena College (Ed.), *Liberal education and the new economy*. Loudonville, NY: Siena College.

National O*NET™ Consortium (2001, May). *O*NET occupational listings*. Raleigh, NC: Author.

National Science Foundation (2002). *Graduate students and postdoctorates in science and engineering, Fall 2000*. Arlington, VA: Author.

Newman, J. H. (1852/1960). *The idea of a university* (Edited by M. J. Svaglic). New York: Rinehart Press.

Norcross, J. C., & Castle, P. H. (2002). Appreciating the PsyD: The facts. *Eye on Psi Chi, 7* (1), 22–26.

Occupational Outlook Handbook (1998a, January 15). Social and human service assistants. Retrieved September 20, 1998, at http://www.bls.gov/oco/ocos059.htm.

Occupational Outlook Handbook (1998b). Social workers. Retrieved September 20, 1998, at http://www.bls.gov/oco/ocos060.htm

Occupational Outlook Handbook (2004a). *Counselors*. Washington, DC: U.S. Bureau of Labor Statistics.

Occupational Outlook Handbook (2004b). *Psychologists*. Washington, DC: U.S. Bureau of Labor Statistics.

Osborne, R.E. (1996, Fall). The "personal" side of graduate school personal statements. *Eye on Psi Chi, 1(1)*, 14–15.

Perlman, B., & McCann, L. I. (1998a). *The most frequently listed courses in the undergraduate psychology curriculum*. Paper presented at the meeting of the American Psychological Association, San Francisco.

Perlman, B., & McCann, L. I. (1998b). *The structure of the psychology undergraduate curriculum*. Paper presented at the meeting of the American Psychological Association, San Francisco.

Peterson, D. R. (2003). Unintended consequences: Ventures and misadventures in the education of professional psychologists. *American Psychologist, 58*, 791–800.

Pinkus, R. B. & Korn, J. H. (1973). The preprofessional option: An alternative to graduate work in psychology. *American Psychologist, 28*, 710–718.

Plous, S. (1998a). Advice on letters of recommendation. Retrieved September 28, 1998, at http://www.wesleyan.edu/spn/recitips.htm.

Plous, S. (1998b). Tips on creating an academic vita. Retrieved September 28, 1998, at http://www.wesleyan.edu/spn/vitatips.htm.

Plous, S. (1998c). Sample template for creating a vita. Retrieved September 28, 1998, at http://www.weslyan.edu/spn/vitasamp.htm.

Prickett, T. J., Gada-Jain, N., & Bernieri, F. J. (2000, May). *The importance of first impressions in a job interview*. Presented at the Midwestern Psychological Association, Chicago, IL.

Psi Chi (2004a). Becoming a member. Retrieved July 18, 2004, from http://www.psichi.org/about/becomember.asp.

Psi Chi (2004b). Benefits of membership. Retrieved July 18, 2004, from http://www.psichi.org/about/benefits.asp.

Reingold, H. (1994). *The psychologist's guide to an academic career*. Washington, DC: American Psychological Association.

Rewey, K. (2000, Fall). Getting a good letter of recommendation. *Eye on Psi Chi, 5* (1), 27–29.

Robinson, F. P. (1970). *Effective study* (4th ed.). New York: Harper & Row.

Roediger, R. (2004). Vita voyeur. *APS Observer, 17* (1). Retrieved April 8, 2004, from http://www.psychologicalscience.org/observer/getArticle.cfm?id=1498.

Rosnow, R. L., Rotheram-Borus, M. J., Ceci, S. J., Blanck, P. D., & Koocher, G. P. (1993). The institutional review board as a mirror of scientific and ethical standards. *American Psychologist, 48*, 821–826.

San Diego State University (1998). SDSU criminal justice program. Retrieved January 6, 1999, at http:/www.sdsu.edu/academicprog/crimjust.html.

Shepard, B. (1996, February 12). Employment opportunities for psychology majors. Retrieved March 30, 1998, at http://www.cs.trinity.edu/~cjackson/employ.html#employ-top.

Singleton, D., Tate, A. C., & Kohout, J. L. (2003). 2002 master's, specialist's, and related degrees employment survey. Washington, DC: American Psychological Association.

Slattery, J. M., & Park, C. L. (2002, Spring). Predictors of successful supervision of undergraduate researchers by faculty. *Eye on Psi Chi, 6* (3), 29–33.

Smith, D. (2002, June). Where are recent grads getting jobs? *Monitor on Psychology, 33* (6), 28–29.

Sternberg, R. J. (Ed.) (1997). *Career paths in psychology: Where your degree can take you.* Washington, DC: American Psychological Association.

Super, C. M., & Super, D. E. (1994). *Opportunities in psychology careers.* Lincolnwood, IL: VGM Career Horizons.

Tarsi, M., & Jalbert, N. (1998). An examination of the career paths of a matched sample of Psi Chi and Non-Psi Chi psychology majors. 1997–98 Hunt Award Research Report. Retrieved July 18, 2004, from http://www.psichi.org/awards/winners/hunt_reports/jalbert.asp.

Task Force on Undergraduate Psychology Major Competencies (2002, March). *Undergraduate psychology major learning goals and outcomes: A report.* Washington, DC: American Psychological Association.

Taylor, R. D., & Hardy, C.-A. (1996). Careers in psychology at the associate's, bachelor's, master's, and doctoral levels. *Psychological Reports, 79*, 960–962.

The Chronicle survey of public opinion on higher education (2003, May 2). *The Chronicle of Higher Education*, p. A11.

Thomas, J. H., & McDaniel, C. R. (2004). Effectiveness of a required course in career planning for psychology majors. *Teaching of Psychology, 31*, 22–27.

TMP Worldwide (1998). Action verbs to enhance our resume. Retrieved September 28, 1998, at http://www.aboutwork.com/rescov/resinfo/verbs.html.

Trials of War Criminals Before the Nuremberg Military Tribunals Under Control Council Law No. 10 (1949). *Nuremberg Code* (Vol. 2, pp. 181–182). Washington, DC: U.S. Government Printing Office.

Turabian, K. L. (1982). *A manual for writers of term papers, theses, and dissertations* (5th ed.). Chicago: University of Chicago Press.

United States Department of Labor (1991a). *What work requires of schools, A SCANS report for America 2000.* The Secretary's Commission on Achieving Necessary Skills. Washington, DC: Author.

United States Department of Labor (1991b). *Tips for finding the right job.* Employment and Training Administration, Washington, DC: Author.

University of California–Berkeley (1998). Taking tests—general tips. Retrieved September 28, 1998, at http://www-slc.uga.berkeley.edu/CalREN/TestsGeneral.html.

University of California–Santa Cruz (1998). Choosing a topic. Retrieved October 27, 1998, at http://bob.ucsc.edu/library/ref/instruction/research/topic.htm.

University of Michigan at Dearborn (1998). Benefits to the student. Retrieved December 1, 1998, at http://www-personal.umd.umich.edu/~pdjones/benef_s.html.

University of Oregon (2001). Policy on academic dishonesty. Retrieved July 22, 2004, from http://www.uoregon.edu/~conduct/sai.htm

Vanderbilt University (1996). How to select a research topic. Retrieved October 27, 1998, at http://www.library.vanderbilt.edu/education/topic.html.

Vittengl, J. R., Bosley, C. Y., Brescia, S. A., Eckardt, E. A., Neidig, J. M., Shelver, K. S., Sapenoff, L. A. (2004). Why are some undergraduates more (and others less) interested in psychological research? *Teaching of Psychology, 31,* 91–97.

Wahlstrom, C., & Williams, B. K. (2004). *College to career: Your road to personal success.* Mason, OH: South-Western.

Walfish, S. (2001). Developing a career in psychology. In S. Walfish & A. K. Hess (Eds.), *Succeeding in graduate school: The career guide for psychology students* (pp. 385–397). Mahwah, NJ: Erlbaum.

Walfish, S., & Hess, A. K. (Eds.) (2001). *Succeeding in graduate school: The career guide for psychology students.* Mahwah, NJ: Erlbaum.

Ware, M. E. (2001). Pursuing a career with a bachelor's degree in psychology. In S. Walfish & A. K. Hess (Eds.), *Succeeding in graduate school: The career guide for psychology students* (pp. 11–30). Mahwah, NJ: Erlbaum.

Waters, M. (1998, July). Naps could replace coffee as workers' favorite break. *American Psychological Association Monitor,* p. 6.

Webb, A. R., & Speer, J. R. (1986). Prototype of a profession: Psychology's public image. *Professional Psychology: Research and Practice, 17,* 5–9.

Weinstein, C. E., Palmer, D. R., & Schulte, A. C. (1987). *Learning and study strategies inventory.* Clearwater, FL: H&H Publishing Co.

Wilson, D. W. (1998). It takes more than good grades. *Eye on Psi Chi, Winter,* 11–13, 42.

Wolfle, D. L. (1947). The sensible organization of courses in psychology. *American Psychologist, 2,* 437–445.

Wood, G. (1981). *Fundamentals of psychological research* (3rd ed.). Boston: Little, Brown.

Wood, M. R., & Palm, L. J. (2000). Students' anxiety in a senior thesis course. *Psychological Reports, 86,* 935–936.

Yancey, G. B., Clarkson, C. P., Baxa, J. D., & Clarkson, R. N. (2003). Examples of good and bad interpersonal skills at work. *Eye on Psi Chi, 7* (3), 40–41.

Zuckerman, R. A. (1995). Doc Whiz's 40 ways to P.O. the prof. Retrieved July 21, 2004, from http://www.educ.kent.edu/community/DOCWHIZ/poprof.html.

Index

*Page numbers with *f* indicate figures; page numbers with *t* indicate tables.